POPULAR MUSIC AND HUMAN RIGHTS

This book is dedicated to those who understand the importance of the right to imagine an individual will, the right to some form of self-determination, and the right to self-legislation

Popular Music and Human Rights

Volume I: British and American Music

IAN PEDDIE

Routledge
Taylor & Francis Group

LONDON AND NEW YORK

First published 2011 by Ashgate Publishing

Published 2017 by Routledge
2 Park Square, Milton Park, Abingdon, Oxon OX14 4RN
711 Third Avenue, New York, NY 10017, USA

Routledge is an imprint of the Taylor & Francis Group, an informa business

British Library Cataloguing in Publication Data
Popular music and human rights.
  Volume 1, British and American music. -- (Ashgate popular and folk music series)
  1. Popular music--Great Britain--History and criticism. 2. Popular music--United
  States--History and criticism. 3. Popular music--Social aspects--Great Britain.
  4. Popular music--Social aspects--United States. 5. Human rights--Great Britain--Songs
  and music. 6. Human rights--United States--Songs and music.
  I. Series II. Peddie, Ian.
  306.4'8424-dc22

Library of Congress Cataloging-in-Publication Data
Popular music and human rights / [edited by] Ian Peddie.
    p. cm. -- (Ashgate Popular and folk music series)
  Includes index.
  ISBN 978-0-7546-6852-7 (v. 1 : hardcover : alk. paper) -- ISBN 978-0-7546-6853-4
  (v. 2 : hardcover : alk. paper) -- ISBN 978-0-7546-9512-7 (v. 1 : ebook) --
  ISBN 978-0-7546-9513-4 (v. 2 : ebook) 1. Popular music--Social aspects. 2. Human
  rights. I. Peddie, Ian.
  ML3918.P67P66 2011
  781.64'1599--dc22

2011004394

ISBN 13: 978-1-4094-6406-8 (Set)
ISBN 13: 978-1-4094-6404-4 (Volume 1 - pbk)

Contents

List of Contributors

Ian Peddie has taught at Florida Gulf Coast University, the University of Sydney, and West Texas A&M University. His edited collection, *The Resisting Muse: Popular Music and Social Protest* (Ashgate), a finalist in the Association for Recorded Sound Collections book of the year, was published in 2006. He is an avowed humanist, and one of the harmonizing themes in his work is the way in which human interaction is governed by a cohesive inequality, and these sentiments inform his book *The Hunted Revolutionaries: Narrating Class in Twentieth Century American Literature* (VDM Verlag, 2009).

He has published numerous essays on authors such as Irvine Welsh, Langston Hughes, T.S. Eliot, and Thomas McGrath, as well as on topics such as class, poverty, and radicalism. These topics influence his approach to popular music, where he has written on Led Zeppelin, Goldie, and Billy Bragg.

Kieran Cashell is a Lecturer in the Critical and Contextual Studies Programme in the Limerick Institute of Technology, Ireland. He is the author of *Aftershock: The Ethical Analysis of Contemporary Transgressive Art* (I.B.Tauris, 2009) and "Sing Me To Sleep: Suicide, Philosophy and The Smiths," in S. Campbell and C. Coulter (eds.) *Why Pamper Life's Complexities?* (Manchester University Press, 2010). He has also published several articles in journals of philosophy.

Kevin C. Dunn is Associate Professor of Political Science at Hobart and William Smith Colleges in Geneva, NY. He is the author of *Imagining the Congo: Identity and International Relations* (Palgrave Macmillan, 2003) and co-editor of *Identity and Global Politics: Theoretical and Empirical Elaborations* (with Patricia Goff; Palgrave Macmillan, 2004). He has published several pieces on punk rock and international relations, including "Never Mind the Bollocks: The Punk Rock Politics of Global Communication," in *Review of International Studies* (vol. 34, 2008) and "The Clash of Civilization: Notes from a Punk/Scholar," in Marianne Franklin (ed.) *Resounding International Relations: On Music, Culture, and Politics* (Palgrave Macmillan, 2005).

Deborah Finding completed her Ph.D. at LSE's Gender Institute. Her work focuses on narratives of sexual violence in popular music, and draws upon trauma theory and feminist cultural studies, as well as many years of NGO work with abused women. Her research interests include gender and psychoanalysis, mediated post-trauma discourses, and fan/community identifications. She also writes more widely on popular culture, including two publications in I.B.Tauris's "Reading Cult Television" book series and several pieces for *The Guardian*.

Professor John Hutnyk is Academic Director of the Centre for Cultural Studies at Goldsmiths College, University of London. He has written many articles on popular music and he is also the author of several books, including *The Rumour of Calcutta* (Zed Books, 1996), *Critique of Exotica* (Pluto Press, 2000), and *Bad Marxism: Capitalism and Cultural Studies* (Pluto Press, 2004).

Stephen A. King earned his Ph.D. in Speech Communication at Indiana University in 1997 and is currently a Professor of Communication Studies at Delta State University, in Cleveland, Mississippi. His book *Reggae, Rastafari, and the Rhetoric of Social Control* was published by the University Press of Mississippi in December 2002. King's work has been published in a variety of journals, including the *Southern Communication Journal, Journal of Popular Culture*, and *Popular Music and Society*. He is currently working on a book project that examines how blues music is being promoted as part of Mississippi's cultural heritage.

Stefan Mattessich is a Professor of English at Santa Monica College in California. His monograph on Thomas Pynchon, *Lines of Flight* (Duke University Press), which was a finalist for the MLA First Book Award, was published in 2002. He has published several articles on contemporary culture, including essays on Don DeLillo, Stanley Kubrick, and Gabriel Garcia Marquez in such venues as *Theory and Event, English Literary History*, and *Postmodern Culture*. He also writes on contemporary politics and theory, especially in terms of their impact upon human agency. Currently he is at work on a book-length project that explores cultural representations of the relations between subjectivity and public space.

Neil Nehring has been a Professor of English at the University of Texas since 1986. He teaches undergraduate and graduate courses on academic approaches to popular music and youth subcultures, as well as the history of revolutionary avant-garde movements in the arts. He also teaches and writes about the intersections of literature, popular music, and youth culture in Great Britain. His published work includes the books *Popular Music, Gender, and Postmodernism: Anger is an Energy* (Sage, 1997) and *Flowers in the Dustbin: Culture, Anarchy, and Postwar England* (University of Michigan Press, 1993), and recent essays in *Popular Music and Society*.

Sam O'Connell is currently completing his doctoral dissertation on twenty-first-century rock concerts as hybrid events (theatrical, media, and musical events). Sam received his A.M. in Drama from Washington University in St. Louis where he was the Editor-in-Chief of *Theatron*, a graduate theatre journal. He has presented on a variety of popular culture issues such as Spike Lee's *Inside Man*, The Dixie Chicks, and "America: A Tribute to Heroes." Sam has also served as the Editorial Assistant for the collected volume *Considering Calamity: Methods for Performance Research* (Assaph Books, 2007), co-edited by Tracy C. Davis and Linda Ben-Zvi, that came out of a conference of the same name held at Northwestern University in September 2005.

Christopher A. Scales is an Assistant Professor of Ethnomusicology at the College of William and Mary, Williamsburg, VA. His research focuses on contemporary Native North American popular music and culture. Aspects of this work have appeared in *Worlds of Music*, the *Canadian University Music Review*, and the *Journal for the Society of Ethnomusicology*. He is currently completing a manuscript entitled *Recording Culture: Powwow Music and the Aboriginal Recording Industry on the Northern Plains*, an ethnographic account of contemporary powwow music culture and the development and increasing importance of the Aboriginal recording industry within this social network. He has also been active in collaborating with Native musicians and has produced, recorded, or performed on several powwow and "Contemporary Native music" CD projects for Arbor Records and War Pony Records, independent record labels specializing in North American Aboriginal music.

David Thurmaier is Assistant Professor of Music Theory at Florida Gulf Coast University. He received a Ph.D. in Music Theory from Indiana University in 2006, where his dissertation focused on time and compositional process in the music of Charles Ives. In addition to Ives, his research interests include musical temporality, pedagogy of twentieth-century music, and American Experimental music.

Sheila Whiteley is Visiting Professor in Media at the University of Brighton. She is author of *The Space Between the Notes: Rock and the Counter Culture* (Routledge, 1992), *Women and Popular Music: Popular Music and Gender* (Routledge, 2000), and *Too Much Too Young: Popular Music, Age and Identity* (Routledge, 2005), and editor of *Sexing the Groove: Popular Music and Gender* (Routledge, 1996). She co-edited (with Andy Bennett and Stan Hawkins) *Music Space and Place: Popular Music and Cultural Identity* (Ashgate, 2002) and (with Jennifer Rycenga) *Queering the Popular Pitch* (Routledge, 2006). She was Chair of Popular Music at the University of Salford (1999-2006), and is a member of the Advisory Board of the Music as Performance Working Group (MAP).

Foreword

Billy Bragg

If I was asked what, in my opinion, was the most potent political song ever recorded, I would have no hesitation in naming Chuck Berry's "Roll Over Beethoven." Recorded in early 1956, this song is both a clarion call to a new generation and a startling declaration of a seismic change in the cultural hegemony. Imagine the reaction of middle America to this song blasting out of the radio, joyfully celebrating the decline of a high-brow white culture of the elite and its replacement by an electrifying black culture, accessible to all.

With this song, Chuck Berry hits his stride, finding a way to distance himself and his audience from the culture of previous generations. And once they had found the means to question the culture of their parents, it was only a matter of time before this new breed of teenagers would use music as a medium through which to question their parent's values as well.

We still live in the shadow of the great creative out-pouring that occurred when the bands that followed the original rock'n'rollers applied their songwriting skills to address the issues of the day. In the 1960s, young people had no access to the mainstream media. Their only platform for communication—to one another and to the outside world—was pop music.

The popular music of the 1960s more than lived up to Berry's vision, sweeping away the old order, crossing barriers of race and class, giving voice to those who had previously been excluded. The idea that music should be a force for social change took root during that decade. Artists, who previously had been inanely quizzed about their favorite colors, were now sought out for their political views and an entire counter culture was created around pop music with its own media and markets.

However, as this was a revolution based mainly on consumer choices, the changes wrought were cultural and social, rather than political. Yet, four decades after the high water mark of the 1960s, the notion that music can change the world remains a tantalizing notion to artists and audiences alike.

Chuck Berry caused more real outrage than a thousand Lady Gaga's by simply questioning, as a black man, the validity of contemporary culture in Eisenhower's America. It is questionable whether any young artist today could start a cultural revolution by singing "Roll Over John Lennon." Due to the ubiquity of popular music, the gap between the generations has never been so small.

Yet, in a post-ideological society, where individualistic self-interest is the default position and any attempt at political discussion is likely to be met with cynicism, the potential for music to once again become a medium with a message is apparent. Without an over-arching ideology such as socialism to express the compassionate will of the collective, leaving individuals with nothing to protect them except their basic human rights, music can act as the glue that binds us together in our struggles for a fairer society.

The essays collected here set out to explore both the potential and the pitfalls of utilizing popular music as a method of creating cultural, social, and, ultimately, political solidarity.

General Editor's Preface

The upheaval that occurred in musicology during the last two decades of the twentieth century has created a new urgency for the study of popular music alongside the development of new critical and theoretical models. A relativistic outlook has replaced the universal perspective of modernism (the international ambitions of the 12-note style); the grand narrative of the evolution and dissolution of tonality has been challenged, and emphasis has shifted to cultural context, reception and subject position. Together, these have conspired to eat away at the status of canonical composers and categories of high and low in music. A need has arisen, also, to recognize and address the emergence of crossovers, mixed and new genres, to engage in debates concerning the vexed problem of what constitutes authenticity in music and to offer a critique of musical practice as the product of free, individual expression.

Popular musicology is now a vital and exciting area of scholarship, and the *Ashgate Popular and Folk Music Series* presents some of the best research in the field. Authors are concerned with locating musical practices, values and meanings in cultural context, and draw upon methodologies and theories developed in cultural studies, semiotics, poststructuralism, psychology and sociology. The series focuses on popular musics of the twentieth and twenty-first centuries. It is designed to embrace the world's popular musics from Acid Jazz to Zydeco, whether high tech or low tech, commercial or non-commercial, contemporary or traditional.

Professor Derek B. Scott
Professor of Critical Musicology
University of Leeds

Acknowledgements

My thanks go to my fellow contributors, each of whom has brought something new to the study of music and human rights. Heidi Bishop, Senior Editor at Ashgate Publishing and Sophie Lumley, Editorial Assistant, have shown much patience and understanding as this two-volume project has come together.

There are countless human rights. Yet arguably it is extremely difficult to conceive of human rights without at one stage or another thinking hierarchically. This point is important if we are to grasp the connections between power and rights, an association which now defines rights discourse. For all the presence of "inalienable rights," "absolute rights of man," "states of freedom," and other expressions of liberty and self-determination fundamental to the discourse of rights, the idea of some form of mutually respectful ensemble of social relations still remains a distant hope. Along with its companion volume, this book examines the many ways in which popular music has responded to the issues of human rights.

Introduction

Long synonymous with the conditions necessary for a life of dignity, human rights provide a moral standard of national political legitimacy. Implicit in that moral standard is the possibility that human rights may provide a vehicle for the inclusion of a range of voices hitherto long silent. As scholars often point out, human rights can play a significant role in providing a range of discourses that embody power for the powerless. The same claim might be made about popular music: substituting the phrase "human rights" for that of "popular music" in the above statement suggests that the two possess a mutual affinity worthy of sustained investigation.

Given the contemporary relevance of human rights—and we recall UN Secretary-General Kofi Annan's initiative in 2006 to create a Human Rights Council based upon the conviction that "lack of respect for human rights and human dignity is the fundamental reason why the peace of the world today is so precarious, and why prosperity is so unequally shared"—their absence in studies of popular music is all the more surprising. While statements such as Annan's are public articulations meant to address deep and profound problems, the articulation of such issues, the creation of a "Human Rights Council," signals the very absence it seeks to assuage at the same time as it reveals how high the stakes are. For worryingly, the serious consequences of human rights violations suggest that their scarcity as a topic of critical focus for scholars of popular music is an omission with potentially alarming ramifications. Whether, for instance, it may be stretching the boundaries of credibility to suggest that the absence of human rights as a topic of critical focus for popular music scholars is in some immeasurable way a contributory factor to the kind of atmosphere that prompted Mary Robinson, former Irish Premier and UN High Commissioner for Human Rights, to remind us that "today's human rights violations are the causes of tomorrow's conflicts" is debatable. On the other hand, it is undeniable that the sins of omission *do* have an impact more complex and more recondite than out of sight, out of mind platitudes. With this in mind it is worth remembering that because in many parts of the world music is one of the few avenues of public expression, it is therefore a vital means through which ideas are disseminated and opposition organized; to proceed from such a departure point invites examination of the ways in which popular music addresses many of the most important aspects of human rights. For too many of those who comprise the audience of the musicians who will be discussed in this volume, the dream of human rights remains a daily ideological struggle. That rights remain such a pressing concern reiterates the cavernous gap between the theory and practice of self-determination.

At a time of such uncertainty and confusion, with human rights currently being violated all over the world, music, which of course is always produced in a social context, is an extremely useful medium; in its immediacy music has a potency of expression with a reach long and wide. For so many, then, music is a medium of hope. As Jimi Hendrix, one of the icons of Western popular music put it, "music doesn't lie. If there is something to be changed in this world, then it can only happen through music."

Billy Bragg's position in the vanguard of informed, politically aware musicians is firmly established. Kieran Cashell's approach to the bard of Basildon's work considers how and why Bragg, although heavily influenced by punk, tapped into the rich tradition of British folk. What emerged from this melding of the electric guitar-driven punk-like social realism of Bragg's work and English folk was a revitalization of the latter, effectively a form of punk-folk which exposed traditional forms to new audiences. Using the theories of Benjamin and Adorno as a guide, Cashell suggests that Bragg has played a crucial role in transmitting the folk tradition and disassociating it from the forces of consensus and returning it to the province of radicalism from whence it emerged. This act, the author argues, led to the development of new ways of expressing activism in music.

Kevin Dunn's chapter on punk, globalization, and human rights advances the notion that the widespread prevalence of punk ensures that it is truly a world music, albeit one with scenes and networks that encourage the articulation of human rights in local terms of reference. Tracing the rise of punk to New York in the early 1970s, Dunn examines the genre's social beginnings, its DIY ethos, and its challenges to the status quo. In discussing different scenes, Dunn suggests that punk's value lies in its ability to provide a means of engagement with rights, and, in keeping with one of the central tenets of its ethos, that punk is a "DIY vehicle for empowerment and political action."

Beginning with the conviction that sexual violence may be the most prevalent human rights violation, Deborah Finding's chapter examines the connections between art and trauma. Using Tori Amos's 1992 song "Me and a Gun" as a key text, the author surveyed over two thousand listeners, many of whom indicated a profound connection to Amos's narrative of sexual violence. Paradoxically perhaps, in a song which is considered anxiety provoking, listeners find plenty to identify with in "Me and a Gun," particularly in terms of the absence of superficial resolution which invites comparisons with the listener's own life—and this is where the song's power lies. That the song has inspired countless support networks is testament to its importance as a piece of trauma art just as it points to the pervasiveness of sexual violence.

Written in the context of restrictions on civil liberties, global terror wars, and the paranoia endemic to contemporary London, John Hutnyk contends that space for meaningful debate is under serious threat in Britain. The erosion of human rights, the author implies in his argument, necessitates a re-examination of culture, while the gap between political expression and diluted versions of multiculturalism demands a more engaged critique of culture. In this discussion, Hutnyk uses the work of Fun-da-Mental and drum and bass outfit Asian Dub Foundation to examine anticolonialism, insurgency struggles, and political freedom in the UK, suggesting ultimately that "difficult" music can offer new ways of countering infringements of human rights.

From whatever angle one considers the blues, for African Americans it has been a medium of protest through which they have sought their basic human rights. Stephen A. King considers the blues player Willie King's political narratives and particularly his comments on trauma, connecting both to a public memory dominated by the brutality of Jim Crow. Willie King's songs also point to contemporary oppression, especially through his deployment of the word "terror," a term that has significant contemporary ramifications just as it remains an indelible part of the lives of those forced to live in the American South in the early twentieth century. This chapter, then, examines the interrelationship of Willie King's political narratives, public memory, and human rights.

Stefan Mattessich's theoretically informed discussion of the film musical *Hedwig and the Angry Inch* (2001) concentrates on the performative notions of self. Noting the antagonisms between communal needs for love and justice and the desire for recognition or prestige, the author suggests that the transgendered protagonist Hedwig is an exemplary reflection on cultural politics over the last 50 years. By way of cultural/political initiatives like the "Velvet Revolution," Charter 77, and influential essays such as Vaclav Havel's "The Power of the Powerless," Mattessich uses Hedwig to consider the construction of human rights discourses. More specifically, he connects the malleability of Hedwig's identity to the question of how authority might be contested, suggesting, *à la* Rancière, that it is only at the level of subjective identity that this question can be meaningfully considered.

The checkered history of political benefit albums is the subject of Neil Nehring's chapter. With an impressively broad sweep through the genre, Nehring considers whether consciousness-raising, one of the chief goals of such albums, is actually attainable or whether the plethora of benefit albums has trivialized the genre to the extent where it functions as a form of compensation for the political cowardice of musicians' work. In questioning the dubious quality of many benefit albums, the author suggests that the genre has been mundane and predictable even if some benefit albums do raise money. Their impact in terms of human rights, on the other hand, remains open to question.

The achievements of benefit concerts, the subject of Sam O'Connell's chapter, are as ambiguous as those of benefit albums. In addition to providing a site of collective mourning, benefit concerts bring to national attention events and causes in a culturally and socially contained manner. As O'Connell intimates, benefit concerts also prescribe and model appropriate social responses. While concentrating on *America: A Tribute to Heroes* (2001) and *A Concert for Hurricane Relief* (2005), the author contends that 9/11 provided a context around which sanctioned responses to Hurricane Katrina were built. How these and other concerts were framed is fundamental to understanding the extent to which the music and genres deemed appropriate—and those excluded from the process—are part of scripted attempts to direct and define how concerts are interpreted.

Ian Peddie's chapter argues that the impetus provided by postwar independence movements in Africa and Asia was crucial to the US civil rights movement and to the work of Gil Scott-Heron. Independence movements provided the ideological framework through which Scott-Heron formulated a body of music that celebrated the incipient power of the black diaspora, especially its ability to effect change. In the music of Scott-Heron, Peddie argues, the impetus for change in former colonies resonated with black Americans in terms of the struggle for equality and rights. That is, Scott-Heron effectively domesticated international independence movements as reminders of communal obligations, with exhortative calls to struggle, encouraging collectivist notions of diasporic identity. Scott-Heron's work, Peddie concludes, is a crucial bridge between narratives of rights, civil and human.

Christopher Scales makes a compelling case for popular music as a significant catalyst for Native American ethnic identification and political participation. The rise of Red Power activism, the author contends, is articulated through various sociopolitical projects, not least the memorialized atrocities that occurred at Wounded Knee in December 1890, where 146 Lakota Sioux were shot. As a site of Native American resistance, Wounded Knee is also a symbol of Native political unity and strength, as well as a key feature of activism in the imagination of Native musicians and writers. Using the music of XIT, Scales teases out how indigenous nations forge political alliances across tribal and social divides and through this process assert their rights to the collective place of Native Americans within the US and Canada.

After establishing an unlikely identity of interests between Bruce Springsteen and F.D. Roosevelt regarding their respective positions on rights, David Thurmaier proceeds to examine some of the salient musical characteristics in Springsteen's work and how they apply to human rights. Thurmaier suggests that FDR and Springsteen were both concerned with how rights might be safeguarded and the importance of rights to the ideals of American nationhood. Given that both FDR and Springsteen agree that rights are contingent upon how society treats its less fortunate members, the implication is that a safe, secure, and content populace is likely to foster ideas of compassion and understanding and equality and, by extension, of a fully realized notion of human rights.

Beginning with the premise that "women's rights and human rights are viewed as distinct," Sheila Whiteley argues that the cultural norms surrounding sexuality and freedom of choice are all too often bounded by both class and ethnicity. As such, the female body becomes the terrain upon which the struggle for liberation is contested. While analyzing some of the historical problems that surround bodily autonomy, Whiteley considers the influence patriarchy, rape, abortion, and shaming have had on the female form. Through analysis of the work of artists including Joni Mitchell, Jamelia, and Tracy Chapman, Whiteley examines the nature of subjugation and how the female musico-political voice is important in questioning power and status, oppression and subordination.

Chapter 1

More Relevance than Spotlight and Applause: Billy Bragg in the British Folk Tradition

Kieran Cashell

Politics is an ethical practice that arises in a situation of injustice which exerts a demand for responsibility.—Simon Critchley

Routinely (and often casually) categorized in the folk genre, Billy Bragg has recently become associated with what some have begun to regard as a third folk revival.[1] To a large extent this is attributable, ironically, to his role in the project of composing music for Woody Guthrie's back-catalogue of "lost" song lyrics. Following two acclaimed albums of material (recorded with Chicago rock institution Wilco) and the epithet a "Musical Elder Statesman" (dubbed by one US music critic), it is no surprise that discussion of Bragg tends to overstate the American influence.[2] An unfortunate consequence of this, as Mark Willhardt observes, is that the British tradition "almost never appears": Bragg is frequently identified "as the inheritor of the legacy of Guthrie and Dylan, not Harry Cox or Bob Copper" (2006, p. 40). The political commitments of his music may have a more familiar and well-defined precedent in the American than the British tradition. To critics, if Bragg's musical activism seems more closely related to the US protest movement, the genealogy of the English folk song appears, in contrast, a more erudite and less accessible, less obviously political inheritance: "Whereas the Americans pushed for a politics of opposition, most of the British work tended toward the Lomaxian authenticity of genre, conveying generations-old song." Willhardt concludes that, "Although Bragg's concerns and political context [may be] English, his musical antecedents are found in North America" (2006, p. 40).

---

[1] See for example, BBC4, *Folk Britannia*: www.bbc.co.uk/bbcfour/music/features/folk-britannia.shtml. *The Imagined Village* project (Virgin, 2007). See also Harper (2006, p. xii).

[2] *Mermaid Avenue* (1998) and *Mermaid Avenue Volume II* (2000); Nora Guthrie, Woody's daughter, selected Bragg to tackle the lyrical archive because she wanted a musician who was sympathetic to the protest ethos yet had the distance to bring something new to the legacy. Bragg also recorded some Guthrie songs with The Blokes. The US critic is Harvey Pekar (2004, p. 56).

As a result, there have been few systematic attempts to contextualize Bragg in the British folk tradition. In response to this deficit, I locate his work apropos the British tradition by surveying its originary field of influence and unearthing what Bragg himself, on the sleeve of *Back to Basics*, calls the "roots of [his] urbane folk music" (1987). First codified by source revivalists Cecil Sharp, Alan Lomax, and Percy Grainger, and augmented, most importantly for our purposes, by revivalists A.L. Lloyd and Ewan MacColl, the British folk song has also been preserved through the performance and recording of Martin Carthy, The Watersons, Dick Gaughan, Anne Briggs, Tim Hart and Maddy Prior, June Tabor, Shirley Collins, Bert Jansch, Nic Jones, and Martin Simpson.[3]

Examination of Bragg in this relation must also appreciate that, without the influence of punk culture, his unique contribution to the folk tradition in the UK cannot be adequately assessed. Thematizing Bragg apropos the British, as opposed to the American tradition, however, uniquely allows us to incorporate the value of punk for his socially-engaged music without either diminishing its radical political dimension or minimizing the influence of the English folk song. For US audiences may not be aware that the dimensions of British folk and punk are not as incompatible as they might *prima facie* appear.

Bragg's autobiography *The Progressive Patriot* contains an account of his commitment to the punk "cultural revolution," which gave the young singer, as it did so many others inspired by its anger and energy, the impetus to want to get out and say something—or at least make some noise: "Can't sing? Who cares? It's what you're singing *about* that matters" (2006, p. 241). The value he acquired from punk was an all-important attitude. Intuiting in the movement a powerful ethos by which to convert the anarchic aggression of disaffected youth into legitimate oppositional and political expression, Bragg felt that "By taking control of the means of production of all things that were important to us, we were going to change the world" (2006, p. 242).

More than the Sex Pistols (of whose project Bragg remained skeptical) it was The Clash that inspired the development of his particular means of organizing the scatter-bomb anarchism of punk into a coherent "aesthetics of resistance" (Weiss, 2005). For him, Joe Strummer and Mick Jones's band epitomized the punk manifesto with regard to this ambition. Bragg's early confidence that punk had the capacity to change the world was soon eroded, however; and a resolution to act on the political convictions finding increasing expression in his songs followed. The Clash's "failure to engage fully with politics" was, he explains, a crucial factor in his later decision "to work closely with the Labour Party in the hope of defeating the Tories in the 1987 election" (Bragg, 2006, p. 247). Yet his engagement with left-wing politics to mobilize culture for social change is still directly influenced,

---

[3]   Andy Irvine, Johnny Moynihan, Christy Moore, and Paul Brady should also be mentioned. Despite their Irish heritage and *sean-nós* singing styles, included in their repertoires are many fascinating interpretations of English and Scottish songs.

he claims, by the lessons he learnt from the "mistakes" of The Clash (2006, p. 247).

Later, in the Acknowledgements, Bragg reflects that his initial intentions in authoring the book were to "reconcile" his "love of folk" with his commitment to punk. In light of this, Norma Waterson's regrets about the failure of the folk movement to assimilate punk as a new form of popular expression in the 1980s are interesting. "When punk came about," she says, "it should have happened in the folk clubs. But the punks weren't allowed in and that's why folk music stagnated for a time in the 1980s" (quoted in Morrish, 2007, p. 45). Yet there *is* evidence, despite this, that punk did, at least to a limited extent, inform the development of folk music; if some traditional singers embraced the punk ethos, certain punks, like Bragg, became increasingly attracted to the radical elements sublimated in the tradition. Many second-generation Irish immigrants in the UK, in particular, finding themselves informed by both cultures, developed a unique intergenerational fusion of contemporary and traditional influences. Most notable in this context is Shane MacGowan whose songs, inspired by the experience of the second-generation Irish émigré, achieve an unprecedented synthesis of punk and folk. His Gothic imagery and Banshee screaming (in picked-up Cocknified accent) interleave the Irish céilí-house dance tradition with a darkness that suggests the nightmare of the Industrial School and the inheritance of abuse.[4] And Bragg's relationship with the English tradition, as revolutionary in its way as MacGowan's, is perhaps also more intricate and subtle, and therefore more difficult to assess. Indeed, Andrew Collins provocatively states, in his "official" biography of the singer, that Bragg's music is "more punk than folk (he has often described his earliest incarnation as 'a one-man Clash')" (2002, p. 87).

The objection that Bragg has nothing whatever, not even at the most superficial level, in common with the British folk heritage can be sustained. Yet I remain convinced that Bragg's music is profoundly, if tacitly, associated with this tradition; this association is, with some surprising exceptions, most profound in the songs of his early period, that is, when his punk sensibility was also at its most visceral. This is, of course, a controversial claim; but we need to go further here if the significant political value of Bragg's music is to be acknowledged (and, of course, it must be). Assimilating Bragg to the most recent British folk revival, alongside Eliza Carthy, Kate Rusby, Seth Lakeman, Chris Wood, and as epitomized most recently by the *Imagined Village* (2007) project, is problematic; it reveals the disquieting phenomenon that when overtly identified with (even in the company of the Copper Family, Carthy, Waterson et al.), the English tradition cannot but appear an ersatz commercial category recuperated for the commercial

---

[4] The Pogues are typically associated with The Dubliners and the Clancy Brothers. Neither the optimism of the New World emigrant expressed in the Clancy's Irish-Americana nor the metropolitan drinking milieu of The Dubliners seems apposite here. Rather the relevant influence is the céilí band (playing at wakes and in dance-houses around rural Ireland).

interests of the entertainment industry (the *Imagined Village* CD is distributed by Virgin). Listening to Bragg's modification of "Hard Times Old England," one is reminded of Steeleye Span's terminal collaboration with Status Quo on *All Around My Hat*[5] 20 years earlier.

In this chapter, contra identification with new genre folk, I will suggest another way of thematizing Bragg's place in the tradition. To make this plausible will require the critical political dimension of Bragg's music to be made explicit.

Of course, the first and most controversial issue in this project of explication is the conflict between Bragg's authored lyric and the oral transmission criterion (OTC), a consensually accepted standard that the defining characteristic of the "genuine folk song" is its intergenerational dissemination by mouth and, as Vic Gammon importantly adds, by ear (quoted in Morrish, 2007, p. 13). Cecil Sharp (1965, p. 4) argued that the OTC denotes more than the social milieu in which the folk song thrives; for him, it connotes, rather, both the method of its creation and the entire "process by which it grows" (quoted in Howes, 1969, p. 7). According to Howes, Sharp's defense of the OTC accounted "for the communal character of the folk-song, even of its natural flavour, for in passing through many minds it has taken on the character of communal authorship—many minds have, in fact, contributed to its creation" (1969, p. 7).

In 1955, at the International Folk Music Council's seventh conference, the OTC was enshrined as a foundational principle, stating that it is precisely the "re-fashioning and re-creation" of the song by the "community that gives it its folk character" (Howes, 1969, p. 11). Yet, it should be pointed out that the OTC should not be assumed to preclude creativity. A.L. Lloyd has identified what he refers to as the social "dialectic" of communal and individual in the folk tradition by noting that the "talented performer, in reproducing the songs of his group, would make certain personal suggestions which, if adopted by the community, become part of the collective inheritance, to reappear subsequently as a nameless and respected part of communally sanctioned tradition" (1967, p. 321). The folk tradition, Lloyd concludes, constitutes an utterly public form of musical and lyrical synergy: "There is nothing private or exclusive about a folksong" (1967, p. 65). Preserved by branch instead of root, not by mindless imitation, the tradition survives through a process of sublation: new challenge, formative augmentation, radical questioning—all contribute to the final assimilation into the canon. Theodor Adorno goes further, "Only that which inexorably denies tradition," he insists, "may once again retrieve it" (1993-94, p. 81).

It is simply not possible to categorize a Bragg composition, according to the oral criterion, as a folk song. Indeed, it is difficult to imagine traditionalists like Sharp, or revivalists like Lloyd, recognizing Bragg as a folk singer from any, even the most charitable perspective. But one reason why it is difficult to assess Bragg's engagement with the British folk tradition is because it refuses to be reduced to

---

[5]   A Status Quo-influenced soft-core rock version of "Hard Times Old England" appears on *All Around My Hat*.

a single criterion. In a way remarkably similar to Nottinghamshire singer Anne Briggs, for instance, Bragg's bond with the tradition is more fundamental and intuitive than a convention like the OTC can accommodate.[6] "I never found a single thread," Anne Briggs explained in an interview broadcast on British Television, "apart from a gut feeling. The only thread that ran through it all was that direct line that some singers ... had to human emotion."[7] She added: "I immediately felt 'that's my music, that's what I should be singing'. I didn't know it was called folk music, I just heard it and it was mine" (Briggs, 1999). Briggs's impact on the folk scene of the early 1960s, as acknowledged by Harper, was phenomenal. Referring (importantly in this connection) not only to her visceral delivery and singing style but also to her intoxicated performances, Harper quotes Bert Jansch: "you've got to understand that at that time, her impact in that world, she was more akin to punk than anything that had gone before" (2006, p. 113).

Bragg, like Briggs, intuitively tapped into some deep resource in the tradition; not by gullibly accepting what is regarded as "traditional" but rather by way of challenge and question, he augments this heritage, realizing that without critical confrontation, it cannot have contemporary relevance. Adorno's dialectical argument claims that renunciation is, paradoxically, crucial for the continuing survival of tradition. If the folk tradition, in particular, fails to be critical then it risks violating the vital impulse from which it originated in the first instance.

If OTC provides a means of identifying the folk song on the basis of a criterion of authenticity, modern revivalist performers tend to be hostile to this prerequisite. "It is utterly ridiculous to try to keep folk music pure," Martin Carthy insists, "because it has never been pure." "The idea of there being a folk pedigree," he adds, "is a joke" (1987, p. 6). A folk song is relativized by how (and when) and by whom it is performed; singing a folk song necessarily involves the singer in a personal, emotionally-invested and therefore positional interpretation. Even Child's collection (1882-98) transcribes three or four different versions of the (same?) song. And yet: certain singers, although they may have a completely opposed outlook (believing, for example, that the preservation of tradition is a conservative tendency), can still, despite this attitude, attune to the tradition in a *fundamental* way, expressing this connection by composing new songs that yet, by their form, are recognizably folk songs.[8] Many of Bragg's compositions (especially 1983-88) reveal such a visceral engagement with, and instinctive understanding of, the British folk tradition. Songs such as "The Man in the Iron Mask," "The Myth of Trust," "The Saturday Boy," "Greetings to the New Brunette," and some later songs such as "The Short Answer," "Northern Industrial Town," and "Take Down

---

[6]   BBC4, *Folk Britannia*; Briggs is arguably the most influential singer of the folk revival. Harper regards her as "the greatest English traditional singer" (2006, p. 61).

[7]   At some point in the 1970s she ceased singing and has never recorded since; she explained this in *Folk Britannia*, saying that she had given herself up so entirely to becoming a "vehicle for the material" that it had consumed her and left her exhausted.

[8]   The songwriting of Irish singer Andy Irvine should be included in this category.

the Union Jack" manifest that thread of audible influence grounded in a tacit familiarity with the musical structures of the folk tradition that Briggs refers to.

Apart from the authored lyric, the other prominent difficulty in associating Bragg with the English tradition is his guitar playing. It is his electric guitar playing that distinguishes Bragg from most—if not all—exponents (source, revivalist, and contemporary). It also differentiates him, significantly, from the Guthrie-Dylan protest singer-songwriter—an archetype still affiliated with the instrument.

Moreover, the electric guitar has only very reluctantly, if at all, been accepted in the folk genre. Since the Newport Festival fiasco of 1965, when Dylan provoked outrage by plugging in, the instrument has been treated with extreme prejudice. Bragg confronted the archetype by taking to the stage with an electric guitar and nothing else. "The conceit of bastardizing the stand-up folkie tradition by swapping the acoustic guitar for an electric," Collins recalls, "was fairly radical at the time" (2002, p. 86). Representing a conscious identification with his punk "sensibility," his audience is compelled, moreover, to understand it as oppositional, an attitude emphasized by his often angular and spiky, ragged playing style.

Early in his career, Bragg allegedly, and provocatively, promised that "he would never play an acoustic guitar in public" (in Alfonso et al., 2003, p. 246). He has, of course, since reneged on this promise. With his technique of electric playing, with struck open chords ringing out into the space around him, a figure admonishing from the stage, Bragg takes an aggressive position precisely *contra* the tradition. Even those guitarists and sophisticated singers in the English and Scottish folk tradition that he most closely resembles—Martin Carthy, Nic Jones, Bert Jansch, and Dick Gaughan—Bragg seems to stand *against* in this respect. Yet it is possible to imagine Ewan MacColl listening to *Brewing Up* and coming to appreciate the steely resonance of Bragg's guitar as an appropriate accompaniment to the industrial song—providing, as it were, the iron tracks along which the lyrics travel.

Unlike the musicians mentioned, all of whom have experimented with complex alternative tunings to facilitate the unusual modes and rhythms associated with British folk (see Sharp, 1965) Bragg is not a virtuoso guitarist. His playing is unsophisticated and certainly within the capability of an amateur fan to master without trauma. Yet this flexibility is fundamental to his utilitarian ethos. *Back to Basics*, the 1985 songbook, which included a flexi disc entitled "Play Guitar the Billy Bragg Way," epitomizes this democratic attitude.[9] I don't mean to suggest that Bragg's playing is unoriginal. On the contrary, his style is remarkably creative, and, as an accompaniment to the semantics of his songwriting, highly

---

[9]   The utilitarian design of his records belongs in this sociocultural sphere; the sleeves were two-tone with wood-cut graphics or primitive black-and-white photography and included the much discussed (and much admired) use-value exhortations to "Pay No More Than £2.99 for this 7 Track Album" or "£3.99 or Less" (mysteriously disappearing, however, after 1990's *The Internationale*).

appropriate. Bragg treats the guitar as an instrument: not in the musical but rather in the *industrial* sense. Handled without ornamentation, and using basic chords connected by complex (often damped) bass lines, the guitar adds an industrial ambience to the song (complementing the motifs of wet streets, red-brick terraces, hardware in the night skies, fire escapes, etc.).

"The essence of what I play," Bragg replied to my attempts to fathom the originality of his style, "is percussive." That is to say, the focus of attention is on the *right* hand as it rhythmically impacts the strings. "A lot of what I play is not clear notes," he went on, "it's all clicks and clunks" (Bragg, 2008). I put it to him that Nic Jones and Martin Carthy's styles have been characterized as percussive; Carthy favors heavy-gauge strings and restricts the melody to the bottom four while playing damped bass drones and Jones developed a distinctive right-hand percussive beat in his playing style.[10]

"Fundamentally," Bragg says in response to this suggestion, "the voice is the melody, and the guitar is the rhythm; I'm basically a rhythm guitar player." It is tempting to compare this statement, particularly in the present context, with Carthy's claim (made in 1971 when his seminal *Shearwater* was recorded) not to be "a solo guitarist." He continues: "I'm an accompanist, which is a recently developed style in England, and I'm interested in finding a way of doing it in an appropriate way" (Carthy, 1972). I view Bragg's playing as a rhizomatic development of precisely this objective, which, having responded to the cultural influence of folk, also desires to acknowledge the paradigm shift of punk, and therefore must change in order to stay attuned to the ethos of both. Thus Bragg's guitar may express fidelity to punk yet it is also where his connection to the English folk tradition is, paradoxically, most audible.

Rooksby identifies the "bare fact" of the solo performance as characteristic of the singing tradition in England (2007, p. 57). Solo delivery facilitates performative variations and specific manipulation of the lyrical and semantic as well as formal structure to suit vocal range, personal investment in the song, and mode of address. And the solo performance remains the keystone of Bragg's craft. It represents fidelity to the DIY ethos of punk culture; politically, it expresses an expression of aggressive autonomy in satirical defiance of Thatcher's glorification of free enterprise, an attitude embodied by the backpack PA system for electric buskers-cum-social agitators (designed by Kenny Jones) he sported in the early 1980s (Collins, 2002, p. 137). Yet, again this defiant solo attitude connects in a serendipitous way with the tradition (witness his free interpolation of lyrical novelties into "Waiting for the Great Leap Forward" and "Greetings to the New Brunette" in performance).

"Before punk," Bragg explained to me, "I was listening to The Watersons, Shirley Collins, Martin Carthy, Anne Briggs, Simon and Garfunkel" (2008). Yet, he continued, "what happened was punk swept it all away and I turned my back on all that; I didn't want to play in folk clubs, I wanted to play in rock

---

[10] See interview with Mark Tucker in *Acoustic*, 1 (2005): 16-20.

clubs" (Bragg, 2008).[11] In *The Progressive Patriot* (2006) the genealogy of his discovery of English folk is delineated in the context of his musical development as a whole. Interestingly, it was his discovery that Dylan had creatively tracked song lyrics onto traditional English melodies ("Lord Franklin" ["Bob Dylan's Dream"], "Scarborough Fair" ["Girl from the North Country"], and "Nottamun Town" ["Masters of War"]) on *The Freewheelin' Bob Dylan* that stimulated Bragg to revisit the music of his "own country" which he then systematically "immersed" himself in, "borrowing album after album from the folk section of Barking Central Library: industrial ballads sung by Bert Lloyd and Ewan McColl [*sic*]; Shirley Collins's plaintive voice, framed by her sister Dolly's haunting pipe organ; the Watersons, like a force of nature, with their roaring harmonies" (Bragg, 2006, p. 160). A moment of epiphany followed when Bragg, familiar (as everyone was) with Simon and Garfunkel's popularization of "Scarborough Fair," encountered Martin Carthy's first milestone recording. He could now appreciate Simon and Garfunkel's profound indebtedness (as with Dylan's "Girl from the North Country") to Carthy's treatment of this strange, fundamental song, and how insipid their version sounded in comparison.

This early listening regime has left distinct traces on Bragg's punk-influenced material that are everywhere audible to the trained ear. On *Brewing Up*, for instance, the descending melody with damped base drone that constitutes the intro and coda of "The Myth of Trust" closely replicates Carthy's version of MacColl's "Springhill Mining Disaster." Similarly, the guitar voicing on "Ideology" rhythmically follows Briggs's arrangement of "Blackwaterside"; the overdubbed parallel vocals on "Love Gets Dangerous," and the unaccompanied "I Don't Need This Pressure Ron" as well as "Ye Thatcherites by Name," are influenced by The Watersons' monodic singing style; *a cappella* songs, "Tender Comrade," "I Dreamed I Saw Phil Ochs Last Night," and "You Make Me Brave" (arguably a response to "My Husband's Got No Courage in Him"), are also sung in the monodic solo style of unaccompanied folk singing. As well as this, some of his songs set original lyrics to traditional melodies in the Dylan schema (for instance, "There is Power in a Union," "Ye Thatcherites"). Finally, for the moment, the introduction of the F chord at the end of "It Says Here" identifies the mode as Mixolydian (with flattened seventh note) and therefore links it melodically to the English musical tradition (similarly in "Strange Things Happen" and in the recent "I Keep Faith"[12]).

One striking feature of the first 21 songs (*Life's A Riot*, *Brewing Up*, and *Between the Wars*[13]) is their structure: Bragg's early songs deviate (in lyrical as well as melodic form) significantly from the commercial song; few of them adhere

---

[11]   Elsewhere he suggested that he didn't want to be "a Nick Drake and play in folk clubs" (in Goddard, 2006, p. 71).

[12]   I.e., the middle 8's C in the key of D.

[13]   Collected on *Back to Basics* (1987); the 1985 *Days Like These* should also be included in this catalogue.

to the verse-chorus format and (if, for argument's sake, the instrumental bridges are ignored) there are usually no middle 8 sections.[14] Typically, an early Bragg song is composed of two or three stanzas sometimes with a chorus, but more often a coda ("Island of No Return," "Days Like These"), concluding couplet ("It Says Here"), or last-line refrain. The latter, another significant difference, is prominent in "Like Soldier's Do," "The Man in the Iron Mask," "Between the Wars," "Days Like These," and later songs like "The Marriage," "Ideology," "There is Power in a Union," "I Dreamed I Saw Phil Ochs Last Night," and "Northern Industrial Town." Such peculiarities may make the songs less accessible to audiences habituated to the commercial song structure. Yet these, while far from standard in the folk tradition, are nevertheless assimilated more readily because of the variable structure of the folk song (Rooksby, 2007, pp. 56-7): on this point, "Ontario, Quebec and Me," a later Bragg song, is paradigmatic.

In "St Swithin's Day," which opens side two of Bragg's 1984 LP, *Brewing Up*, the various dimensions identified here are crystallized. Sounding *very like* a folk song, it is in fact reminiscent of several English ballads (notably "Little Muzgrave and Lady Barnard," "Bill Norrie," and "John Barleycorn"), the calendrical marker situating the song at a seasonal point (i.e., every July 15th) giving it a continuing, cyclical relevance and allowing for semantic flexibility. Reference to the weather in the first verse does not solely function as a "reality effect" but sustains the key allusion of the song. The final stanza returns to the song's title marker, just like "Little Muzgrave," and thus the seasonal circle, although consummated, begins all over again: "Like the love we spoke of *forever* on St Swithin's day."

Bragg's accompanying chords are voiced in a rhythmic mixture of plucked arpeggios and pesante strumming near the bridge—prior to a sudden choked caesura before the verse begins. The melody is carried across the bass strings and repeated cyclically, with the held bottom C (and open G) remaining unchanged throughout, providing a treble drone: this creates an effect similar to the dropped tunings favored by folk guitarists (for instance, most famously, D Modal or DADGAD,[15] which, when played open, sounds a Dsus4 chord without the third note). F is the fourth note in the key of C and the chord is voiced, at least initially, without the third (E).[16]

Bragg's voice (like Dylan's) lacks chromatic subtlety. Recall that he came to prominence with his counterhegemonic decision to sing in a markedly against the pop-cultural norm (recognizably East London) accent. In this, he follows the British punk (and mod) vocal attack of John Lydon, Joe Strummer, and Paul Weller with a voice mandated to critique, primed for the delivery of an immediate polemic.

---

[14] The middle 8 proper is introduced to the Bragg structure in "Levi Stubbs" and "Greetings" (both on *Talking With the Taxman about Poetry*, 1986).

[15] See discussion in Harper's *Dazzling Oh anyan*, which quotes Martin Carthy: "When [Davy] invented DADGAD that was the moment life got interesting" (2006, p. 88). See also p. 325.

[16] He advises, in the disc that accompanies *Back to Basics*, that the lower E in "St Swithin's Day" (key of C) "should not be played."

This point cannot be overstated because, in this context, the accent marks the song as indigenous and vernacular (*à la* punk). In rejecting the mid-Atlantic neutral accent normalized in the pop/rock context (because of American pop-cultural hegemony) it also, again surprisingly, connects with the British folk tradition (which is, it should be remembered, both indigenous *and* vernacular). Nic Jones, Briggs, Carthy, Martin Simpson, and June Tabor, when singing indigenous songs, also sing in the vernacular. This phenomenon, I would argue, above everything discussed so far, epitomizes the visceral expression of the folk-punk nexus at the point of emission of the song: the vocal chords of the singer.

Above all, Bragg's songs are influenced by a committed political consciousness which implicitly determines their structure at a deep level. They can be considered "political" (or, more accurately, perhaps, because their response to injustice makes a claim on the listener, "ethical") not principally because they are didactic but rather because the themes of social class and injustice, as mediated by the lyrics' imagery and mode of address, constitute the essence of his songs. To appreciate this, it is plausible to situate Bragg's music in the context of the neorealist (characteristically British), working-class aesthetic that extends from L.S. Lowry and the Pitmen Painters to Alan Sillitoe and the kitchen sink realism of the 1950s and 1960s, and includes Ewan MacColl, and, more recently, The Smiths,[17] Pulp, Mike Leigh, and the art of Richard Billingham and Tracey Emin: "I'm celebrating my love for you with a pint of beer and a new tattoo"; "It's amazing how quick a little rain can clear the streets"; "She was married before she was even entitled to vote"; "between Marx and marzipan in the dictionary there was Mary"; "brutality and the economy are related"; "in the end compassion must be the greatest family value"; "I steal a kiss from you in the supermarket." This post-industrial, realist, working-class aesthetic takes inspiration from the rich history of the labor movement in Britain and can be considered to derive from the same cultural foundation from which the English industrial song emerged (as charted by Lloyd and MacColl). This indigenous culture developed a powerful, inherently oppositional expression, what Weiss describes as the "aesthetics of resistance": a cultural form of life to which struggle is intrinsic, an art form that "makes its task the solution of an oppressive or difficult situation" (2005, p. 110).

Bragg's pragmatic guitar playing is again relevant here. His insistence on the electric guitar deployed in the industrial sense expresses the tacit proposition that art is another means of production, "just as the tools and machines [are]" (Weiss, 2005, p. 308); but it is also a means that has the capacity to express opposition to ideological apparatuses that operate to disempower, exploit, and dominate: for the worker: "culture is lugging, pulling, and lifting, tying together and fastening" (Weiss, 2005, p. 310). But it is not only the lyrical content of Bragg's songs that mine this rich seam of (post-industrial) working-class culture, the melodic

---

[17] It is no accident that Bragg covered Morrissey's most kitchen-sink inspired song, "Jeane." I haven't the space to include the rich culture of antiwar songs in the folk tradition that Bragg's work clearly continues.

structures of his songs are also informed by it. Dave Woodhead's trumpet (as heard in "The Saturday Boy," "The Marriage," "The Home Front," "Valentine's Day is Over") is crucial in this connection. Evoking the colliery brass bands, or the Salvation Army, Bragg's arrangement marks the influence of Robin Dransfield's version of "Spenser the Rover" as well as Martin Carthy's collaboration with trumpeter Howard Evans on *Out of the Cut* (1981), his most polemic recording.[18]

Coal not Dole: The Event of the Miners' Strike

It was when he traveled to the picket lines to support the unionized miners of the British coal industry during the 1984-85 strike that Bragg was compelled to acknowledge the importance of folk and, specifically, the radical dimension of the British tradition for his musical development. "I came to play in the coalfields," he says, "and the folk singers were there before me—they were more radical than me" (Bragg, 2008). If any incident could be identified as responsible for his radicalization, both politically and musically, it was the miners' strike (Bragg, 2008). Obviously, his early songs express an oppositional attitude, but as Ian Peddie observes, it was the strike that "galvanised" this attitude "into action" (2000, p. 2). Bragg performed in Sunderland alongside Scottish singer (and Harraton "Nova Scotia" Colliery deputy) George (Jock) Purdon: "an old geezer with these incredibly powerful songs like 'The Blackleg Miners'." As a result of this formative experience he realized that "we're not the first people to have come across this problem" (Bragg, 2008).

In response to the National Coal Board (NCB)'s announcement of the intention to decommission 20 coalmines across England and Wales with estimated job losses of 20,000, Arthur Scargill, head of the National Mineworkers' Union (NUM), called for nationwide industrial action. On discovering that the call was issued without holding a ballot of members, the Thatcher administration (having identified public sector industries with powerful trade unions as key obstructions to its economic program) deemed the strike "unofficial." Funding was confiscated and armed riot-police battalions were enlisted to escort strikebreakers ("scabs") across picket lines, leading to sporadic outbursts of violence, widespread embitterment, and the renewal of social class divisions in the UK—all of which was premeditated to turn public opinion against the union.[19] Made into ideological scapegoats of economic impediment, as encapsulated in Thatcher's bellicose epithet "the enemy within."[20]

---

[18] Witness, for instance, "Rigs of the Time," "I Sowed Some Seeds," and "Song of the Lower Classes."

[19] Speaking to the secretary for the Miner's Wives Support Group, Bragg realized: "They forced the miners to strike—none of it was chance. It was deliberate Tory policy, like the Falklands War" (in Salewicz, 1989, p. 16).

[20] Following the Falklands conflict, the Conservative Government, then in its second term of office, had instigated an aggressive economic project of the denationalization

Returning from Europe in September, 1984, Bragg went to South Wales and north-east England to support the miners: "I started doing gigs outside of London in the coal fields and found that I was able to articulate what I believed in so that these people that we were doing the benefits for—the miners—didn't think I was just some fashionable pop star from London trying to enhance my career by doing a few fashionable benefits" (quoted in Willhardt, 2006, p. 41).

Collins cites a particular benefit in Sunderland (at Wearmouth pit) where NUM members pressurized Bragg to defend his position on the class struggle, Marxism, and the labor movement—a crucially important "catalyst" in the singer's political education. Indeed he sarcastically credits Thatcher for this: "she made me a socialist" (in Salewicz, 1989, p. 16). Bragg was particularly impressed by the solidarity and activism of the Miner's Wives Support Group, a coalition of the wives, mothers, and sisters of imprisoned miners (in Salewicz, 1989, p. 16).[21] Members would address the audience between acts, and speak, impassioned and fierce, at the picket lines: "This was something," Bragg says, "you couldn't get doing gigs in London" (quoted in Collins, 2002, p. 144).

During the strike the singer came into contact with exponents of the English and Scottish traditions and came to appreciate their common radical left-wing (Lloyd-MacColl) heritage. In this connection, many assume that Bragg first met Leith folk singer Dick Gaughan at the coalfields (Collins, 2002); but Gaughan, to his own regret, was not able to participate in the gigs at the height of the strike due to illness (serious voice problems).[22] In the use of folksong as a vehicle of social

---

of private industry. Historically, the most powerful of the trade unions was the NUM (a previous strike brought down the Heath administration in 1974). In March, 1985, after 51 weeks, multiple imprisonments and 10 fatalities, a delegation of the NUM elected by 98 votes to 91 to end industrial action. The demoralized miners had been returning piecemeal to work from January. By then Thatcher had incapacitated the trade union movement; the hitherto powerful working-class culture in Britain was in decline. Indeed, in the expedient path-clearing for her economic program, an entire form of life was eradicated. Now, some 25 years later, "many don't know," Tom Nairn writes, "or have forgotten, how badly traditional mining communities suffered from the closing of the pits, and the move to neoliberalism" (2009, p. 29).

[21]   Weiss acknowledges the importance of the participation of women in the history of political activism: "Women, in fact, always played an important role in the resistance movement; this is why Lotte Bischoff [German activist] was so important to me ..." (2005, p. 117). A visit to the People's History Museum in Manchester will also evince the centrality of women to the labor movement in the UK.

[22]   According to Gaughan's comprehensive website: www.dickgaughan.co.uk; he did some benefit work but was mainly confined to Edinburgh. His voice had recovered by early 1985 sufficiently to play live again (*Live in Edinburgh* [1985]) at the end of the strike (at which time—January, February—thousands of strikers had returned to work). Bragg and Gaughan, although aware of each other's work, first met in Berlin in 1986 (clarified by email; Bragg, 2010), although according to Salewicz (1989, p. 17), he billed (and may have briefly met) with Gaughan in Edinburgh in 1985.

activism,[23] Gaughan is exemplary and has had a profound formative influence on Bragg. He would have been familiar with Gaughan's splenetic interpretation of Leon Rosselson's ballad "The World Turned Upside Down"—narrating the defeat of the Essex Commune Diggers' Rebellion of 1649—from his 1981 album *Handful of Earth*; he would also have heard Rosselson himself sing it (with Roy Bailey) at the benefits (and earlier that year at the Labour Party's Euro-election gig at the Free Trade Hall in Manchester). Bragg's version of Rosselson's song, as unique as Gaughan's but clearly influenced by his rendition, appears on the *Between the Wars* EP (1985).[24] When I inquired about this influence, Bragg replied: "The difference between me and Dick Gaughan is that Dick never saw The Clash—that's all it is. Apart from that, we're more or less the same" (Bragg, 2008). Indeed, the entire argument is condensed in this statement and is audible in Bragg's folk-punk rendition of "World Turned Upside Down."

"*Between the Wars* was my signal," Bragg recalls, "for those people who had ears to hear, that I recognized the tradition and that I was willing to be accommodated by it" (Bragg, 2008). The four-track EP was released in March, 1985, just after the cessation of industrial action. Dedicated to the Miners' Wives Support Group, it remains Bragg's most trenchant political statement; it also constitutes his first structured response to a violation of human rights he witnessed at first hand. At the time Andy Kershaw suggested that "*Into Battle with the Art of Song*" would have been a title more appropriate to its uncompromising activist status (Collins, 2002, p. 12).[25]

Surprisingly the EP includes two cover versions and an alternative interpretation of one of his previously-recorded songs. However, he has subjected these tracks to the utilitarian treatment of his freshly-forged industrial folk-punk form. These songs, as a result, assume an unexpected yet deeply affecting resonance in the aftermath of the miners' strike. Reinforcing the idea that the significance of

---

[23] In 1986 Gaughan released an album of Scottish mining songs in memoriam of the strike. His intention was to record "as representative a selection ... of songs which come from or are about the Scottish mining communities" (Gaughan, 1986). *True and Bold* is dedicated to "the value of [the miners'] work for the rest of us" as well as to the "spirit of working class solidarity" (1986). Among traditional (Lloyd-sourced) songs like "Collier Laddie" and the "Blantyre Explosion," it also includes songs by Jock Purdon and Ed Pickford's "Pound a Week Rise." A version of Florence Reece's "Which Side Are You On?" is credited to Gaughan on the album. Bragg's own reworking of Reece's song appeared on his *Between the Wars* EP in 1985 (i.e., a year before Gaughan's album was released). However, Gaughan did perform his version at MacColl's seventieth birthday gig in the Royal Festival Hall in January, 1985 and it is also recorded on *Live in Edinburgh* (1985).

[24] Bragg recorded a Gaughan composition, "Think Again," on the B-side of "Greetings to the New Brunette" (with a live version on the *Live and Dubious* EP).

[25] A scene of children at lunch on the sleeve provided a critical commentary on defense spending by way of reference to a Tory MP Bragg witnessed expressing his views in a television debate during the Cold War: "What good are free school dinners if they are being fed to our children by Russian paratroopers?" (Collins, 2002, p. 142).

the folk song is determined by the moment of its singing, Bragg's industrialization of "World Turned Upside Down" effects a particularly disturbing parallax: for did they not, in 1984, "send the hired men and troopers to wipe out the [miners'] claim"? Were the working class not the new "dispossessed," divested of rights by free market deregulation and systematic union disempowerment? And, in 1985, after the defeat of the miners, only "the vision lingers on."

"The vision," according to Peddie (2000, p. 5), refers to "the tradition of organized resistance endemic to the labour struggle." He quotes Bragg: "the importance of tradition to the labour movement can't be underestimated" (in Peddie, 2000, p. 5) because it is in the collective memory that the vision remains. Interestingly, the most militant track on Bragg's EP, and the only one considered to make unambiguous reference to the strike, is an adaptation of Florence Reece's "Which Side Are You On?" a pro-union solidarity anthem originally composed in support of the Harlan County (Kentucky) miners' strike of 1931:[26] "We set off to join the picket line/ And together we cannot fail./ We got stopped by police at the county line/ They said go home boys or you'll go into jail." Also Bragg's reworking of "It Says Here" (from *Brewing Up*), in the company of the other tracks on the EP, becomes a satirical critique of the media's complicit role in the scapegoating of the miners during the strike: "It says here that the unions will never learn ... It says here that we should be proud that we are free/ And our free press reflects our democracy."

In the face of Thatcher's project of de-industrialization and the aggressive valorization of private-for-profit free-market fundamentalism, Bragg's product, as an archival document, marks the passing of the industrial labor movement and the termination of the politics of class consciousness. Like "society" in 1985, class supposedly now no longer exists: something new (the vacuous crisis of identity) has emerged from the political fallout. Moreover, the 1984-85 strike represents, perhaps ironically, the greatest disaster in mining history: the final disempowerment of the trade union movement and the collapse of that social unanimity that hitherto consolidated communities in a common consciousness of class identity and cultural purpose. "What was it all for?" (as Bragg sings in "St Swithin's Day").

During its year-long deadlock, the miners' strike became more than an industrial dispute; it became, to quote Tom Nairn, a *war*: "Something vital was at stake and then lost in the defeat" (2009, p. 29). In the spring of 1985, following the violent suppression of the picketing miners, it became clear that the stakes of this conflict were the future of socialism and, ultimately, the destiny of the working class. The strike therefore stands as a critical moment in the decline of the European labor

---

[26]   Reece (1900-1986) was the wife of a United Mine Workers' Union organizer. During the 1931 dispute with mine owners, her family was intimidated by company-hired men. After one episode in which Florence and children were terrorized by deputies who entered their house illegally, she wrote "Which Side Are You On?" and set it to the melody of a Baptist Hymn, "Lay the Lily Low."

movement (which cleared a path for the unregulated ascendance of neoliberalism and financial capitalism). So, what it was for was the powerful indigenous working-class culture, the aesthetics of resistance, which was subsequently lost in the defeat.

The Iron Muse and the Aesthetics of Resistance: Industrial Folk Song in Britain

Distinguished by its occupational hazards and hard labor, noted for conflict between unionized workers and industrialists, and associated with "Disasters, death and diseases like pneumoconiosis," the British coal mining industry, in the words of Melvyn Bragg, "makes for a bitter heritage" (2009). Yet despite this legacy, the industry produced one of the richest sources of social expression in indigenous music. Credit for reclaiming and publicizing this cultural heritage is due to the research of the postwar ethnomusicologist A.L. Lloyd. One of the key motivators of the second folk revival, Lloyd first officially acknowledged the "industrial folk song" as an important part of British culture with the publication of two seminal song anthologies in 1952: *Come All Ye Bold Miners* and *Coaldust Ballads*.

Contrary to the prevailing conviction that folk culture was bucolic in essence, Lloyd's research confirmed that "the urban proletariat was active in creating its own folk songs" and, in fact, revealed that "the actual creation of folk song survived better in the mining and mill areas than in the rural districts" (1967, p. 30). He discovered that "far from being destroyed by the industrial revolution," this kind of social expression "was actually created by its conditions" (1967, p. 298). As a committed Marxist Lloyd was sensitized to the sociological dialectic of cultural production (1967, p. 315); and the industrial folk song preserves the expression of a group that although disenfranchised by the Industrial Revolution was yet crystallized, especially through the union movement, by a steadfast solidarity, common purpose, and sense of social community. Such a culture constituted for Lloyd a powerful conduit to a sociopolitical reality which he sought to elaborate by focusing on vernacular songs specifically about labor in the industrial era (Morrish, 2007, p. 29).

He characterized the industrial tradition as "made by workers themselves directly out of their own experiences, expressing their own interests and aspirations, and incidentally passed on among themselves mainly by oral means." However, he adds significantly (and militantly), "this is no *sine qua non*" (Lloyd, 1967, p. 298). He argues indeed that the industrial songs, many of which were composed by known authors, were "far more collective in expression than the more anonymous rural songs that preceded them" not because they are passed on by word of mouth but rather because "social cohesion is their great motive and method" (1967, p. 321).

Because they have not undergone the process of refinement characteristic of the anonymous songs, Howes claims that Lloyd was forced to admit that the industrial song was "artistically" inferior. Howes misses Lloyd's point. Aesthetics, he clearly states, is not judged in the conventional (artistic) manner here; for it is rather the "crudity" of the industrial song that is essential to its mode of expression; and it is a category error to consider this an aesthetic defect. Rather it ought to be recognized instead as its deepest (aesthetic) value: "insofar as the voice that speaks in them is of work and joy and disaster and struggle is the hoarse, hard-bitten voice of the miner himself" (Lloyd, 1952, p. 11). In assessing the significance of the genre, rather than focusing on the Lomaxian issue of authenticity, Lloyd changes the focus of attention from the song (like MacColl) to the singer and applies a simple methodological hypothesis: "who uses the song and for what purpose"? It is the *worker* who uses it to "express solidarity with work-mates" (Lloyd, 1967, p. 310). Above all the industrial song possesses a pragmatic function: to express collective experience of the social conditions of labor and to communicate specific injustice with the intention to raise consciousness and influence workers to unite in resistance; the meaning of many songs is simply that "something be done to set wrongs right" (1967, p. 304). Lloyd continues: "The singers' first aim was to describe the hard condition of life in their own locality, the exploitation and disasters, the strikes and lock-outs affecting their relatively small community, and to explain and criticize the reasons to their comrades in the clearest, most digestible way" (1967, p. 320). Despite his unfair reputation as a conservative traditionalist, Lloyd unequivocally supported the composition of original material in the idiom. For instance the introduction to *Come All Ye Bold Miners* explicitly expresses hope that this collection will encourage readers to compose songs based on their own work experience. "Here then are the pit-songs of the past," he says, "We await the pit-songs of the future" (Lloyd, 1952, p. 17). And in *Folk Song in England* there is a prolonged discussion of the "synthesis of professional and traditional folk culture" in the post-oral industrial period by way of the individually created authored lyric (especially notable in the labor ballads of the working class).[27]

Five years before the publication of *Folk Song in England*, Louis Killen and Johnny Handle recorded (with Colin Ross) three EPs of Northumberland-Durham coalfield ballads for Topic: *The Colliers' Rant*, *Northumbrian Garland*, and *Stottin Doon the Waall*. These were later assembled on a compilation, *Along the Coaly Tyne*

---

[27]   Apart from MacColl's compositions ("Springhill Mining Disaster"), of the new contributions two stand out: Frank Higgins's "Testimony of Patience Kershaw (Child Miner)" (1969) and Rosselson's "Palaces of Gold"—a response to the Aberfan disaster of 1966, in which 144 people were killed (including 116 schoolchildren) when a slagheap collapsed on a village in South Wales. Carthy sings this song on *Crown of Horn*. The lyrics of Higgins's song derive from historical documentation: the Children's Employment Commission (1842). One document—referred to, incidentally, in Lloyd's *Folk Song in England*—contains a statement from an underage mineworker taken by the Ashley Mines Committee: "The bald place upon my head is made by thrusting the corves" (Lloyd, 1967, p. 327).

in 1968.[28] In 1967, the Ian Campbell Folk Group recorded an album of pit-songs for Transatlantic based on Lloyd's research (*Coaldust Ballads*) which included the songs "The Blantyre Explosion," "The Sandgate Dandle," and "Collier Laddie," and two industrial songs written by MacColl in the pitmatic idiom, "The Plodder Seam" and "Come All Ye Gallant Colliers."[29]

It is in this context that Billy Bragg's relationship to the tradition should be thematized. Enabling us to position his music within the British folk movement, it also provides for its key political dimension. His song "Between the Wars" begins with the declaration: "I was a miner" which immediately situates the song in the environment of the industrial ballad.[30] Its proper site, in other words, is among the songs collected by Lloyd which in his estimation are "close to the heart of the common people" and therefore not intended "to decorate life, as to make it bearable" (Lloyd, 1952, p. 11).

It would be mistaken, therefore, to consider "Between the Wars" an unequivocal celebration of labor. For, as Weiss observes, the glorifying of "honest" industry conceals the truth that work in capitalist economies is sold at the lowest wage for the highest profit. Trade unions were organized in the first instance to limit and regulate (by mass withdrawal of labor if necessary) the injustices perpetuated and standardized by this system and to establish a charter of rights that would protect the worker from exploitation. In this context, "The praise of labor" can be nothing but "a praise of subordination" (Weiss, 2005, p. 311). Bragg's song, however, realistically acknowledges the workers' position: "But they [the Government] brought prosperity down at the armoury," he sings and ironically adds, "we're arming for peace me boys, between the wars." Bragg has always avoided romanticizing labor as heroic (something probably learned from MacColl). In the *Aesthetics of Resistance* Weiss details how the workers between the wars "devoted their concentrated energy to manufacturing the iron blocks, which became rails, gun mounts, cannon." He continues, in a sentence that supports the sentiments expressed in "Between the Wars" that they were busy reconstituting "their peacefulness into a force that would turn against them ..." (Bragg, 2005, p. 311).

What needs to be emphasized here is that Bragg's response is structured by the way in which his mode of expression, both musically and rhetorically, draws on that rich and bitter heritage referred to by Melvyn Bragg and culturally delineated

---

[28] It includes "The Trimdon Grange Explosion," by Thomas Armstrong (1848-1919), the "Tanfield Colliery poet," following the Co. Durham colliery gas explosion in 1882 in which 74 miners died (Lloyd, 1967, p. 338).

[29] It featured another famous Durham song (also recorded by Killen), "Blackleg Miners," a "fierce" trade union song that dates back to the establishment of the NUM (Lloyd, 1952, p. 136).

[30] Three other trades are inventoried in "Between the Wars" in the mode of ballads like "The Dalesman's Litany": "I was a docker," he states, "I was a railwayman ... I raised a family in time of austerity with sweat at the foundry." These trades had the most famous and biggest unions (their banners can be viewed in the People's History Museum).

by Lloyd, and mediated through the folk tradition by MacColl, Killen, Handle, Rosselson, and Gaughan. In other words, Bragg identified within the British industrial folk tradition the appropriate cultural framework for commenting on and condemning contemporary instances of injustice. He achieved this mediation by forging a new sociopolitical genre from the traditional ore of the English folk song but tempered in what John Harris refers to as "the righteous fire of punk rock" (2004, p. 4). Indeed it is revealing that Bragg should have focused on this epoch, as Lloyd claims it was the very time when the industrial song went into decline in Britain: and here, conditions have conspired for its unexpected post-punk renaissance.

"I kept the faith" the second verse of "Between the Wars" begins, "and I kept voting." Yet the faith referred to here is qualified a little later as a political fidelity (faith, Bragg insists, in my fellow men) and hence it expresses the socialist convictions that have eclipsed former religious beliefs. The entire product expresses disillusion with state institutions, not just with the political economy, but also with organized religion and suggests a search for a new project of secular faith in society. "Between the Wars" therefore subtly draws the consequences of the defiant attitude of "World Turned Upside Down": "We will not worship the god you serve/ The god of greed who feeds the rich while poor men starve." Disillusioned with a political system that seems only to breed cynicism and resignation, the song expresses a fidelity that transcends local injustice: despite the adversity and disillusionment, in which even the gods turn against the faithful, it is nevertheless necessary to *keep faith*. As the refrain is iterated for the last time the final descending motif from C to G is left to ring on elliptically into darkness and silence: *we are between the wars* ....[31]

On March 21, 1985 Bragg made his debut appearance on UK chart program *Top of the Pops*. Against programming policy he insisted on playing "Between the Wars" live and the resultant performance remains a decisive moment for the dialectic of aesthetics and politics. Those who saw witnessed, for the first time ever perhaps, musical opposition to the political status quo enacted on a commercial, music industry-endorsed chart show. Considering the events that transpired in Bragg's appearance, remembering, for instance, that communities in the north of England, South Wales, and Scotland had been eliminated over the course of the previous cold black year, this performance rang out a shrill wake-up call. Being compelled to acknowledge their individual contribution to the ideology that added up to public opinion's ostracizing of the miners, the audience could not have witnessed this show without shame. Even if the miners and the NUM were defeated and the Tories were in the ascendant, and a victorious

---

[31]   A close connection with Ewan MacColl's song, "The Ballad of Accounting," composed for a BBC radio series *Landmarks*, is evident. Gaughan recorded a version of MacColl's song on *Kist O' Gold* (1976): "We hardly saw the crossroads and small attention gave to the landmarks on the journey from cradle to grave." The final verse closes with the question: "Did you reach some understanding of your fellow men?"

Thatcher was ushering in her "no-society" New England dressed up in the Tories' myth-of-progress, the singer stands, alone, pointing out, "we are *between the wars*." In the end, the performance of this new radical "folk-song-with-teeth" epitomizes everything Bragg stands for, namely, the search, to use Lloyd's words, "for some less transitory satisfaction than is offered by the masters of mass entertainment" (1967, p. 371).[32]

Bragg's performance on *Top of the Pops* in 1985 remains a subversive and inspiring event. Indeed, I would go further, and suggest that this performance constitutes an "event"—in the sense given to this concept by French philosopher Alain Badiou (1999, 2005a). His appearance (pale, skinny, short cropped hair, grey Fred Perry shirt, and Dr. Martens boots under turned-up Levi's) eventuated in the activation of everything the song represents: an expression of solidarity with the working class, a public commitment to the principles of socialism in the wake of the miners' defeat, promotion of resistance to every value espoused by Thatcher; Bragg's provocation to an amnesiac audience is to face up to political reality, acknowledge the violation of human rights that had occurred in the UK (during an edifying show of humanitarian concern for others inspired by Geldof's Band Aid),[33] and react to it. To be precise, Bragg's *Top of the Pops* appearance is not the *événement* per se; strictly speaking, it represents the enactment of what Badiou calls "*fidelity* to the event" (1999). *This* is what Bragg *uses* his song for; this is its purpose: to reaffirm everything that the miners' strike, as an *event*, stands for (i.e., commitment to socialism in a sociohistorical environment that has never been more hostile to it).

The meaning of the event, Badiou insists, is "determined only by the activity of those faithful to it" (1999, p. 81). Although it is easy for those in power to (mis-) quote historical failures to abrogate responsibility and promote agendas, what is impossible to do is completely erase the traces of the event (for we can always quote back *ideas worth fighting for*). Despite the best efforts to spin a hermetic consensual hegemony, the vision associated with the event, and the ethic linked to this lingering vision, can never be suppressed.

Indeed, the success or failure of actual historical events may not be, in itself, politically important. According to Badiou, some of the most significant events for political change were conspicuous failures (the 1916 Easter Rising in Ireland for instance). Rather, the criterion of success is how the people inspired by the event commit themselves to its political legacy, regardless of its *actual* outcome; those who, responding to the promise of the event, dedicate their lives to realizing its "unfinished project." Because its traces continue to reverberate in social consciousness, the event cannot be completely extinguished; it always preserves

---

[32] Of course we could have used Bragg's own words which uncannily parallel Lloyd's when he sings of "Seeking some more relevance than spotlight and applause" (Bragg, 1985).

[33] Taking attention away from the miners' strike; but also distracting from the claims of political prisoners in the Maze Prison (Northern Ireland) in the wake of the high-profile death of Nationalist hunger-striker Bobby Sands.

the power to reignite the flame of resistance in the conscience of later generations. Yes, perhaps "Nothing is gained by remaining in the trenches of 1984," yet we only gain control of the disputed territory if the "experiences and memories" are faithfully held and retrieved for the education of the coming generations (Routledge in Nairn, 2009).

In light of this, Bragg's recent song "I Keep Faith" makes a significant political statement. Revisiting the exact lyric from "Between the Wars," commitment to socialism, as a response to injustice and the violation of human rights, as first expressed in that appearance on *Top of the Pops* in 1985, is reaffirmed. It has, once again, become politically decisive to express fidelity to the event. Yet again, 25 years after the strike, historical conditions have come to pass wherein the "tradition of the oppressed," as Marxist critical theorist Walter Benjamin writes, "teaches us that the 'state of emergency' in which we live is not the exception but the rule." Benjamin's claim rings, like a fire alarm, yet again, eerily true (Löwy, 2005, p. 392). In an ideologically confused and politically bankrupt epoch, when received wisdom suggests that "capitalism is indestructible"[34] (despite overwhelming evidence to the contrary), and social justice and the democratic mandate are again contemptuously disregarded in the aggressive protection of toxic financial institutions, with unions demonized (or bought off) amid calls for the illegalization of industrial action,[35] Bragg's act of fidelity to the event, "I Keep Faith," could not more precisely mark the reiteration of this political and, I would also argue, ethical commitment to socialism, or what I have been calling, after Weiss, the "aesthetics of resistance." The kind of secular faith Bragg emphasizes in this song is precisely that fidelity to the event that he has, to his immense credit, sustained even through the several disappointments of left-wing politics and the labor movement in the recent past: from the defeat of the miners to the loss of the 1987 election, from the disintegration of Red Wedge to the fall of communism and the rise of far-right nationalism to the ultimate failure: New Labour's capitulation to Thatcherite neoliberalism and its betrayal of the principles of democratic socialism.[36] "'I Keep Faith' is the key song in the set," Bragg claims. "I'm now explicitly asking the audience to engage: I give it [responsibility] to the audience, I connect with them, I empower them. Yet the lyrics of 'I Keep Faith' also mean that it could be a love song ... it's about the very thing that keeps me doing this ... my faith in the audience. It's an effort to personalise the struggle by saying look y'know, it's only our own cynicism that stops us from making our politicians

---

[34]   This, believe it or not, is from "Resistance is Surrender" (Žižek, 2007), illustrating, I suppose, Althusser's thesis that ideology is impossible to resist.

[35]   In Ireland, as I write, there have been suggestions from government ministers and industry officials for rewriting of public sector contracts that would make strike action illegal.

[36]   "It was Tony Blair," Žižek argues, "who was able to institutionalise it ... Thatcher wasn't a Thatcherite, she was merely herself; it was Blair (more than Major) who truly gave form to Thatcherism" (2007).

accountable ... that's why they get away with this shit" (Bragg, 2008). Prior to headlining a gig organized by Hope not Hate (a group opposed to the far-right British National Party) in central London, he says: "tonight the way I'm going to introduce ['I Keep Faith'], it will be about us as a group of anti-fascists keeping faith in the people of Barking [Bragg's home town in Essex] and Dagenham and not dismissing them just because the BNP are targeting them" (Bragg, 2010, p. 17).

It is this expression of faith, representing as it does the gesture of fidelity to the original event that is, I believe, ultimately of political significance in this context: "I know it takes a mess of courage to go against the grain," Bragg sings, "I know it takes great sacrifice for so little gain" (2008).

I don't know if Bragg had Thesis VII of Benjamin's "On the Concept of History" in mind when composing "I Keep Faith," but this text proposes that the historical materialist should endeavor to document history "against the grain" (*gegen der Strich*) (1975, p. 248). "To brush cultural history *gegen der Strich*," Michael Löwy comments, suggests viewing "it from the standpoint of the defeated, the pariahs" (Löwy, 2005, p. 55). It is politically necessary to repossess the tradition in this political and economic environment, for it is in danger of becoming "a tool of the ruling classes" (Benjamin, 1975, p. 247). As Benjamin cautioned, it is the responsibility of "every era" to renew "the attempt ... to wrest tradition away from a conformism that is about to overpower it" (quoted in Buck-Morss, 2002, p. 247).

Billy Bragg's music, in its unique development of a form through which the punk attitude has facilitated the revitalization of the British folk tradition, has managed to make the passing on of tradition into a radical act, and has succeeded, to that extent, in wresting tradition away from the powers of conformity.

A vision of the singer, spot-lit and framed by the dark auditorium is hereby invoked, black and white, like the photograph credited to Jayne Creamer on the inside sleeve of *Back to Basics*: this "dialectical image" precipitates a memory that flashes up and must be grasped before it disappears (Benjamin, 1975, p. 247). The task of the materialist historian is to seize upon such configurations in which an event from the past becomes relevant to the present. In them the revolutionary chance to retrieve the oppressed past lives: the potential to change *not the present* but the *future* (Benjamin, 1975, p. 254). And the image of the event flickers again. And with it is expressed, at one and the same time, and for the reasons examined above, a continuing fidelity to the event of the miners' strike, that historical moment in which social conditions conspired to enable Bragg to consolidate his political commitment to socialism and, at the same time, mark his cultural initiation into the British folk tradition in a way that could be reconciled with his radical punk attitude, finally leading to the development of a unique framework through which to express social activism in musical form.

Chapter 2

"Know Your Rights": Punk Rock, Globalization, and Human Rights

Kevin C. Dunn

In 1977, punk rock emerged as a major disruptive force within both the established music scene and the larger capitalist societies of the industrial West. This chapter explores the contours and content of punk's subsequent engagement with discourses of human rights. The core argument is that punk provides individuals, groups, and communities with resources through which they can articulate and actualize a localized understanding of human rights. As a cultural field, punk tends to have three core elements: an anti-status quo disposition, a pronounced do-it-yourself ethos, and a desire for disalienation (resistance to the multiple forms of alienation in modern society). While punk cannot be reduced to one specific political agenda, these three elements provide actors with significant tools for possible political interventions and actions. The first section of the chapter discusses the evolution of punk as a musical and cultural field, emphasizing the ways in which punk is both a means of global communication and a counterhegemonic message in its own right. The rest of the chapter focuses on four different British and American punk bands to illustrate the diversity of understandings about human rights. The first case looks at The Clash, one of the original British punk bands. The second band, Crass, was a British anarchist punk band that was both inspired by and a reaction to liberal bands like The Clash. In both cases, The Clash and Crass produced an articulation of human rights that was informed by their own social and cultural context of the late 1970s/early 1980s. The chapter then turns to two bands with roots in the Washington, DC punk scene of the 1980s, Bad Brains and Bikini Kill. The former articulated an understanding of universal human rights rooted in a spiritual worldview informed by Rastafarianism, while the latter was deeply involved in the feminist Riot Grrrl movement of the early 1990s. These four cases provide examples of the various ways actors have employed elements of global punk to produce their own discourses on human rights, informed by their local context and struggles.

Most conversations about human rights are centered around the three "generations" of rights: 1) broadly political, such as freedom of speech, assembly, and so forth; 2) economic and social; and 3) rights of the people. While rights can be understood as claims, liberties, powers, and immunities, there are tensions about where they originate. They tend to be framed as either "natural rights," reflecting universal moral values, or "charter of rights," particularist notions based on positive law. The standard liberal position combines both universal and particularist thinking, making it somewhat of a mish-mash of ideas perched on a shaky conceptual foundation. At the same time, claims to "universalism" are often challenged for masking partial interpretations prone to intolerance. As this chapter will illustrate, punk bands have engaged with all three generations of human rights and tend to reflect a diversity of opinions regarding how those rights should be framed. There is not one given "punk perspective" on human rights. Rather, the main argument here is that punk provides actors and communities with musical and cultural resources that can be employed in local political struggles around how rights should be understood and realized.

Punk as a Global Phenomenon

The term "punk rock" first emerged regularly in accepted terminology in the late 1970s with regard to the music scene in New York City's Lower East Side, which included bands such as the Ramones, Television, Blondie, Richard Hell and the Voidoids, and others. But punk music and style gained international attention largely through the emergence of a scene in the UK, particularly in London, and specifically around the well-publicized antics of the Sex Pistols (Savage, 1991). Heavily conditioned by class politics and working-class culture, the original British punk scene both reflected and mocked the disintegration of British society in the late 1970s. Led by bands such as the Sex Pistols, The Clash, The Slits, the Buzzcocks, X-Ray Spex, The Raincoats, Gang of Four, the Mekons, and The Damned, British punks tended to view established social conventions as hypocritical obfuscations obscuring the brutality of real life. The punk culture that emerged out of Britain and New York quickly spread and evolved, and major punk scenes were created in cities and small towns across the globe, from Mexico and South America to Africa, the Middle East, and Asia. Greil Marcus argued that punk provided "a surge of new voices unprecedented in the geopolitics of popular culture—a surge of voices that, for a time, made a weird phrase like 'the geopolitics of popular culture' seem like a natural fact" (1989, p. 65).

From its inception, punk sought to challenge and reject the world as it is. For many, this critical opposition to the status quo is a defining element of punk. As Guy Picciotto of the seminal Washington, DC band Fugazi observed: "The whole concept of punk was something that was against whatever seemed normal or whatever seemed kind of handed down. To me the basic tenets of punk have always been: no set of rules, no set of expectations, and that it always challenges the status quo" (personal interview with author, March 30, 2007). Pat Thetic of the Pittsburgh punk band Anti-Flag notes "Punk rock is about fighting against the status quo and trying to find other ways of seeing the world that are more productive and less destructive to people" (personal interview with author, May 12, 2005). Dedicated to the process of disalienation, punk emerged in a late 1970s social context in which the youth in numerous Western industrialized countries struggled with feelings of alienation from the social, economic, and political forces around them. For many, punk offered powerful resources for participation and access in the face of the alienation that is cultivated by the dominant culture (Davies, 2005, p. 126).

Disalienation and anti-establishment thought have resulted in the privileging of a do-it-yourself (DIY) attitude in punk. The DIY ethos reflects an intentional transformation of punks from consumers of the mass media to agents of cultural production. As Legs McNeil wrote in his low-budget, self-produced fanzine *Punk*: "Punk rock—any kid can pick up a guitar and become a rock 'n' roll star, despite or because of his lack of ability, talent, intelligence, limitations and/or potential, and usually do so out of frustration, hostility, a lot of nerve and a need for ego fulfilment" (quoted in Leblanc, 1999, p. 35). An example of the DIY ethos is represented in a well-known, widely circulated drawing of how to play three chords on a guitar, accompanied by the caption "Now Form a Band." Zines carried similar messages, informing readers how to play chords, make a record, distribute that record, and book their own shows. *Punk Planet* magazine carried a special section in which contributors offered their own DIY input, and the magazine *MaximumRockNRoll* created a resource guide to the global punk scene called "Book Your Own Fucking Life," which is online at http://www.byofl.org. Daniel Sinker, founder of the magazine *Punk Planet*, points out that "Punk said that *anyone* could take part—in fact, anyone *should* take part" (2001, p. 9; original emphasis). He continues, "Punk has always been about asking 'why' and then doing something about it. It's about picking up a guitar and asking 'Why can't I play this?' It's about picking up a typewriter and asking, 'Why don't my opinions count?' It's about looking at the world around you and asking, 'Why are things as fucked up as they are?' And then it's about looking inwards at yourself and asking 'Why aren't I doing anything about this?'" (Sinker, 2001, p. 10).

It is not my contention that these three elements are exclusive to punk. Indeed, over its three decades of existence, punk has been influenced by a wide array of other genres, some of which have also been typified by a tradition of musical resistance and a DIY ethos (e.g., folk music, reggae, hip-hop), while others have provided outlets for anger of a more apolitical bent (e.g., some forms of heavy metal). My point here is to suggest that punk provides individuals with resources for agency and political expression where other musical genres and cultural fields may only passively communicate dissent (see Dunn, 2008). This is evident in the following exploration of human rights discourses across four different punk bands.

Punk and Human Rights: Four Snapshots

The Clash: "These Are Your Rights!"

The Clash established themselves as a politically astute and socially conscious band, distinguishing themselves from other early punk bands that were (often mistakenly) characterized as nihilistic and apolitical, to become regarded as one of the most influential bands of the UK punk scene. The band was formed in London in mid-1976 when singer/guitarist Joe Strummer joined the London SS, a group composed of Mick Jones (guitar/vocals), Paul Simonon (bass), and Terry Chimes (drums). Changing its name to The Clash, the band landed a spot opening for the Sex Pistols on a few UK dates, leading to a record deal with CBS in early 1977. The Clash combined their critical, leftist political commentary with an optimistic idealism. While the Sex Pistols may have been content to destroy the status quo, The Clash sought to lay the groundwork for a new order built on equity and social justice. With the 1979 release of their third and most critically acclaimed album, *London Calling*, the band had pushed punk in numerous different musical directions, from rockabilly to ska to reggae. After several more releases and some personnel disputes, the band broke up in early 1986. But their impact was phenomenal, helping to shape the sounds of Western rock, not only punk but its various distant musical cousins (such as ska, rockabilly, and alt.country) as well. The Clash were also one of the most successfully exported UK punk bands, impacting musical scenes from Jamaica to Japan.

In their engagement with political issues, The Clash regularly employed a cosmopolitan understanding of human rights, while heavily framing that around the socioeconomic context of late 1970s Britain. Faced with collapsing welfare and social structures and the rise of Thatcher's free-market economic policies, The Clash's discourse on human rights had a pronounced socialist flavor, with a defense of the welfare system. Central to the discourse was a critique of the capitalist system. For The Clash, discussions of human rights centered primarily on the rights of humans to get access to basic human needs, like food, clothing, and shelter (see "Clampdown," "Broadway"). This distinctly liberal conception of human rights is best reflected in the sarcastic lyrics of "Know Your Rights" from their 1982 album *Combat Rock*: "Know your rights, all 3 of them! Number 1: You have the right not to be killed. Murder is a CRIME! Unless it was done by a policeman or aristocrat. Number 2: You have the right to food money, providing of course you don't mind a little humiliation, investigation and, if you cross your fingers, rehabilitation. Number 3: You have the right to free speech as long as you're not dumb enough to actually try it."

What often made The Clash distinct from many of their punk contemporaries was their global sensibility. Their awareness of Third World political and economic issues partly stemmed from the influence that reggae and other immigrant music was having on their own musical evolution. But it was also informed from an awareness of problems facing the immigrant community in the UK. The Clash famously played an early show at the 1978 Rock Against Racism concert and continued to be active in antiracist causes, and they often sang about global, non-UK issues (see "Spanish Bombs," "Washington Bullets," "Rock the Casbah"), providing commentary for contemporary Third World developments. The Clash made explicit reference to human rights in their critique of US involvement in Central America on the song "Washington Bullets," on 1980's *Sandinista!* album, name checking Víctor Jara, the Sandinistas, and then-President Jimmy Carter's rhetorical promotion of human rights.

The final theme in their articulation of human rights was a critique of the structural violence inflicted on the population by a repressive police state and the fear of nuclear war made real by the presence of US military and weaponry in the UK. The Clash repeatedly spoke out against police violence and brutality, as well as the ravages of modern war (see "The Call Up," "Stop the World," "Straight to Hell"). Often these discussions were framed explicitly by assumptions that people have the right to be protected from the various forms of structural violence inflicted by the state, whether it be police violence or warfare. Ironically, their response to these structural threats tended to be a call for greater government intervention and responsibility, reflecting a continued commitment to liberalism (see D'Ambrosio, 2004).

Crass: "White Punks on Hope"

Partly inspired by The Clash and similar bands, Crass helped foster the anarcho-punk movement in the UK. Rejecting what they regarded as the "selling out" of the initial punk movement, Crass and like-minded bands sought to live their lives closer to an idealized punk ethos. In many ways, however, Crass was a rejection of The Clash as much as they were inspired by them. The seeds of the band were planted when members of the Dial House collective went to see The Clash in Chelmsford on May 29, 1977. The members of the commune were electrified by the energy and potential they saw in The Clash and in punk in general (Berger, 2006, pp. 75-80). But Penny Rimbaud, who in many ways became the heart of Crass, was conflicted: "I thought The Clash were very exciting, but when I started looking at what they were doing, I couldn't continue my interest. It was another piece of pantomime" (quoted in Berger, 2006, p. 76). As they mockingly sang on "White Punks on Hope," a blatant swipe at The Clash's "White Riot": "Black man's got his problems and his way to deal with it,/ so don't fool yourself you're helping with your white liberal shit./ If you care to take a closer look at the way things really stand,/ You'd see we're all just niggers to the rulers of this land. For Crass, the DIY, disalienation, and anti-status quo elements of punk were not just topics for songs, but a template for how one should live. As Crass wrote in the liner notes for their album *Best Before*:

> When, in 1976, punk first spewed itself across the nation's headlines with the message "do it yourself", we, who in various ways and for many years had been doing just that, naively believed that Messrs. Rotten, Strummer etc. etc. meant it. … By now we had realised that our fellow punks, The Pistols, The Clash and all the other muso-puppets weren't doing it at all. They may like to think that they ripped off the majors, but it was Joe Public who'd been ripped. They helped no one but themselves, started another facile fashion, brought a new lease of life to London's trendy Kings Road and claimed they'd started a revolution. Same old

story. We were on our own again. ... we determined to make it our mission to create a real alternative to music biz exploitation, we wanted to offer something that gave rather than took and, above all, we wanted to make it survive. Too many promises have been made from stages only to be forgotten on the streets.

While never achieving—or seeking—the commercial success enjoyed by The Clash, Crass had a significant impact on the creation of a global anarcho-punk movement (Glasper, 2006). As they note,

The true effect of our work is not to be found within the confines of rock'n'roll, but in the radicalised minds of thousands of people throughout the world. From the Gates of Greenham to the Berlin Wall, from the Stop The City actions to underground gigs in Poland, our particular brand of anarcho-pacifism, now almost synonymous with punk, has made itself known. (liner notes, *Best Before*)

Given their philosophical roots, it is not surprising that Crass's articulation of human rights reflected this anarchist sensibility. Three points are notable. First, Crass's human rights discourse was framed primarily as a critique of capitalism. More explicit in their criticism than The Clash, Crass fired most of their salvos against the dehumanizing elements of capitalism in general, and Thatcher's "free market" policies in particular. As one of their earliest songs asked: "Do they owe us a living? Of course they fucking do!" ("Do They Owe Us a Living?"). Linked to their critique of capitalism's assault on basic human rights was a blasphemous critique of organized religion ("So What," "Reality Asylum," and *Christ—The Album*). The main theme of this critique was that organized religion was a form of structural violence against both individuals and humanity. Indeed, like the numerous anarcho-punks to follow in their wake, Crass generally offered a systemic critique, eschewing what they regarding as liberalism's faulty emphasis on government programs as solutions.

The second notable point is that Crass focused on gender and women's rights. While always a part of their philosophy from the outset (see "Big Man, Big M.A.N."), Crass's feminism was placed at the forefront of their 1981 album *Penis Envy*. As they noted,

It now seemed time to launch a feminist attack. For some time we had been aware that we were being labelled as a bother band and that the feminist element within our work was largely ignored. We released *Penis Envy* and the music press, missing the point entirely, heralded it as having been made by "the only feminists physically attractive enough to make you sure they're singing out of choice rather than revenge." What do you do with these guys? (liner notes, *Best Before*)

For Crass, their conception of human rights recognized that the liberal discourse around human rights privileged a particular account of human dignity and worth that was partial and masculinized, based on traditional gender roles and the subordination of women within a patriarchic family structure.

Finally, Crass's articulation of their political message, including their articulation of human rights, was framed in the DIY ethos of punk. While The Clash and many other bands in the first wave of punk had signed to major corporate record labels, Crass explicitly adopted a do-it-yourself approach, recording and releasing their music on their own label and sharing resources and expertise to encourage others to do likewise. This DIY attitude permeated their political philosophy, as it resonated with anarchism's core message of taking charge and directly addressing the immediate issues in one's life rather than asking for some governmental solution to a problem (see Williams, 2007, p. 308). As they sang on "Angels": "Be an example in virtue and in deed./ Put into practice the words that you read." While other bands and activists in the punk scene paid lip service to the concept of self-reliance, Crass made it a touchstone of their daily lives. This is a significant point for Crass: human rights are not things to be demanded from the state, as is the typical liberal disposition. This attitude is shared by most other anarcho-punk bands. For instance, Deek Allen of the Scottish anarcho-punk band Oi Polloi, a band that considers itself largely influenced by Crass, argued: "Don't expect other people to do stuff. It's not a case of petitioning politicians to please change things for us. We have the fucking power to do it" (personal interview with author, April, 2009). As such, human rights are goals to be achieved from personal politics at the immediate local/personal/communal level. Crass wrote,

> We have all been guilty of defining the enemy, and indeed there are those who would obstruct the course of liberty, yet ultimately the enemy is to be found within. There is no them and us, there is only you and me. We need to consolidate, reassess, reject what patently does not work and be prepared to adopt ideas and attitudes that might. We need to find the "self" that can truly be the authority that it is. We need to look beyond the barbed-wire and the ranks of police for a vision of life which is of our choosing, not that which is dictated by cynics and despots. (liner notes, *Best Before*)

As the banner Crass often hung on the stage proclaimed, "There is no authority but yourself."

Bad Brains: "I and I Survive"

Bad Brains were one of the earliest bands that emerged out of the influential Washington, DC punk scene, which included Minor Threat, Fugazi, Rites of Spring, and Youth Brigade. The band was made up of four black youths who had been converted to the power of punk through exposure to such bands as the Ramones. As vocalist HR observed, "When we heard punk rock, we said, 'That's where the energy is!'" (quoted in Anderson and Jenkins, 2001, p. 34). Bassist Darryl Jenifer commented: "We dug the militancy happening in punk rock. It said,

'If you have something to say, say it'" (quoted in Anderson and Jenkins, 2001, p. 34). Virtually inventing the genre of hardcore, Bad Brains also drew from reggae, Rastafarianism, and the concept of "Positive Mental Attitude." As Darryl Jenifer quipped in an interview, "We're a gospel group ... preaching a word of unity" (interview with *Damaged Goods* zine; quoted in the liner notes of *Attitude: The ROIR Sessions*).

Bad Brains became massively influential, not just within the DC scene (where they shared a practice space with Minor Threat, greatly influencing that band's sound and disposition) but across the US, as their music became a template for other punk bands. Playing fast, loud, and musically-sophisticated songs (as opposed to simple three-chord tunes), Bad Brains became known for their explosive energy, eventually getting banned from clubs because the crowds often became unmanageable (see "Banned in D.C."). The band would often slow the energy down at live shows with slower reggae numbers. Indeed, as the band embraced Rastafarianism early in their career, their songs were deeply religious and spiritual.

Reflecting these Rastafarian beliefs, a discourse of human rights and positive political change was at the center of Bad Brains's message. Lead singer Earl Hudson adopted the punk moniker HR to reflect this dedication to human rights, even naming his reggae side-work "Human Rights." Bad Brains's articulation of human rights was usually vaguely defined. But at the center was a belief in universal moral values, stemming from the Rastafarian belief that all people enjoyed God-given natural rights.

Bad Brains often promoted political resistance, empowerment, and activism in their songs (see "We Will Not," "Destroy Babylon"). In this way, they were not much different from other punk bands, such as The Clash or Crass. But their calls for rebellion and revolution were complemented with songs about Jah's love (see "God of Love," "Give Thanks and Praises"). Thus, Bad Brains, like other punk bands informed by a devout religious belief—whether Christianity, Islam, Judaism, or Hare Krishna—reject particularist notions of rights based on positive laws. Rather, they frame their understanding of human rights and human dignity through an understanding of a universal "natural" law.

Bikini Kill: "Revolution Girl-Style Now!"

Bad Brains also reflected a notable masculinist shift in the American punk scene that occurred in the 1980s. The initial punk scene was extremely diverse, drawing in males, females, transgendered individuals, straights, and homosexuals (see Lee, 1983, p. 20; McNeil and McCain, 1996; Spitz and Mullen, 2001). After several years, however, punk became less hospitable to women. This was particularly pronounced on the West Coast, where hyper-masculine bands such as Fear and Black Flag became leaders of the new American punk scene of the 1980s (Leblanc, 1999, p. 50). But by the early 1990s, a female-led backlash was underway, aimed at reclaiming the multi-gendered spaces of the initial punk movement.

The clearest manifestation of this movement was Riot Grrrl, which came into existence in the Spring of 1991. Allison Wolfe and Molly Neuman (members of the band Bratmobile) worked with fanzine editor Jen Smith to establish a collectively-authored feminist zine called *Riot Grrrl*. At the same time, Kathleen Hanna (of the zine *Bikini Kill*) began organizing weekly "Riot Grrrl" meetings with about 20 other women. Hanna joined forces with Kathi Wilcon and Tobey Vail (with whom she edited the zine) and Billy Karren to form a band, also called Bikini Kill. Bikini Kill and their Riot Grrrl compatriots (such as Bratmobile, Calamity Jane, Heavens to Betsy, Huggy Bear, Tribe 8, Cunts with Attitude, and Team Dresch) played aggressive punk rock with a pronounced feminist agenda, placing gender issues at the forefront. Bikini Kill's song "Double Dare Ya" became a rallying cry for many in the scene, with its opening line: "We're Bikini Kill and we want revolution girl-style now!!" Politically charged, Riot Grrrl bands directly challenged the physical marginalization of women in the punk scene. Bikini Kill, for example, encouraged women to come to the front of the stage, and the band also passed out lyric sheets to audience members in order to focus attention on the feminist messages of their songs. For Riot Grrrls, the response to traditional patriarchy in the immediate punk community and in the larger society was "girl power."

Riot Grrrl bands like Bikini Kill articulated a discourse of human rights within punk rock that placed gender issues at the forefront, again using punk to articulate a response to local issues and problems. Songs focused on issues central to Riot Grrrl such as rape, domestic abuse, women's health, sexuality, and, above all, female empowerment. Bikini Kill's Kathleen Hanna saw girl bands as a way for women to take ownership of their own bodies:

> It's a good way to act out behaviors that are wrongly deemed "inappropriate." This is a refutation of censorship and body fascism. This can deny taboos that keep us enslaved ... To discuss in both literal and artistic ways those issues that are really important to girls. Naming these issues, specifically, validates their importance. (Hanna, c. 1991)

Bikini Kill, their Riot Grrrl compatriots, and like-minded bands critiqued liberal conceptions of human rights by pointing out its particularist notion of human dignity, its masculinist underpinnings, and its privileging of traditional gender roles.

Bikini Kill's articulation of a human rights agenda also emphasized a critique of liberal individualism and a privileging of community. Kathleen Hanna has discussed how some of her work draws from the feminist concept of "autokeny," meaning "the self in community." As she argues,

> In Western culture, there's this whole thing of how it's the individual versus the community. People get freaked out when there's any kind of political movement because they're going to lose their individuality. But autokeny is about how your individuality can reinforce your sense of community and your sense of community can reinforce your individuality. (quoted in Sinker, 2001, pp. 63-4)

This leads to a pluralistic understanding of knowledge production—and a critique of "universalism." As they sang on "Resist Psychic Death": "There's more than two ways of thinking./ There's more than one way of knowing./ There's more than two ways of being./ There's more than one way of going somewhere."

While most Riot Grrrl bands focused on the violent and destructive aspect of patriarchy in everyday life, Bikini Kill also incorporated a critique of capitalism into their discourses of human dignity and rights. As Hanna stated,

> I'm really frustrated with feminism that doesn't have an analysis of capitalism, or anti-capitalism that doesn't have a racial, feminist, or real class analysis ... If we don't challenge the unhealthy forms of competitiveness that capitalism breeds, or the way it teaches us to objectify ourselves and each other, then we're just selling ourselves out. Nothing is going to change. (quoted in Sinker, 2001, p. 67)

Reflective of punk's rejection of the status quo, Hanna believed that the system itself had to be replaced. Thus, Bikini Kill had little patience for liberalism's faith in reform and progress. As she notes, "I don't believe in reformism. I don't just want my piece of the pie. I believe in revolutionary action" (quoted in Sinker, 2001, p. 67).

Conclusion

Since its inception, punk has spread across and beyond Britain and the United States, becoming a truly global phenomenon with bands and local scenes emerging in Asia, Africa, Europe, the Middle East, and Central and South America. These local scenes are usually connected to other scenes through informal networks and circuits of exchange, ranging from touring bands to personally circulated zines (see Dunn, 2008). In each of these scenes, local youths have drawn upon the global cultural field of punk to help make sense of their own issues, and to devise potential solutions. Thus each of these punk scenes, while recognizable as "punk," has its own distinctive flavor or "accent." In these scenes, bands and punks articulate a discourse of human rights and human dignity through a local frame of reference, informed in part by their own contemporary socioeconomic conditions and historical context. Like the four bands discussed in this chapter, local actors draw upon the global cultural field of punk to empower themselves to be active participants in their own local struggles. Punk's anti-status quo orientation and advocacy of DIY empowerment turn it into a potentially powerful mechanism for disalienation and political critique.

The four punk bands examined here show that there is no single "punk perspective" on human rights. While there is often a general critique of liberal conceptions of rights, that critique is certainly not universal. Rather, there is a tension between privileging the three "generations" of human rights, and a wide diversity on how human rights conversations are framed. While some bands like The Clash may appeal to the state for the protection of human dignity through positive laws, other bands such as Crass reject such state-centrism outright. At the same time, there is a diversity of opinion about the source of human rights, with bands such as Bad Brains advocating universalism, while other bands such as Bikini Kill and Crass explicitly reject such a position.

While punk does not offer a singular answer to questions about human rights, it does offer everyone a set of resources to *engage* in that conversation in the first place. In our late-modern/postmodern society, politics often presents itself as a field made up exclusively of experts, far removed from the average person and the reality of everyday life. Such distance is exacerbated when discussions of human rights are framed in obtuse legal jargon or cumbersome philosophical rhetoric. Punk has allowed these four bands to articulate and circulate their own interpretations of those conversations, and—perhaps most importantly of all—with the belief that their interpretations are as equally valid as those of the "professionals" and the "experts." Simply put, punk is a DIY vehicle for everyday empowerment and political action.

Chapter 3

Unlocking the Silence:
Tori Amos, Sexual Violence, and Affect

Deborah Finding

> It was like I instantly knew what she was talking about. I locked my door, put
> the song on repeat, and just sat on the floor and absolutely sobbed. It was just so
> amazing to suddenly feel like I'm not all alone, and this is normal—to be feeling
> this way.—Shannon Lambert

This is how Tori Amos fan Shannon Lambert described the experience of hearing
Amos's rape-narrative song "Me and a Gun" for the first time.[1] Shannon was raped
at the age of 15 at a friend's party by an older boy from her school. For four years,
she tried to "forget" the experience, an endeavor which left her depressed and
suicidal. Then a university friend lent her Amos's debut album *Little Earthquakes*,
and Shannon connected with Amos's narrative of sexual violence in a profound
way. In 2005, I surveyed over 2,000 Tori Amos listeners, and found that the sort
of connection Shannon described was a common and vital experience for them.
This chapter aims to explore the ways in which these connections happen—by
examining the song itself, Amos's personal role, and the chains of support that
have sprung up in communities connected to Amos and her work.

Sexual Violence as a Human Rights Issue

Though this chapter aims to shine a light on the support so many have found
through a song and an artist, it is important to note that the lack of support
elsewhere is particularly shocking, given the ubiquity of sexual violence. Sexual
violence is arguably the most pervasive human rights violation of our time, based
as it is on the structural gender inequality that necessarily affects 50 percent of
the world's population. In 2005 Amnesty International concluded, based on an
amalgamation of 50 surveys from around the world, that at least one out of every
three women has been forced or coerced into sex, beaten, or abused in some
other sexually violent way in her lifetime. Similarly, the WHO World Report on
Violence and Health in 2002 showed that one in four women experiences sexual
violence at the hands of an intimate partner, and that one-third of girls are forced

---

[1]   From *Little Earthquakes* (Atlantic Records, 1992).

into their first sexual experience. The Council of Europe cited domestic violence as the primary cause of death, disability, and ill-health for women aged between 16 and 44, overshadowing cancer and traffic accidents. In addition to highlighting individual personal and familial experiences, there are many other sexually violent acts constantly occurring worldwide, such as the trafficking of women and young girls for prostitution, female genital mutilation, and rape as a weapon of war and conflict.

The pervasiveness of sexual violence is reflected in the sheer number of sexual violence representations in the media. Stories about rape appear not just in news media, but also in film, television, literature, and music. Much work has been done showing the ways in which an unrealistic view of rape is presented in the media (e.g., by predominantly showing stranger rape when the majority of rapes are committed by someone close to the victim, or by suggesting that false rape accusations are just as common as genuine rapes, when in fact they represent a maximum of 3 percent of cases reported to the police). These incorrect assumptions about rape, commonly referred to as "rape myths," were explored by a UK survey commissioned by Amnesty in 2005. The results of the survey showed that a third of all respondents thought a woman was partially or totally to blame for rape if she had flirted, more than a third thought she was partially or totally responsible if she was drunk, and a quarter thought she was partially or totally responsible if she was wearing sexy or revealing clothing. Research has also shown that those who believe in rape myths are far more unlikely to be able to identify sexual violence, and frequently blame the victim (e.g., Varelas and Foley, 1998; Estrich, 1987). Moreover, findings reveal that jurors in rape cases are more likely to rely on popular understandings of rape (e.g., those they find in media representations and rape myth "talk"[2]) than on legal definitions (Epstein and Langenbahn, 1994).

Despite these disheartening conclusions about media and sexual violence, there are instances that do not fall into this pattern. In popular music, there are many women singing about sexual and domestic violence in ways that illuminate both the trauma itself and its long-term impact. These songs are often based on the artist's personal experience, and examples of these artists include (but are not limited to): Suzanne Vega, Tracy Chapman, Ani DiFranco, Heather Nova, Christina Aguilera, Jamelia, Bananarama, Alanis Morrisette, Sheryl Crow, and Tasmin Archer. However, the most significant song about sexual violence, in terms of its impact, is undoubtedly Tori Amos's "Me and a Gun." This chapter focuses on how "Me and a Gun" functions as a piece of trauma art, as well as looking at the work done by the song, by Amos herself, and by other connected chains of support, with regard to sexual violence.

---

[2]   See also Soothill and Walby (1991), Benedict (1992), Greer (2003), and Gill (2007) for further analysis of the deployment of rape myths in news reporting of sexual violence.

Trauma Art and Affect

Jill Bennett's work on trauma, affect, and art (2005) is fascinating in its suggestion that memory through "trauma art" may actually be able to move the trauma from the body into a distinctive (and potentially global) political framework. In her analysis, which draws heavily on postcolonial theory to explore our interconnectedness, she suggests that in realizing a particular way of seeing and feeling, trauma art may allow certain critical and affective interactions to take place, which in turn constitute what she calls "empathic vision."[3] This interaction of affect is reminiscent of Deleuze's notion of "the encountered sign" (2003), in which the art manifests itself in our senses, emotions, or bodies, and this experience pushes us into an intellectual inquiry. This intellectual inquiry forces us to examine the issue the art raises afresh, which may lead to a different understanding, and/or to the conclusion that some kind of action must be taken. This action can take several forms, ranging from an active remembering (like the post-Holocaust mantra "never forget") to a political protest for social change, or practical alleviation of the suffering of others. In addition to these potential consequences, there is one further type of affect to consider, that of the possibility of individuals *feeling better* as a result of their interactions with Amos's work. Such outcomes are, of course, deeply personal to the individual, but can include: feeling heard and having their emotional responses validated, finding others who have shared experiences and feelings, and "speaking out" about their experiences of sexual violence. These, in turn, can be connected to the less obviously personal responses, such as activism and work with other survivors, however, the chain begins with a strong emotional connection to the song. There are precedents to this in other art forms; for example, of Paul Celan's concentration camp poem, "Todesfuge" (Death Fugue), Primo Levi said, "I wear it inside me like a graft" (2001, p. 198). Trauma art, like trauma itself, can be (in the titular words of Jeanette Winterson's 1992 novel) "written on the body" and incorporated into the self, to such an extent that it resembles the graft Levi suggests. In short, there are three types of affect to consider when approaching Amos's "Me and a Gun": first, discomfort or anxiety leading to empathic thought and improved understanding or insight, second, validation of one's own experiences and "healing," and third, motivation to take action, such as helping others.

---

[3] Bennett's "empathic vision" borrows from Dominic LaCapra's notion of "empathic unsettlement" (1994), which he defines (in relation to his work on representing Holocaust experiences) as an aesthetic experience in which "I" simultaneously *feel* for the other, *and* am aware of the gap between my perception and the other's experience.

"Me and a Gun": How It Functions

In assessing "Me and a Gun" as a piece of trauma art, it is important to look at the ways in which the song works on its listeners. The song is essentially a descriptive narrative of an experience of sexual violence, without a great deal of room for interpretation. However, there are aspects of the song worth drawing out for particular examination. First, with regard to the song's presentation there are two important points to note: the *a cappella* nature of the song, and the fact that the experience is described in the present tense. Both of these qualities render the song immediate, unsafe, and uncomfortable to listen to.

The narrator takes the listener deep into the heart of the violation by describing both the physical nature of the attack as well as her state of mind and thoughts during the attack. The listener is invited to join in with the narrator's analysis of her own internal experience: "You can laugh/ It's kind of funny/ The things you think/ At times like these/ Like I haven't seen Barbados/ So I must get out of this." Many people who have experienced some sort of life-threatening, or suddenly serious incident, whether it is an assault or a car accident, will know the ironic laughter the narrator reports here. Reactions to severe negative stimuli cannot be known in advance, and as a result, the thoughts that do occur can seem very random in retrospect. In this case, the narrator latches onto places she has never been as a reason she must stay alive; the recurring motif in the song is Barbados, but later she also mentions "Carolina/ Where the biscuits are soft and sweet."

Amos moves from the general to the specific by returning to the very physical nature of the assault. This is best illustrated with the lines, "These things go through your head/ When there's a man on your back/ And you're pushed flat on your stomach/ It's not a classic Cadillac." When Amos sings the line "And you're pushed flat on your stomach," she emphasizes "flat" in a way that makes it sound as though she is being pushed down at that moment. She also uses "you" to its greatest effect here, making the listeners have some of the narrator's experience for themselves. It is a lot easier for the listener to be included in "the things you think at times like these," than it is when the narrator changes "a man on my back" to "a man on your back/ And you're pushed flat on your stomach." Whether the listener likes it or not, Amos is taking them into the depths of that experience with her narrator.

Although the song stands primarily as a personal narrative, there is one overtly political (feminist) comment about the politics of sexual violence which is worth including here: "Yes I wore a slinky red thing/ Does that mean I should spread/ For you/ Your friends/ Your father/ Mr. Ed?" The narrator is challenging the "she was asking for it" rape myth by saying that however provocatively she was dressed, she did not deserve to be assaulted.

The song ends with as much discomfort as it began. The final lines, "And I haven't seen Barbados/ So I must get out of this," leave us stranded with the narrator in the car, not knowing whether she gets out alive or not. Arthur Frank (1995) suggests that illness narratives fall into three categories: the restitution narrative, in which the main focus is a return to health, the chaos narrative, in which there is a lack of order or mediation, and the quest narrative, which takes the form of illness as a journey with something to be gained at the end. Though sexual violence experiences are not "illness," the ways in which both can affect mind as well as body, self-identification, and relationships with other people, mean that work on illness narratives is particularly relevant to work on trauma narratives.[4] "Me and a Gun" takes the form of the chaos narrative, because of its immediacy and its nonresolution. The listener does not find out at the end of the song whether the narrator escapes her attacker or not, and is left with the details and the emotional panic of the experience, but no comforting, or otherwise explanatory context. Frank argues that the chaos narrative is the most embodied narrative of the three, existing as it does "on the edges of a wound" (1995, p. 101). It is the most difficult narrative for an audience to hear, because its lack of structure and resolution provoke anxiety, leaving the listener to face the narrative as a possible reality in their own lives. The story is unresolved and due to this, and the present tense used, the experience remains *currently happening* every time the song is played. The power of the song is undeniable.

What Has Changed as a Result of "Me and a Gun"?

For Deleuze, the "encountered sign" in trauma art that is felt or sensed, rather than recognized on a purely cerebral level, is the spark in a narrative that allows an affective connection to take place. Once this connection has been made, the listener is propelled into deep thoughts, engaging in the narrative with both mind and body, in a way that could not have happened without the spark of the encountered sign. In terms of "Me and a Gun," this could be any part of the song that resonates with, or in some other way significantly touches, the listener. However, the outcome of this connection with the sign is that the listener, in encountering Amos's narrative in these visceral and personal terms, is pushed toward a deeper understanding not just of Amos's narrative, but of rape itself. Using questions from the Amnesty survey of (UK) public opinion and understanding of sexual violence, the listener survey sought to establish whether or not this was the case. That is, were Amos's listeners less likely to accept rape myths than the general public? Across all of the rape myths that were explored (for example, that women bore some responsibility for being raped if they wore sexy clothing, flirted, or were drunk, etc.), the Tori Amos listenership consistently rejected these in significantly higher numbers (between 11 and 24 percent more, depending on the rape myth). Though further research would be needed before a claim that this link is causal could be made—and the survey established Amos's listenership as a left-leaning, well-educated, liberal group—it is still worth noting the differences between the two sets of responses, especially with Deleuze's notion in mind.

---

[4] Also see Elaine Scarry's *The Body in Pain* (1985), for further work in this area.

Though the song has been discussed here on its own merits, there is no doubt that its impact, and the amount of media attention it generated, was greatly increased by Amos's revelation that the song was based on her own experience of sexual violence. This experience occurred when Amos was in her early twenties and playing in piano bars in Los Angeles. She gave a fan a lift home one night after the show and the fan kidnapped and raped her. It was the combination of the starkness and honesty of "Me and a Gun" and Amos's own willingness to speak out about her own experience that brought the issue to the fore. However, when Amos helped to set up the first national sexual violence helpline in the United States, RAINN (Rape, Abuse and Incest National Network), her position as patron saint to the sexually abused was firmly established.

At the time of setting up RAINN, Amos gave a number of interviews in which she discussed the response to her song and her speaking out as her motivation for doing so. For example:

> I got so many letters, not just from women, saying if they could have just had somebody to talk to ... and not just somebody who talks on the phone and goes, "Oh God, I know what you mean. I'm so sorry this happened to you." But someone who can give you steps toward healing, not just commiserating. And that's what this number will do. Wherever you are in the country, you can call the 800 number and be put directly in contact with (a professional) who lives close to you. I had to do something, because you wouldn't believe how many letters come in. It would blow your mind how many.[5] (quoted in Morse, 1994, p. 63)

Though Amos often spoke in these general terms, there was one specific incident that remained at the heart of her decision to set up a more official, stable, and appropriate support than she could offer herself:

> This girl showed up backstage. ... She just stood there and said, "Last night my stepfather raped me. He's been raping me every night for seven years." I said, "Get her on the bus!" When we were crossing the state line that night, [the tour manager] said, "The FBI's going to be on your ass so fast." And I'm like, wait a minute, what is right and wrong here? Where has the law failed? That this girl's only hope is an artist.[6] (quoted in Press, 1996, n.p.)

---

[5]   Amos has stated on many occasions that at one point she was receiving hundreds of letters a week from listeners who had experienced some form of sexual violation.

[6]   Amos also recounted this story on the American news show *20/20* in 1999 (*20/20*, ABC, 1978- current). Amos said that the girl was so overcome during the show that she collapsed. After being brought backstage, Amos remembers, "I said, 'What's going on with you?' and she said 'I want to come and join the tour.' I said, 'what's so bad that you want to do that, now?' and she said, 'Because my stepfather raped me last night, he'll rape me tomorrow night, and he's going to rape me tonight when I get home.'"

Though Amos gave this interview in the context of her motivation to set up RAINN, it is interesting to see that there are several other things at work here. First, the point Amos makes about the law having failed can be taken in a wider context than simply an interpretation of being stopped by law from helping someone being victimized by something that is against the law. When Amos says "That this girl's only hope is an artist," she is referencing not just the failure of the law to protect this girl, but also the lack of service provision for those experiencing sexual violence, given the fact that this girl had come to Amos, a recording and performing artist, for emotional and practical support with sexual abuse that had been taking place for seven years. Second, it is clear that the girl felt that she could come to Amos personally and share her experience, as all the others who wrote letters had also felt. Third, it is also plain that it was Amos's first instinct to help the girl personally. Only Amos's tour manager prevented Amos from allowing the girl to come on tour with them, on the grounds that they could be arrested for kidnapping her, as she was underage and they would be crossing US state lines.

However, despite helping to establish an official source of support, Amos's unofficial role as personal confidante to the sexually abused was, and to a large extent still is, overwhelming. It is very rare for an artist as successful as Amos is to meet fans before every show. Yet, Amos's Meet and Greets have been a feature of her whole touring life, and are very important to her fans. They provide an opportunity for anyone who is willing to turn up a few hours before the show (usually just before sound check) to meet Amos and speak to her. This opportunity is often used by fans to request a song for that evening's performance, have an album signed, or hand a letter or gift to Amos. However it also provides a space for other, more personal interactions. In attending several of the Meet and Greets in both the United States and the UK in 2005, I witnessed people telling Amos deeply personal things about themselves and their experiences, including narratives of abuse, rape, and attempted suicide, in this forum.[7] Amos herself seemed to be touched by these interactions, and to engage with each person and their story, fully. On several occasions, I noticed Amos's eyes well up with tears, or observed her taking and clasping the person's hand as they told her their story.

Although I witnessed only a few Meet and Greets, the survey confirmed that these experiences are quite standard for Amos. Respondents were asked if they had felt supported by Tori Amos *in person*, and 22 percent said they had. This question was answered by 1,969, and 439 of them answered "yes." Given that each person who answered "yes" had a personal interaction with Amos, in which

---

[7] There is a significant degree of discomfort in "eavesdropping" on interactions as personal as this. However, the nature of the Meet and Greet makes it virtually impossible not to do so. An area is usually fenced off for the Meet and Greet by Amos's security so that there is some sort of barrier between Amos and the fans. After each person has their interaction with Amos, they move away to let someone else take their place. The fenced area is usually crowded and somewhat pen-like, and a truly "private" conversation would be very difficult to achieve with this degree of proximity to others.

they spoke to her about emotional issues, and were responded to in such a way that they felt supported, the work Amos has done in this regard herself is something quite extraordinary (especially when taking into account the fact that the survey respondents only represent a small fraction of Amos's listenership). Twenty-two percent of respondents had also written a letter to Amos, and 8 percent of respondents said that they had told Amos something that they had never told anyone else in their lives.

The personal interactions between Amos and her fans on this issue have had quite extraordinary consequences. When Shannon Lambert, whose experience of listening to "Me and a Gun" was quoted at the beginning of this chapter, created a personal website, "Welcome To Barbados," peppered with Tori Amos lyrics and telling her own story of sexual violence, she received a huge response, including an invitation to speak about her experiences on a US national news show, *20/20*.[8] After the *20/20* segment was filmed, Shannon and the two other sexual violence survivors who were with her were taken backstage to meet Amos. Of the experience, Shannon wrote:

> I followed him into Tori's dressing room and there she was ... right next to me, the woman who has saved my life so many times, the woman whose voice helped me to find my own. For so long she has been my best friend, the one who keeps me company when I have nightmares, the one who validates every emotion I feel. I hugged her and introduced myself. We all sat down and she asked how we were ... I said I was terrified. Tori decided we needed a lip gloss boost so she dug through her purse to find some delicious vanilla flavored gloss which she shared ("don't worry, I don't have any diseases you can see"). I felt a lot better with Tori-lip gloss on :) We spent a few moments just chatting, looking at Tori's wedding ring, and talking about random things.
>
> Kellie, another survivor, asked Tori a question, and then it was my turn. I needed to thank Tori for all she has done for me. The tears were rolling down my face as she held my hand and told me that I was strong, that I was amazing, that I saved myself. For a while, at least, I believed her. The 20/20 cameras were asked to leave, and then the real magic began as we all shared with each other. The four of us were sitting there, clutching each other's hands and strength, drying each other's tears, and we were all equal. It wasn't Tori, the musical superstar, and three of her obsessed fans; it was four equals, all fighting the same demons and holding on to each other. Tori shared with us so much, and that meant more to me than anything else. She convinced me that she needed us just as much as we needed her. All four of us were sobbing, and that beautiful moment will remain in my memory forever. (http://welcometobarbados.org/goodyear.html, April 5, 2010)

---

[8] The segment can be viewed here, in two parts: Part 1: http://youtube.com/watch?v=UXKK2JeC_tY; Part 2: http://www.youtube.com/watch?v=oBO9LTeBW-k, both accessed April 5, 2011.

Shannon described the conversation with Amos as "very healing, private and emotional." After it was over Amos autographed a photograph for Shannon with the words "We'll get there together," a phrase Shannon admits became something of a mantra to her as she developed an idea for a support network for others going through similar experiences. Knowing that she would not be able to respond personally to everyone who would write to her after the *20/20* show aired, Shannon wanted to create a space in which people could talk to each other, rather than just to her. Originally integrated into her "Welcome to Barbados" site, that space eventually became "Pandora's Aquarium" (named after Amos's song of the same name), a significant and effective nonprofit organization. Since its inception, over 20,000 people have registered with the site for support. In addition, Pandora's Aquarium runs a lending library of sexual violence resources for its members, provides factsheets and articles to rape crisis centers, and organizes survivor's retreat weekends. In 2009, Lambert, now 30, was named one of L'Oréal's ten national "Women of Worth," and, after a public vote, was declared the overall winner, thus awarding Pandora's Aquarium (now "Pandora's Project") $25,000 to continue its work with survivors.

Lambert's mission statement reads: "My hope is that Pandora's Aquarium will be a place where rape and sexual abuse survivors break the silence, tell their stories, heal those most invasive, unseeable of scars, and begin to live again." One such person who accessed Lambert's forum for just these reasons was Lindsay, now 24. Lindsay was abused between the ages of 3 and 15 by her grandfather, and also raped by a family friend she was babysitting for when she was 13. The experiences had left her feeling that she had no one to trust or turn to, until she discovered Pandora's Aquarium at the age of 17. Lindsay wrote:

> I did not have much support in my real life, and Pandy's [pet name for Pandora's Aquarium among forum members] became my one main outlet. I found so much support around the social isolation I felt once I told about the rape at 13, and I began to make friends online, some of who became my friends in my life outside the boards. (quoted in Finding, 2010, p. 243)

Though Lindsay found Pandora's Aquarium through chance and not via a prior relationship with Amos's music, the other members of the forum quickly recommended Amos's debut album *Little Earthquakes*, among others, to her. Lindsay found Amos's music to be a great source of help in her recovery. Though Lindsay still struggles, she now feels that she has come through her darkest days, with a great deal of thanks to Amos, her music and Pandora's Aquarium, and is now happily engaged to her long-term girlfriend and is studying to be a social worker:

> There are still challenges that I face, particularly still having to deal with some of the aftermath of being a sexual assault survivor, but I am stronger than ever and love the fact that I am soon going to have my master's in social work. I

may not have musical talent like Tori, but I know how important having a good therapist who is empathic to the needs of survivors is to the healing journey. I hope to be that therapist to many people, particularly to survivors of sexual violence. (quoted in Finding, 2010, p. 244)

Lindsay met Amos at a book signing, and was keen to tell her about the role that Amos had played in both her recovery and her life choices:

I went on to say: "Your music and story has been an inspiration to me on my healing journey. I have been able to turn my pain into activism, which includes participating in fundraisers for RAINN and by participating in a local colleges' coalition against sexual assault, and I have you as a role model. I owe part of my journey to you." Tori said, "Thank you Lindsay. You know, we survivors need to stick together and work with others to make sure this never happens to anyone else. I'm glad you are doing this work." I about nearly died that I got that recognition for the activism I had done up to that time by one of my heroes. (quoted in Finding, 2010, p. 244)

The Interconnected Chains of Affect

Both Shannon's and Lindsay's narratives illuminate the fact that there are three distinct but interconnected sources of support for survivors of sexual violence who come to be caught up in the music of Tori Amos: the music itself, Tori Amos herself, both in person and as an iconic survivor/healer figure, and the community of fellow survivors that springs up around them. In both stories, it is clear that the three sources of support *are* both distinct and connected. For example, though most people who received support from Pandora's Aquarium did so by first discovering the music of Tori Amos, and then being referred to the forum, or finding it through an internet search connected to Amos, Lindsay discovered Pandora's Aquarium by chance, and then came to the music, and Amos in person, as secondary sources of support. In comparing Lindsay's trajectory of Tori Amos-connected support to that of Shannon, who found Amos's music first, started writing about it online, and then received support from Amos herself, it is clear that the chain of support works in both directions.

The interconnectedness of these three modes of support is vital. For example, Amos would not be as iconic as a sexual violence survivor/healer without her music, but at the same time, she also offers both Lindsay and Shannon something more than is offered in her music alone. The connection that transpires between Amos and both Lindsay and Shannon transcends the expectation that both women seemed to have before the meeting—that they were fans meeting a singer who has also become the patron saint of sexual violence survivors. Rather, what happened in both cases, cements and deconstructs this role for Amos. Both Lindsay and Shannon get things autographed by Amos in their meetings—a marker of the star/

fan relationship at work there. However, in both meetings, it is Amos who takes a step away from that relationship, and toward a much closer one. In Shannon's story, after the cameras stop rolling, Amos shares her lip-gloss with the women, before all four tell their stories, hold hands and cry together. It is interesting to note that Amos shares two personal things with the women: the lip-gloss and her own story. We might discount the lip-gloss as trivial while lauding the story as significant, however, I believe there is more at stake here. In sharing something feminine, physical, and personal with the women, Amos underlines the message she might like to give in words ("you are not dirty," "you can still be a sexual being," "you did not cause this by making yourself look attractive") with her actions. The parallel with the Bible story in which Jesus heals the leper (Mark 1: 40-45) is clear: though Jesus does heal the leprosy, the significance of the story is often seen in his willingness to touch the man, which was forbidden, at a time when the disease was associated with a great degree of shame and social stigma. Likewise, for these women, that someone in Amos's position of power, both as a star and as the "patron saint" of sexual violence, showed willingness, not only to talk to them about sexual violation, but also to share with them something physically intimate, is as clear a message of acceptance as they could receive.

In Lindsay's story, Amos tells her, "We survivors need to stick together," which is reminiscent of Shannon's "we'll get there together" autograph. These words have resonance with both women's stories, as well as with the many other narratives that were shared during the research process about people's personal experiences with Amos. It seems that one of the major ways in which Amos has helped people with their experiences of sexual violence lies in her willingness to align herself with her listeners. Because of this, people are able to feel part of a community of which Amos is not just the figurehead, but also a member, living with and struggling with the aftermath of her own experiences. However, it seems to me that Amos's role as figurehead of this community is just as important as her role as active participant in it. Though it may have been both healing and useful, it seems unlikely that the *20/20* private meeting would have had such significance for the women involved had Amos not also been present and participating in it. Likewise, when Amos affirms Lindsay's work in their face-to-face meeting, Lindsay says, "I about nearly died that I got that recognition for the activism I had done up to that time by one of my heroes." It is Amos's status as "hero," both in terms of her music and in terms of her iconic stature with regard to sexual violence, that makes both women feel especially validated, heard, and supported.

Though both Shannon's and Lindsay's stories are, of course, deeply personal and individual, they are also representative. During the course of my research, I met many of Amos's listeners who also shared personal stories about their encounters with Amos, her music, and the communities around them, with me. A common thread running through almost all of these stories was the (almost incredulous) gratitude that *someone like Amos* had taken the time to hear their story, interact with it in an emotional way, and offer some kind of personal support, in addition to the music that had already supported and sustained them. Their narratives, and many of those written on the survey by respondents, had many structural similarities, as well as similarities in trauma-content. They began with a sense of (usually teenage) isolation, before moving to the ways in which Amos's music had made them feel not alone. After discovering the music, they attended live shows and Meet and Greets, which performed two functions. The first of these was to access Amos herself and get support that way. The second was to meet other like-minded, people with whom they formed friendships and in many cases, surrogate families. In the preface to his book, *The Wounded Storyteller*, Arthur Frank writes,

> In wounded storytelling the physical act becomes the ethical act. Kierkegaard wrote of the ethical person as editor of his life: to tell one's life is to assume responsibility for that life. This responsibility expands. In stories, the teller not only recovers her voice; she becomes a witness to the conditions that rob others of their voices. When any person recovers his voice, many people begin to speak through that story. (1995, pp. xii-xiii)

Frank's image of a chain of silences being unlocked by narratives has particular resonance with Tori Amos's work. Whether in lyrics such as "Sometimes I hear my voice/ And it's been here/ Silent all these years" (from "Silent All These Years," on the album *Little Earthquakes*, 1992) or in her involvement with RAINN (whose subheading is "Unlock the Silence"), Amos has been inextricably linked with speaking out about sexual violence, which, in turn, has encouraged others to do likewise. All three narrators explored in this chapter, Shannon, Lindsay, and Amos herself, as "wounded storytellers," took their experiences of sexual violence and, after accessing support for themselves, went on to help others with similar experiences. Many more of the survey respondents also reported being involved one way or another in "healing work," whether or not they related these roles directly to a connection with Amos. As such, there are now many networks of support in place, both explicitly linked to Amos and only tangentially linked. Once again, these linking chains may have their roots in Amos and "Me and a Gun," but their range and reach now vastly extends this original spark. The ongoing vitality of these support networks, whether or not Amos continues to be directly involved or not, is surely the biggest testament to Amos's work she could receive. As Shannon said, when interviewed on *20/20* about the thanks she owed to Amos, "I won't say that she saved my life, because I don't think she'd like that. But she definitely helped me to find the strength to save myself."

Chapter 4

Pantomime Paranoia in London, or, "Lookout, He's behind You!"

John Hutnyk

Visiting the Kumars

At the end of the last and at the very start of the present century, there emerged a new figure of fun in the British media who has been revealed also to have an ominous underside. Court jesters of culture, the flavor of the month for a short while anyway, South Asian comics and comedians became popular and almost ever-present on our screens. For a while, many of us laughed, and many celebrated a coming of age; daft like everyone else meant visibility at last. The televised hilarity of "Goodness Gracious Me" and the madcap efforts of Sanjeev Bhaskar on his BBC pseudo chat show "The Kumars at No. 42" were welcome insofar as they promoted manifestations of "multicultural comedy" as part of a tolerant and inclusive tradition. But this is not—never—the whole story, and I think the popularity of such shows now reveals in retrospect some disturbing emergent anxieties where the visibility of comic figures does more politically than ever the mischief of the usual court jester as courtier to power achieved.

The question of who comes to visit the Kumars at Number 42 was a matter of mirth on television, and various celebrities from all walks of life sat with an "average"—actually quite wacky—South Asian family to talk about their latest cultural product: promoting a film, a play, their new book, and so on. As a light entertainment early evening format it was a great success. But such questioning of the neighbors and the to-ings and fro-ings of their associates can be a much sharper confrontation elsewhere in Britain, especially in the years after the advent of the War of Terror, attacks on the World Trade Center in New York, and the London bombs of 2005. It could be argued that the figure of the terrorist in Asian garb is a new manifestation of the scapegoat; the Asian next door becomes a stereotype and scare-mongering figure, made all the more suspect by religious incomprehension, language barriers, and ingrained institutionalized xenophobia. A raft of recent studies have pointed out (Wilson, 2006; Kundnani, 2007) that alongside the visit to the Kumars we now also witness special squad investigations, high-profile security raids, and closures of streets; the police cordoning off areas of middle English suburbia; the nightly news interviewing people living on the same streets as suspects, insisting that "he kept to himself" or "they seemed like normal people"; and scenes of the accused being driven off to interrogation and detention under the anti-terror legislation. Or we see average citizens subjected to unprovoked and violent mayhem at the hands of the state, as in Forest Gate (where Mohammed Abdul Kahar was shot in the chest and his brother Abul Koyair kicked and beaten as 250 police stormed their house on June 2, 2006) or the Stockwell tube (where Operation Kratos officers shot-to-kill Jean Charles de Menezes on July 22, 2005), and as planned and prepared for in various terror legislations, police and army procedure manuals, and as called for by right-wing newspapers and talk-back radio shock jocks.

I see the Kumars as the bright side of a sinister kind of theatre that has emerged in Britain today, and I think it can be linked to other seemingly innocent comic aspects of British performance culture, with relevance to similar scenarios throughout the world. This chapter attempts to unpack the scripts.

A Suicide Rapper

In its June 28, 2006 issue, *The Guardian* newspaper found a fairly absurd headline to put above a slightly modified press release Nation Records put out to promote the new Fun-da-Mental album.[1] In effect the headline accused frontman Aki Nawaz of terrorist sympathies, support for Osama bin Laden, un-British sentiments, and punk sensibilities. Despite *The Guardian*'s carefully distanced reporting ("Nawaz says he is prepared to face the consequences"), this story seemed more likely to belong to the *News of the World* than a left-leaning intellectual broadsheet. *The Sun* duly took up the tale the next day with an inflammatory headline which proclaimed the band's "Suicide Bomb Rap" had provoked "fury" and led to calls from MPs for police to arrest Nawaz for "encouraging terrorism."

Some might say Aki Nawaz is a past master of provocation as a sales gimmick (his earlier outings as drummer for the Southern Death Cult give it away). Yet this strategy, out of the Andrew Loog Oldham school of promotional work where "any publicity is good publicity," is still a risky move. Not least because *The Guardian* can turn itself into some sort of sensational tabloid for a day (the headline itself— "G-had and suicide bombers: the rapper who likens Bin Laden to Che Guevara"— is particularly inane, but references all the storm in a tea cup fears that surround us today, and manages to tap Che Guevara on the shoulder as well). Long ago it became standard for critics to question the commitment with which a pop culture personality might profess political sentiments, and there are endless reams of discussion in the annals of the Left concerning the complicity, compromises, and commercialism of avowedly leftist "cultural" interventions. It is also often pointed out that attempts to simultaneously sell progressive politics and culture industry products without getting some sort of molten plastic rancidity all through your clothes are futile. Turning into that which you despise is a common media refrain (fans call this "selling out"). Yet to limit acknowledgement of Nawaz to his role

---

[1]   http://arts.guardian.co.uk/news/story/0,1807542,00.html, accessed March 24, 2008.

as a rapper rather underplays his diverse activities as impresario of the global juke box over the past 20 years. As co-founder of Nation Records, Nawaz has been instrumental (pun intended) in bringing a diverse and impressive array of talent to attention: ranging from the disasporic beats of Transglobal Underground, the drum and bass of Asian Dub Foundation (discussed further below), the hip-hop/quaito stylings of Prophets of the City, and Qawwali artists such as Aziz Mian and more. With co-conspirator Dave Watts, Fun-da-Mental advances alternative and left-oriented versions of populist world music, as a vehicle for a series of targeted provocations against mainstream hypocrisy and racism. Often misunderstood by the music press, there were many who were enamored at first with their radical stance, but this attitude was soon simplified and resolved itself into sloganeering with various versions of the suggestion they were "the Asian Public Enemy" (reported in Sharma et al., 1996; Hutnyk, 2000) and versioning the band, and the Nation label, as a quixotic exotica. No doubt at times Nawaz has played up to this—his persona as rapper "Propa-Gandhi" clearly marks a knowing ambiguity and many of his comments play on, and yet destabilize, conventions of British South Asian identity.

In the *Guardian* piece that broke the story of the suicide rapper, Nawaz is pictured in a post-Propa-Gandhi but still somewhat pantomime pose. This could be called a disgruntled chic/sheik stance if this were not also an awful play on words. The photo *The Guardian* chose to print is particularly revealing of the current iconography of terror and fear in present day Britain. In the print version of this Ladbroke Grove ensemble (the *Guardian Unlimited* web image is slightly cropped) there is an English flag to the right of the picture, alongside a likely looking resident. The bus in the background on the left is behind a young lad with a backpack—this surely refers with pointed significance to the July 7, 2005 London bomb anniversary about a week away when this story was printed. I want to read the bus in this ensemble as of crucial significance. All the buttons of contemporary Islamaphobia, nationalism and transport system vulnerability, and conspiracy theorizing are referenced in this image here—though it's unclear if the photographer Martin Godwin and Nawaz himself contrived to create this scene together, certainly Nawaz in the photograph is trying to look angry—pantomime villain—and we can tell that inside he is smirking at the absurdity of it all.

And the absurdity of it all is certainly present in the iconic bus photograph that is recalled by means of citation. If the backpack behind Nawaz necessarily evokes the Tavistock Square bus bombing, it does so, intentionally or not, ironically or not, in a way at least deserving of attention. That this has been ignored seems a failure of analysis. Instead of any critical indication of the potency of this scene, either by the news reporters Mark Brown and Luc Torres, or by respected commentators, this remains a silent device within the ensemble, associating by visual proximity, Nawaz with the London bombers—connectivity confirmed and mocked in simultaneity and in the anniversary repetition of the media scare.

Yet, it must be said that while Nawaz is portrayed as a cartoonesque suicide rapper in *The Guardian* and *The Sun*, he also uses this notoriety to convey a previously unheard and unwelcome message about the hypocrisy of the so-called "war on terror." The iconography works to open forums previously unavailable for him to raise issues, provoke discussion. Soon he is invited (and invited back) onto BBC news roundtable talk-back, his voice heard because he courts "outrage" with his agitational views. To some degree his provocation does force issues into the open. He is not invited to the Kumars' show to promote the album, but instead appears on BBC2's *Newsnight* in August, 2006 and on *Newsnight Review* in October the same year (and subsequently). Bad publicity enables important interventions on a serious late evening current affairs program. Possibly via a circuitous route, it is in the casting role of pantomime villain that establishment doors were opened to some different ideas—any publicity at all pays off in the end. Several other scenes are worth examining in this process where a former punk drummer with reformed global world music sensibilities coincides with entertainment values and programming requisites to enable political comment with a sharp edge.

Pantomime

My view is that we need to work through the moves as they travel from comic outrage to serious debate. This means a detour through the theatrical, and for the purposes of this discussion, the comic theatre of British pantomime. Thinking about pantomime terrors deserves a little historical play. The popular Christmas and summer holiday entertainment form has roots in vaudeville and melodrama and might also be traced back through French mime, Italian Commedia dell'arte, or even to Roman mythology and the flutes of the god Pan (Miller, 1978.) A more detailed history of course would have to contend with the relation of the Pied Piper of Hamelin to J.M. Barrie's *Peter Pan*, with issues of role reversal, double entendre, drag, slapstick, superstitions (left side of the stage for demons, right side for fairy princesses), and theatre ghosts if not more. The trajectory within the pantomime archive that I find most relevant here would start with Scheherazade and the stories of *A Thousand and One Nights*, the first "proper book" I owned as a child (novelist Hanif Kureishi calls it "the greatest book of all" in *My Son the Fanatic* [1998, p. xii])—illustrated with lavish pictures of Sinbad the Sailor, various alluring princesses on flying horses or magic carpets, Aladdin and his lamp, and of course Ali Baba and the 40 thieves. That Scheherazade had to tell devious stories to evade death at the hands of the despotic King Shahyar is only the first of the points at which Edward Said-style critiques of Orientalism would need to be deployed. Wicked and conniving traders outfoxed by fantastically beautiful maidens told as fairy tales to children, but barely disguising the violence at the heart of the stories themselves, did effective ideological duty (get 'em while they're young). Jacques Lacan also weighs in on this tale, quoting Edgar Allen Poe in "The Purloined Letter," he reminds us that Scheherazade lives from morning to morning, the repetition of her storytelling the gamble of her survival from day to day ([1966] 2006, p. 29). Her gamble risks telling the wrong story, and in Poe on night 1,002 she blunders and must face consequences that are too terrible to tell to kids. My problems with Said and Lacan, however, have always been that these effects are not just literary and historical, even as a wealth of historical research was released in the wake of Said's texts, and Lacan's comments on the gambler's paranoia should indeed make us wary. Today, however, pantomime seems to play an even more sinister role.

The most memorable scenes in panto are the ones of tension. The viewers, children and their parents, watch as the innocent hero is stalked by the dastardly and demonic villain—Captain Hook perhaps, or a demon. The children are encouraged to shout out and expose the impending danger, to call out the threat. This theatrical structure lays out a pattern that repeats. The villain that is "BEHIND YOU" in today's real life panto is the sleeper cell living and working among us, travelling on the tube, plotting next door, preparing to wreak havoc and destruction unannounced (except for the high rotation security announcements at train stations advising us never to leave our belongings untended). Similarly spooky allegories might be evoked from the panto stories, Ali Baba is the despot holding the West ransom to the price of a barrel of oil; Sinbad is Osama, with a secret cave to which only he knows the secret opening code words: "open sesame." The fears that are promulgated here are of course childish terrors and cliché, but the problem with such stereotyping is their maddening ability to transcend reason and keep on popping back up to scare us. This is not a place for thinking; it is just children's theatre. But perhaps we might consider the repetition of the historical as seen in Marx's study of Louis Bonaparte in the *Eighteenth Brumaire*: the second time history repeats it returns as high farce. Marx's *Eighteenth Brumaire* is by far the most eloquent articulation of class and ideological politics available—the classic phrases are well known "they cannot represent themselves, they must be represented" as Bonaparte usurps democracy, the peasants treated as "potatoes in a sack," and Marx wanting to move on and "let the dead bury the dead," and so on. The trouble for Marx, perhaps also for Lacan, was the repetition compulsion built into the story. So much so that this suggests to me a Poe-faced speculative dream version of the story of Scheherazade herself, whom I imagine has this time been detained, rendered, and interned in Guantanamo. Our heroine is kept in isolation in a dank cell, except for a daily interrogation when she is brought before her captors who demand a story. She obliges them with the production of a narrative that provokes ever more draconian civil liberties crackdowns and higher and higher terror alert ratings in the metropolises, but the production of this narrative can never set her free and she will never become queen (the despotic kings are otherwise engaged: Tony Blair and G. W. Bush are already hitched to each other and a legacy in Iraq, and perhaps hitched to history in the same way Nixon was to Watergate and defeat in Vietnam). Of course it's the case that my dreaming of Scheherazade is only a conceit—even as I cannot imagine what so many years in detention can do to anyone. A thousand and one terrors assail us all.

All is War

Thus, the promotional provocation that Nawaz offers on the Fun-da-Mental album *All is War* is a dangerous strategy as well, simply because the authorities that have the power to do such things just may well get the wrong end of the night stick and actually think this father of four is some sort of threat to the nation. There have been times when his friends did think he was destined for Belmarsh Prison on charge of promoting "terror," especially with regard to the album *Erotic Terrorism*, and more recently the track "Cookbook DIY," discussed in a section below. Fun-da-Mental have always pushed hard at the complacencies and hypocrisies of our political servility and this is a good thing too—there are those who argue that we *all* need to threaten a rethink of the dubious policies of Bush-Blair and the clones, of the terror war they are waging worldwide, of the domestic demonization of Muslims, of the crushing of civil society (what civil society? That it's too civil is the problem), and of the stifling numbing dumb dumb dumb of the press. And let's take a lesson from Nepal, which in the same week in which Nawaz was identified by *The Sun* as the pantomime caricature of the "suicide rapper," the Nepalese Government, amid its own Maoist insurgency, still repealed some of its "anti-terror" in the interests of civic freedoms. The Terrorist and Disruptive Activities Ordinance (TADO) was earlier introduced by King Gyanendra in the wake of the 2002 killing of his brother Birendra and ten members of the ruling Rana Royal family. The King was forced to repeal the terror laws by popular pressure from the insurgent Moaist movement, heading (April, 2008) toward democratic electoral victory at pace. Yet beyond Nepal, the war on terror has contracted rather than opened up civic space. It is my view that any exposure of such strictures is to be supported.

Where is the discussion of the repeal of the terror laws and other fear-mongering that is making life in Britain untenable? There are those in the tourist and airline industry who think this offers "a win" to the terrorists. That the terrorists were "laughing at us"—according to Ryan Air chief Michael O'Leary[2]—is only one end of the massive disillusionment of the British public with Bush and Blair's terror war. This laughter readily makes the usual anti-Islamic political editorializing in the media a pro-government panto in itself. Is this just part of show business, the new replacement for *Top of the Pops* perhaps? Of course we can all see that the "banning" of a music track is only a minor power play in an obscure corner of the culture industry. There are a great many other modes of video violence that might much rather take up the time of the self-appointed guardians of propriety in Britain. Certainly there are examples of video images that might give more cause for concern—racist materials proliferate no doubt, and there will be reason to consider training, recruitment, surveillance, suicide, and celebration videos in (forensic) detail. But Nawaz and his "Cookbook DIY" video is just the sort

---

[2]   See http://kavkazcenter.com/eng/content/2006/08/22/5362.shtml, accessed September 23, 2006.

of threat we need much more of, in the sense that we have to debate, discuss, challenge, and change, and absolutely none of this requires any heavy-handed police interventions or worse. No wonder there are concerns about humor; the laughter that ensues is not easily hushed: it reveals much.

The Villains Are Behind You

We must acknowledge that a newspaper publicity event for a culture industry music promo is not really "news," especially while there are more serious debacles to attend to, such as the rise of racism, anti-Islamic profiling, and the anti-people pogroms of the state machine, saturation bombing, occupations of entire nations, war crimes. The gap between music product and international significance surely means it would be a surprise if someone did equate such "cultural" power with the way the war on terror legislates special rules that permit detention without charge or trial in the United States, the UK, Australia, Malaysia, and so on. In his excellent book *The End of Tolerance: Racism in 21st Century Britain*, Arun Kundnani makes an unanswerable case against the erosion of civil rights and for recognition of the way this impacts particularly on minorities, and by extension on us all:

> Never before has such a vast and rapidly expanding accumulation of state power confronted young Asians, Africans and African-Caribbeans, Muslim and non-Muslim, immigrant and British-born. Under anti-terrorist powers, they face mass stop and search without reasonable grounds of suspicion ... They face new powers of arrest that dramatically extend time held in police custody prior to any charges being brought. They face the threat of raids in the early hours ... They face virtual house arrest without the right to defend themselves in court. They face mass surveillance at places of worship, at train stations and airports. They face the risk of armed police deploying shoot-to-kill tactics. They face prosecution for expressing unacceptable opinions, for protesting, for supporting foreign charities, for being members of political organizations deemed unacceptable to the government. Finally, they face the ultimate sanction of having their citizenship itself stripped away! (2007, pp. 167-8)

The news stories referenced obliquely in the above citation would only extend the list if detailed: over-policing and incompetence that leads to the death of civilians like Charles de Menezes on the Stockwell tube, with no police punished; the Forest Gate shooting of innocent brothers, with ongoing harassment; the persecution of the "lyrical terrorist" Samina Malik, with a drawn out court case to examine her crime of writing rhymes on a scrap of paper while at work at Heathrow; a range of other high-profile "cases" and prosecutions, detentions, deportations .... All contribute to a climate of generalized suspicion, such that fellow passengers on the tube are wary, the airport check-in queue is an anxious one, citizens are confronted on the streets, taxi-drivers are beaten, Mosques are attacked, right through to a disproportionate attention to "community cohesion," and the farce of government insistence on British values. This escalation can only be described as a polymorphously perverse new mode of racism manifest in bizarre diverse and ubiquitous forms. To oppose all this is an obligation.

The worldwide erosion of civil liberties under the sign of a perverted new anxiety was already anticipated in Fun-da-Mental's ironic album title reference: *Erotic Terrorism* (1998). Thinking of the detention camps in Afghanistan and Iraq, certainly there is some credence to Fun-da-Mental's pre-September 11, 2001 prophecy that "America Will Go to Hell"—in their antiwar anthem EP release (*America Will Go to Hell*, 1999). The use of the rap form to express a critique of American (and United Nations, NATO, or British military) imperialist activities surely indicates also a more nuanced relationship between politics and content than the unidirectionalist historians of hip-hop might warrant. This not only is a comment on record industry promotional opportunism, but also references the ways commercial imperatives at the same time sanction a certain quietude about the politics of so-called anti-terrorism and the inadequacy of romantic and liberal antiracism. No mere hybrid multiculti cross-ethnic particularity, Fun-da-Mental's call is to fight against the seductive terrorisms of complicity and conformity, the manipulation of market and law, the destruction of culture and civilization in pursuit of oil.

What kind of change in the apparatus of the culture industry would be required to orient attention away from the industrial military entertainment complex? What would displace the ways people in the music press and mainstream academic community consistently deploy categories that are far removed from the actualities articulated in the Fun-da-Mental discussion? The critics appear deaf to ideas. In panto it is tradition for the audience to have to yell loudly: "HE'S BEHIND YOU." This is the classic staged scenario, and so I think what is needed is a more incisive and aggressive denunciation of the performance of well-intended hypocrites such as the singer of sounds of silence. Surely it is clear that many misconceptions come from well-intentioned deployment of arguments around terms like "authenticity," "identity," "appropriation," and "commerce." That it is no surprise that intentions and their effects are readily undone is almost a platitude. The solution is not to insist on the correctness of an alternate interpretation (see Kalra and Hutnyk, 1998; Sharma and Hutnyk, 2000), and it is equally not the case that insistence on fidelity to the source material will redeem all (but a listen to the albums and a check of the websites is worthwhile—combating sanctioned ignorance advanced through media bias is an obligation we must all take up[3]). These are probably the predictable moves that others have already made, but if raising questions about complacency in

---

[3]   The term "sanctioned ignorance" is from the always insightful Gayatri Spivak (1999). The reference to Kalra and Hutnyk (1998) is a special issue on "music and politics" of the journal *Postcolonial Studies*. Sharma and Hutnyk (2000) is to a special issue on "music and politics" of the journal *Theory, Culture & Society*.

commentary adds impetus to the work of showing where a critique of unexamined complicity and marketing zeal restrict possibilities, then the opening is important.

The RampArts Interlude (Notes from a Screening)

Appalled at the carnage on my television screen, I ventured out. I caught the train to Shadwell in East London and walked to the corner of Rampart and Sly Streets (hmmm, significant street names—*Ramparts* was a 1960's magazine of some importance, Sly—well, that's clear enough—at the end of the street there's a great sweet shop ...). So, I arrived at the corner to find Aki Nawaz from Fun-da-Mental slumped in a broken office chair beside a dumpster and a pile of crushed cardboard boxes. "Welcome to my office," he greets me. We sit and chat about the mad media responses to his new album *All is War*; we run through recent events in the horror that is Lebanon; approve the resistance of Hezbollah; and consider the possibility that bruiser John Reid is going gung-ho in his new Home Secretary job because, like an earlier blind incumbent, he is jockeying for position as a possible future leader of the Labour Party, so acting tough is what he thinks will get him noticed in the press. We talk about how the tabloids make public opinion nowadays and his posturing is mainly a way of scaring people into silence, apathy and into nothing but the joys of shopping. Then a Green Party representative comes over and asks Aki what instrument he plays in the band (I only wish Aki had replied, "Hi, my name's Pink").

The then-Home Secretary Reid, believe it or not, was a former CPGBer (Communist Party of Great Britain, old version) and perhaps best noticed for calling current affairs presenter Jeremy Paxman a West London Wanker (aka W-L-W)—Deputy PM John Prescott was at the time trying to remain invisible (with two Jaguar cars) and Tony Blair was off hiding out in some celebrity Bee Jee holiday resort (aka a Florida terror training camp) after paving the way for the Israeli Defense Force to make pavement out of Southern Beirut. An airport carry-on luggage scare and the arrest of a bunch of teenagers is a great service to the no-hoper piggy pollies that need the cover (but *gung ho* is a funny expression; a mix of Bruce Lee and Ho Chi Minh springs to mind, so I best stop using it, because Reid has long ago left the Left behind, and I am told, anyway, that gung-ho was taken up by the US Marines but was originally the abbreviation for a Chinese Communist organization, so using it to refer to the Labour Party is far too uncanny. ... I digress, see http://www.randomhouse.com/wotd/index.pperl?date=19980126 and also contrast the film http://www.imdb.com/title/tt0091159/ and laugh out loud).

Anyway, politics by tabloid. Aki has himself been noticed in the tabloids quite a bit of late; *The Sun* branded him a "suicide rapper" and *The Guardian* had a go as I have mentioned already. The event at RampArts, an anarchist inspired social centre, is to discuss the controversy, and to host the premiere screening of the video for "Cookbook DIY."[4] The evening kicks off in somewhat desultory manner with a half-hour video on the history of Fun-da-Mental that presses various key buttons—"Tribal Revolution," "Dog Tribe," "GODEVIL" clips and plenty of send-up footage of a lame Australian TV interviewer who pretty much can't cope with Aki asking if Australian Aboriginals had rights and land back yet—"what are you doing about it?" "Nothing." The point is didactic and heavy-handed (it's a music talk-back show) but correct.

Slowly the RampArts social center fills up, and people take their seats to find a gift Fun-da-Mental CD—it's not about the sales—and Ken Fero, co-director of Injustice, kicks off proceedings by introducing Aki, John Pandit, and the guy from the Green Party, noting that two other guest speakers were still on their way. Aki starts speaking about how democracy is a weapon that kills, that there is a silencing that is much to blame, that the leader in Downing Street needs to be put on a donkey and paraded through the city, and that he can't understand why nobody is doing anything. He is really angry. The youth in Britain are angry. There are people being killed in their thousands and everyone seems to be going on and on as if there was nothing they could do. They tried to protest against the Gulf War, but were ignored and since then, nothing. Why, he says, aren't people out there burning down town halls and the like? This last comment, almost an aside, will become more and more the hot topic of the night. The Green Party representative speaks next, about free speech—frankly, the usual routines—thank-you Shahrar Ali, invited by the organizers *Red Pepper*. Then Natasha Atlas arrives—her music is also released under Aki's Nation Records imprint—and she talks of her Syrian partner, the troubles musicians have getting visas in Europe, her anger and frustration at the war, and she apologizes for being emotional. In fact it's the most passionate thing I've heard her say ever, and not at all prima donne-esque. Great. Then the final late speaker walks in, Louise Christian, human rights lawyer (and she reminds us the event is organized by *Red Pepper* ... twice ...). She speaks in favor of free speech and against the new additions to the terror laws that will criminalize anyone who speaks in favor of—glorifies, encourages—acts of terror. These laws apply even if the alleged glorifier of terror did not inspire anyone to act, even if they were vague about whether they really intended people to go out and—Louise looks over to Aki—even if they say people should go out and blow up buildings. She supposes these laws will never be tested, that they are like Clause 28, the crime of encouraging homosexuality, or the incitement to racial hatred law, they are a kind of public relations gesture. We should not get paranoid; at least in this country we can have debates like this. There has been no debate as yet, but restlessness in the audience suggests one might start soon—and debate is something we have to cherish, because—here's the clincher—they don't have it in Turkey, Burma, or North Korea.

---

[4] Lyrics here: http://www.dicklaurentisdead.com/fun-da-mental/aiw_lyrics/Cookbook_diy.doc; download track at http://www.fun-da-mental.co.uk/.

John Pandit, from the band Asian Dub Foundation (ADF), speaks next. He quietly points out the need to organize and to do so in new creative ways, to make a new set of alliances. He stresses the need to do the work required to build a movement that is not just protest marches that go from A to B (this will also become a refrain in the discussion, with speakers raising the issue of how the Stop the War coalition does all it can to minimize confrontations and have us all hide in Hyde Park, of course provoking considerable agitation). And it's important, he emphasizes, not to fall for the self-censorship that means that so many musicians who do have media visibility say nothing.

The first question is from the reporter from the *Daily Star*, Neil Chandler, who told me his column appears in the Sunday edition. I think to myself that I might even buy it as his question was OK and in a short exchange with the reporter from the *Morning Star* (and representative of the Stop the War coalition) Neil seemed by far the more credible. But it is the *Daily Star*, so no high hopes, eh (and the subsequent article turns out to be the usual tabloid clichés). In any case, in response to questions, the point was made forcefully by Aki that the issue was British foreign policy. A fairly simple persuasive argument he offers runs: we put up with years and years of racism and it did not mean any young people strapped on jackets and bombed the trains; we endured unemployment and it did not mean anyone went out to bomb buildings [well, Baader-Meinhof excluded, but …]; but the nightly news footage of innocents killed one after the other in their hundreds and no one wants to discuss it, no one listens, no debate, no significant movement to defend Muslims; no defense of mosques from attack; no way the STW coalition was going to deliver on its promise that "if Blair goes to war we will stop the whole country," despite two million marching in February, 2002 … the problem is foreign policy. Change that and it's over.

Some audience members were keen to point out that there were ongoing efforts to defeat Blair. Protests against airports and weapons manufacture, dealers, delivery, sabotage, various campaigns. There was some discussion of how music is important as a way of airing issues, that musicians are more than the soundtrack of a movement; that since the 1960s Vietnam protests music could be something more than entertainment. But so often it's not. I am of course reminded of Adorno saying that the debate was not yet over about art, and perhaps art still carried the "secret omnipresence of resistance" in its hidden core. But this is not enough in a world of shopping. All this is admirable but it does not get to the question of just what kind of organization is needed to defeat the imperialist foreign policy. The questions I ask have to do with this: the need for debate and action on all these points; on what sort of organization is needed; on what sort of action is needed (someone heckles "but not blowing up buildings"); and on what sort of analysis is needed to support both organization adequate to succeed and the actions necessary. This does not get taken up; instead the chair notes there is always resistance, there will always be resistance. Another speaker asks a question about violence, naming Gandhi and the struggle against British colonialism. Aki makes the point that Gandhi was not alone, there was always a range of others involved, from Uddam Singh to

Netaji Subhas Chandra Bose. Gandhi, it is insisted, wanted peace, not blowing up buildings—this is becoming the defining phrase, spiraling into architectural defense. Aki, exasperated, says "you lot care more about buildings than people"—hands thrown up in the air. Everyone wants a say, a filmmaker is shouting from the back, the guy with the roving mike has gone outside to answer a phone call, with the mike still turned on. Chaos. So the movement shall be organized like this ....

Dave Watts from Fun-da-Mental stands up. The discussion has dragged on and his frustration is as clear as that of anyone. He starts by saying he understands why people want to be suicide bombers, he understands the frustration that would make someone want to go out and do it. You can imagine how this rubs up against the Gandhians. Dave says there has to be some understanding of how those who have tried to discuss such things in the past have now ended up ... [pause] ... ready to do violence and blow up buildings [code words]. But then he says he is a man of peace, a lover of peace, but he is angry and we have to fight for peace. The video clip we are about to see is called "Cookbook DIY" and Dave explains it's in three parts, that the person, who in frustration because there is no other avenue for discussion and expression or action has made a home-made bomb for fifty quid, is a small version of the guy who makes a dirty bomb, with materials bought on the black market, but neither are as obscene as the scientist who kisses his wife in the morning—Dave mimes a smooch, playing to the audience—panto—who then goes off to work in a Pentagon lab or some such to make a neutron bomb that kills all the people but leaves the buildings intact. Have a look at the video people ... at which point, the screening.

And that is exactly what "Cookbook DIY" does. Just as it says on the tin. This "suicide rap" exposes the suicide scientist making the neutron bomb, the daisy cutter, the cluster bombs and all those other armaments that the Lords of War, Blair, Reid, etc., threaten us with, under their terror laws, their terror regimes, the bombing runs and their surveillance systems. Their free speech that is no speech, their diplomacy and their democracy. Under the veneer of democracy, the bloodied hands of the piggy pollies; under the musical refrains, the resistance; under the cover of the *Daily* and the *Morning Stars*, another secret possibility. The global resistance, Zindabad!

Pantomime Video

The video itself is pantomime on film.[5] The first verse, about the homemade bomb, is performed, as is the entire clip, by a dress-up figure before the camera. At the very first appearance this figure appears wearing a white rabbit head. This is strange and already disturbing, but I think references in some oblique way a kind of cute or innocent image that belongs to the Britain of pet bunnies, or of the world of Lewis Carroll's *Alice in Wonderland*. That this innocent quickly transforms into a lizard

---

[5]   The video promo was directed by Kashan W. Butt for Nation Films, 2006.

figure is commensurate with the fear that works to suggest a constant vigilance: the otherwise unassuming neighbor becomes a threat. The lizard figure becomes a Zebra, again invoking a kind of infant menagerie, before becoming again the rabbit. But looking more closely, the figure here is wearing a St George T-shirt, thereby clearly signifying nationalism at one level, but also citing the popular World Cup publicity picture of English soccer star Wayne Rooney as dragon-slaying hero, savior to English football fans. This complicates any easy ascription of innocence to the rabbit/zebra/lizard, and, without implicating the English striker, suggests perhaps the home-made bomb is very much home grown. In between the verses, disturbing flashes of dolls tied up, ransom images that tamper with our comforts. Children's toys blasted into the political scene. The graffitist in the Guantanamo jumpsuit works on a banner alongside.

In the second verse, the bomb-maker is now a 31-year-old Ph.D. disaffected with conventional or domestic means of protest, now gone over to the side of organized resistance. Speaking as if to camera at a press conference, or perhaps as if in a video prepared for Al Jazeera broadcast, this figure is insistent, aggressive. Dressed at first as a twisted student in graduation robes, kaffiyeh and graduation hat, half way through the verse this figure changes into someone in a balaclava and the ammunition belt of a mythic revolutionary figure, possibly reminiscent of Pancho Villa or Rambo. This character, the bandit-terrorist, turns the volume of threat up considerably and at the end when the character spins a revolver on his finger and turns to someone in a plain dirty-white hooded sweatshirt: "it takes a dirty mind to build a dirty bomb." But this grubby image surely suggests we are mistaken to locate this threat outside of Europe—in the murky theatres of violence, in the lawless badlands. The point here is to underline the hypocrisy of our geo-political conventions, this image indicative of a failure to appreciate the co-constitution of such badlands with the dubious foreign policy decisions of the imperial powers. In between verses, images of toy cars, computer games, football paraphernalia, and other trinkets from our early adolescent pastimes. The graffiti still not readable.

The final verse clinches the argument about militarism. It depicts the "legitimate scientist" working at his bench in his white lab coat, sponsored by the research funding of the Pentagon, UN flag behind him, developing the most destructive weapons of mass destruction ever known. Half way through the verse this figure transforms into the sinister figure of a Ku Klux Klan member in white hood and smock, then into a suited "Lord of War" wearing a gas mask; presumably only the bureaucrats will survive total war. All this is perhaps heavy-handed, but nevertheless the critical points are not misplaced, the metaphoric substitutions work. The projected indications are sound, the neutron bomb is the violence of racism, of class/bureaucratic inhumanity, the cold clinical cynicism of the (mad) scientist in the employ of even more mad (mutually assured destruction) masters.

By this stage the point is made, finally the full quote is visible from the graffitist. It is a citation from an American president, possibly via the King himself, necessary only to provide a space for reflection while the tune fades. "If we make peaceful revolution impossible, we make violent revolution inevitable"—JFK.

Back to the Kumars

In pantomime one actor can play many roles, often telling their story through rhyme, song, dance, and humor, not necessarily with particularly high literary or artistic pretensions, men in drag, bawdy women, double entendre, burlesque, knowing morals, and audience involvement: "From the very beginning the pantomime was acutely aware of the world around it ... no other form of entertainment has ever devoted itself so wholeheartedly to holding up to the public, for its approbation, censure, or mere amusement, the events, manners, whims and fancies, fads, crazes and absurdities of the time" (Frow, 1985, p. 136).

This could describe Sanjeev Bhaskar's comedy but a return to the heady innocent days of visiting "The Kumars at No. 42" is not possible. In the present era, such comedy is no longer so easy. Fun-da-Mental, however, keep alive incisive critical expression through their oblique angles on world music in a time of war. It is this versus the clash of civilizations rhetoric that animates press interest today. Recall that pantomime, like comedy, sometimes can still speak truth to power, and thereby reveal its hypocritical co-ordinates, but quite often it is only a holiday period entertainment. Though I am still not so sure. I used to think the counter-establishment charge of renegade panto made a lot more sense than the antics of those in power, but now I have to recognize that it is just as much the case that panto has changed, that it has become the News, and the stakes are much higher—and that entertainment must provoke thought and talk, or we die.

In some ways Aki Nawaz has taken pantomime a step further, and managed to raise issues where others have not managed. This does not mean that other pantomime events have been displaced. The spectacle (lower case) of Mr and Mrs G.W. Bush placing a wreath in a wading pool at the base of the former World Trade Center on the evening before the fifth anniversary of September 11, 2001 was somewhat bizarre. This was not cross-dressing, but crocodile tears—the bombing of the Towers was of course reprehensible whoever did it (conspiracy theorists here, there, and everywhere), but rather than offer more images of Bush looking edgy, I think it's more important to listen to Gore Vidal and his concern with the "the destruction of the [US] Republic" as inaugurated after 2001 in the guise of Homeland Security, Guantanamo, Rendition, endorsement of torture etc. (Vidal quips re "Homeland Security" that the term is reminiscent of the Third Reich—"Der Homeland" was not a phrasing he had heard from an American before "it was forced on us" by the government). This was on BBC radio (September 11, 2006), Vidal self-styled as "spokesman for Carthage on Roman radio," defender of "the Constitution" against the oil and gas tyranny, and against the collusive "dreadful media." We have not just lost some buildings, far worse is that we lost the Republic.

This would not be the argument made by Fun-da-Mental or ADF, but the echoes of concerns with buildings, silencing, freedom, and rights recur. I am amazed that the most critical voices that break through the tabloid haze of justifications for war are those of novelists and musicians. Representative politics seems to have avoided such forthright discussion. In the video for "Cookbook DIY" pantomime characters make the argument in each of the three verses. The first entails a cross-of-St-George-wearing youth constructing a strap-on bomb from a recipe downloaded from the internet. That he is dressed as a rabbit and as a lizard in parts of the verse is Fun-da-Mental playing on childlike toys and fears; the second verse references the radical scholar and the figure of the armed guerrilla as the character relates a more cynical employment as a mercenary making a "dirty bomb" with fission materials bought on the black market in Chechnya or some such; the third pantomime figure is the respectable scientist. Here, the scientist in a lab coat morphs improbably-critically into a member of the Ku Klux Klan and then a suited business man, building a neutron bomb that destroys people "but leaves the buildings intact." This outrageous pantomime allows Nawaz to point out the hypocrisy of an empire with no clothes. The terrors we are offered every night on the news are pantomime terrors as well, a performance melodrama, operatically grandiose. The scale they require—weapons of mass destruction, Saddam's show trial—is exaggerated in a way that welcomes oblique internalization. These figures are patently absurd, yet all the more effective as incitements. Perhaps Vidal's Republic was also always a panto scene in the US anyway. But we might also understand the discombobulation of the Presidential bloopers (Bush's varied *faux pas*) as deflection of an otherwise unbearable present; if it were not so serious you would have to laugh; you have to laugh because it is so serious.

The pantomime performance of president and prime minister makes me think also of Alain Badiou, in *Infinite Thought* (2005b), pointing out the non-equivalence of terror directed at a couple of buildings by a nonstate entity ("the terrorists"), and the retribution that is visited on all of our lives by the state terror directed by US forces, directed first at peasants, villagers, and the dispossessed everywhere, but also directed at those in the "we" through security legislation and so on. (Badiou's essay on terror in that book is one of the few good critical academic discussions we have.) That the terror extends to covert activity by secret service agencies, includes surveillance operations, a plethora of dark underworld gadgetry, and so on, removes all vestige of civil liberties, and prepares us for perpetual war is only the logical consequence of our antiwar demonstrations, even when two million, being also only a kind of panto. We marched to hide in Hyde Park ("HE'S BEHIND YOU") and sat down tired to rest, when we should have sat on Blair and not moved till he resigned. This does not mean I want to bring back the days when pantomime was just a cute summer seaside entertainment and music was just an excuse for dancing. I wish it were possible to laugh this away, but it is not. We need to rethink and disrupt the usual categories. As provoked by Fun-da-Mental, music and politics can, I believe, destabilize otherwise dangerous certainties: and that can only be better than the unthinking with which we are often now forced to abide. With a wry smile, I have started to listen once again.

Chapter 5
The Blues, Trauma, and Public Memory: Willie King and the Liberators

Stephen A. King

Following the end of the US Civil War, the newly-emancipated slaves witnessed their own slow return to a "second slavery." During this period of increased repression, blacks were systematically stripped of their rights to vote and hold political office. Many Southern states passed "Black Codes" as early as 1865; these draconian laws were enacted to control, in part, what many whites considered at a time to be a savage, criminally-inclined, inferior species. African Americans were hauled into jail for a variety of "offenses," from violating curfew laws to homelessness. Once imprisoned, many black prisoners were processed through the "convict-leasing" system and bound over to local contractors who forced inmates to engage in harsh, labor-intensive work. With its high mortality rate and lack of financial compensation, the convict-leasing system was, in reality, a return to slavery. Meanwhile, lynching became a spectator sport for whites who believed that the racist and corrupt legal system did not administer "proper" justice. Between 1880 and 1930, an estimated 3,200 African Americans were lynched in the South (Gussow, 2002, p. 45). Men and women were tortured, burned alive or hung from trees or bridges as spectators cheered, laughed, and danced. Many kept amputated fingers and toes as souvenirs. In all, it would be reasonable to conclude that the South at this time was a terrorist state, exacting a sharp and cruel punishment for any perceived enemy that threatened the ideology of white supremacy.

As a product of African American resistance to post-slavery America, blues music—which most likely emerged in the Southern United States during the late nineteenth century—has been a source of protest, a cry by African Americans seeking to secure their basic human rights. Yet, while some blues musicians sang about their second-class citizenship status, the music's protest elements were admittedly covert in nature, certainly compared to other, more aggressive, African American musical genres, including rap. Robert Springer argued that violent retribution by whites against black dissent convinced many blues musicians not to openly express their anger and resentment (1976, p. 281). In fact, some blues musicians camouflaged their message of dissent through allusions to male-female relationships (O'Neal, 2000, n.p.). Blues musician, Albert "Brook" Duck, acknowledged the coded nature of some blues lyrics: "You really had to talk about the woman. But you're talkin' about the boss man all the time, how he treatin' you" (quoted in O'Neal, 2000, n.p.). In other words, a blues singer's excoriation of the "lying" and "cheating" woman ("my baby done mistreat me") was, in some cases, a denouncement of the white oppressor, the "bossman."

While the blues has traditionally served as a medium of protest, very few contemporary blues artists would be characterized as presenting an overt "political" or "revolutionary" message. Alabama-based blues artist Willie King[1] was the rare exception to this trend. With his uncompromising and pointed critique against white supremacy and his call for African Americans to seek their basic human rights, Willie King has been aptly called the "Bob Marley of the Blues." Blues scholars and music critics alike have recognized how King's bold political sensibilities were remarkably different from practically every other contemporary blues artist. Blues scholar, Jim O'Neal, who produced two of King's albums, noted that King was "one of the rare bluesmen to record a body of songs which so pointedly and overtly address the topics of oppression and the battle for human rights" (O'Neal, 2000, n.p.). In his review of King's 2000 album, *Freedom Creek*, former editor of *Living Blues* magazine David Nelson claimed that while King's lyrics focus on the legacy and present-day realities of racism and oppression in rural Alabama, King also "speak[s] to a larger, universal desire for human rights" (Nelson, 2000, p. 50).

This chapter examines the interrelationship between Willie King's political narratives, public memory, and human rights. Although scholars acknowledge the difficulty in developing a consensus on how to define "human rights," the term has, over the years, been associated with the right to life, freedom of expression and movement, protection from persecution and forced occupation (slavery), and freedom to form associations and be granted some form of representation (Benhabib, 2008, p. 102). Through a close textual analysis of his more politically engaging songs, I explore how King framed the concept of human rights as it relates to the history of racial discrimination in the South and the current exclusionary and exploitative practices that still impact the lives of many poor Southern blacks. In songs such as "Stand Up and Speak the Truth" and "Terrorized," King discussed the issue of human rights through an historical narrative that remembers how African Americans were brutalized under a system of white rule. King's songs touch on a host of social evils—slavery, sharecropping, lynching, segregation, and poverty—that worked to maintain a "racial dictatorship" in the South (Omi and Winant, 1994, p. 65). As a musician and human rights activist, King called attention to how the injustices of the past are still embedded in the social and political practices of today. At the same time, his message is a direct repudiation of hegemonic white Southern memories that openly deny the brutality and violence embedded in the social practices of slavery and sharecropping, among other Southern atrocities (Poole, 2006, p. 105). In all, through memory and the narrative

---

[1]   While I was working on this chapter, Willie King died of a heart attack near his home in Old Memphis, Alabama. This chapter is a tribute to his musicianship and his lifelong pursuit to emancipate the oppressed and improve the human condition.

of trauma, King re-centered the blues as an active form of protest, a genre that still agitates for human rights.

Willie King was born in Prairie Point, Mississippi in 1943. His parents separated when King was just a toddler, and he subsequently moved in with his grandparents (Reily, 2005, p. A8). At the age of seven, King relocated with his grandparents to Memphis Town (often referred to as "Old Memphis") in Pickens County, Alabama, just eight miles east of Prairie Point, where his family worked for various plantation owners as sharecroppers (Barretta, 2000, p. 26). With few employment options available, many black families in the South entered into work contracts with white landowners based on the sharecropping arrangement. Laborers farmed a specific plot of land and kept half of the revenue generated from the growing and selling of crops, cotton in particular. Despite the egalitarian tone implied in the name itself, most sharecropping families (both African American and white) ended up falling heavily into debt or just breaking even after a year's work.

King's interest in music started at an early age. Both his grandparents and parents enjoyed listening to blues and gospel music, and his father was an amateur blues musician (Reily, 2005, p. A8). His grandparents would often open up their house for weekend gatherings where local musicians would perform. Before he owned a guitar, the nine-year-old King constructed a diddley bow, an instrument created by distending a steel wire between nails or screws on a wooden board or on the side of a house (Wald, 2004, p. 107). In the mid-1950s, W.P. Morgan, a sympathetic white plantation manager who seemed to pay King and other African American families in the area the kind of respect and generosity almost unheard of in the South at that time, purchased an acoustic Gibson guitar for the 13-year-old musician; King vowed to pay off his debt by helping Morgan milk his cows (Barretta, 2000, p. 26).

Three years later, King decided he had had his fill of field work and left the plantation. Although he had fond memories of his former plantation manager, King realized that the exploitative sharecropping system kept the mostly black labor force in an almost perpetual state of peonage. To ensure his own personal freedom and financial stability, King vowed never to work as "slave" for any "bossman" again. After spending a few years selling moonshine and developing his skills as a musician, King left for Chicago in 1967. King worked at a meat packing plant and a paint factory and became friendly with a number of Chicago blues musicians, including Howlin' Wolf and his house band. Ultimately, however, King found Chicago to be a disappointment and within nine months of his arrival, he returned to Old Memphis, Alabama via a brief stint in Kansas City (Barretta, 2000, p. 29).

By the mid-1970s, King had formed the first incarnation of a band he would later call the Liberators (Barretta, 2000, p. 29). However, it would not be until two African Americans were imprisoned for mail fraud in Aliceville, a small community near Old Memphis, that King's lyrical focus became overtly political and he started to write and compose what he would call his "struggling" or "worried" blues. Maggie Bozeman, a school teacher and local NAACP leader and Julia Wilder, a 70-year-old grandmother, were imprisoned in 1982 for attempting to assist elderly black shut-ins to register to vote (Barretta, 2000, p. 29). "But what they really didn't like that they was goin' around gettin' people signed up to vote," recalled King. "A lot of the whites around there, they just couldn't stand that. So they got 'em up, framed 'em up there" (Barretta, 2000, p. 29).

Like much of Alabama and the South in general, Pickens County has a history of institutionalized racism and fierce bigotry. As late as the early 1980s, Pickens County still maintained segregated waiting rooms, an unfortunate remnant of the South's Jim Crow era. Debbie Bond, a white musician who plays rhythm guitar in the Liberators, arrived in Pickens County in 1979, was threatened at her day job for interacting with African Americans (*Willie King: Down in the Woods*). Even today, Pickens County is still mired in racial strife, as King sadly noted in an interview with *Living Blues* magazine: "I've been here 50 years. It's the same tune, racism, discrimination, but just different people in charge" (quoted in Barretta, 2000, p. 25). As a result, according to Scott Barretta, King's focus on improving the area's black community was not some nostalgic act:

> Willie's music is the music of the civil rights movement. But Willie is in rural Alabama. There was still a lot of oppression going on in the seventies and eighties, and nineties I suppose, probably today, so it's a continuing struggle. The civil rights era is not the past for Willie. So, in that sense, when he is doing these political songs, it's not nostalgia. It's still very relevant. (*Willie King: Down in the Woods*)

Exacerbating the racial strife is the crushing poverty that characterizes Pickens County. Although the county has a relatively large African American population (42.5 percent, compared to Alabama's African American population of 26.5 percent), most of the land is owned by a handful of white farmers (U.S. Census Bureau, Pickens County; Wypijewski, 1997, p. 35). According to the U.S. Census, 22.2 percent of the families in Pickens County lived below the poverty level in 2007, compared to the national average of 12.5 percent (U.S. Census Bureau, Pickens County). It is even worse in Old Memphis. The small community, with an African American population of 97 percent, is shrouded in poverty; in 2000, 33.3 percent of families and 53.1 percent of individuals lived below the poverty level (U.S. Census Bureau, Memphis Town). Although King has had numerous opportunities to leave Pickens County for greater financial rewards elsewhere, he decided to continue to live in Old Memphis in his run-down trailer while continuing to engage in community activism.

In 1983, King formed the Rural Members Association (RMA), a group whose mission is to pass "on the local heritage of traditional African American cultural arts and survival skills to the next generation" (Rural Members Association). Through the RMA, King helped sustain traditional African American "survival skills" through sponsoring classes in woodworking, quilt-making, and food preservation (Wypijewski, 1997, p. 35). At the same time, King was involved in blues education programs sponsored by the Alabama Blues Project, teaching young African Americans—who have largely abandoned the blues for other forms of black-based music—the rich musical and cultural traditions of the blues.

Although King had made only a few recordings since the 1970s, his big break occurred when he met Jim O'Neal, one of the founders of *Living Blues* magazine, at the Black Belt Folk Roots Festival in Alabama, in 1987. O'Neal remembered being bowled over by King's electrifying performance, later claiming that he would have recorded King on the spot if he had the resources to do so (O'Neal, 2000, n.p.). However, it was not until the late 1990s that O'Neal had the opportunity to properly record King; he ended up producing *Freedom Creek* (2000) and *Living in a New World* (2002). King received *Living Blues'* "Best Blues Artist of the Year" award in 2001, an honor he repeated in 2003 and 2004. He was featured in Martin Scorsese's PBS documentary series *The Blues*, in 2003, and in 2005, he was inducted into the "Howlin' Wolf Hall of Fame," an honor he especially cherished since King listed Wolf as one of his most important musical influences. In 2007, a DVD entitled *Willie King: Down in the Woods* was released, which increased King's domestic and international exposure. On March 8, 2009, Willie King died of a massive heart attack on his birthday. He was 66.

Public Memory, Historical Amnesia, and Willie King's Message of Liberation

Within the last 20 years, scholars from a wide variety of disciplines have become increasingly interested in public memory. Public memory, according to historian John Bodnar, is "a body of beliefs and ideas about the past that help a public or society understand both its past, present, and by implication, its future" (1992, p. 15). In a detailed and comprehensive analysis of how public memory differs from other types of remembering, Edward S. Casey highlighted the temporal nature of public memory: "Where other modes of remembering deal primarily with the past ... public memory is both attached to a past (typically an originating event of some sort) *and* acts to ensure a future of further remembering of that same event" (2004, p. 17). In contrast to individual memories, which are often idiosyncratic in nature, public memory is, by definition, a shared experience. It is through remembering the past that a community gains an understanding of the present and a vision for a desired future.

Yet, it would be inaccurate to suggest that all members of a community or society possess identical or congruent memories of the past. Indeed, memory is not history. While "history" has been linked to "truth" and "objectivity," memory is defined by its profound subjectivity because unlike "history," which proposes a singular, "authentic" interpretation of the past, memory is characterized by "competing accounts of past events" (Phillips, 2004, p. 2; Zelizer, 1995, p. 214). In other words, while "history" is transmitted from a seemingly invisible, authoritative source to uninformed auditors, memory is characterized by group conflict. This conflict often arises between vernacular communities, composed of ordinary citizens who reject current ideological practices, and official communities, comprised of individuals and groups concerned with maintaining the status quo. Both groups struggle to persuade listeners to accept a privileged understanding of the past and, by inference, the present and future (Armada, 1998, p. 237).

In the South, whites and African Americans have historically remembered the past in often radically different ways. Not surprisingly, a segment of the South's official culture—political officials, wealthy landowners, tourism operators, and ordinary citizens—have engaged in a kind of historical revisionism by providing a positive and optimistic assessment of slavery, sharecropping, and segregation. For example, the following observations represent, to a certain extent, Mississippi's (King's birthplace) official culture, both past and present. Although the barbaric institution of slavery has been universally repudiated, some observers have argued that slaves were, on the whole, treated with kindness by their owners. Walter Sillers, Sr., a Mississippi landowner and politician, argued in 1923 that slave owners in Mississippi did not tolerate the mistreatment of their slaves and the depiction of slave owners as "cruel" was largely the work of Northern propagandists (1923, p. 9). Meanwhile, some Southern whites have re-imagined sharecropping as a "fair" and "honest" working arrangement. Contemporary accounts find "happy" and "contented" smiling black faces singing joyous and uplifting songs while working as a harmonious, productive unit. For example, one writer fondly remembered the Randle family, a sharecropping family of 13 that lived on his father's farm:

> My daddy had a sharecropping family that lived adjacent to and farmed a piece of land on the west side of Duncan [Mississippi]. ... Chopping cotton can be hard work and is generally considered drudgery, but the Randle family didn't approach it that way. Yes, it was hot and sweaty work, but they removed all the negative aspects by enjoying each other and singing in the field. ... They would sing all day long. Everyone was smiling and enjoying themselves. Their chore was transformed into a pleasant experience by singing in the field. And, besides that, they were very good (talented). As I reflect on those times, I wonder if it was really as good as I remember. You know what? I think it was! Maybe it was better. (Boschert, 2008, p. 15)

While Boschert's rosy narrative puts a "happy face" on sharecropping, other voices have led support for Southern segregation policies. In 1999, Charles W. Capps, Jr.—who served in the Mississippi House of Representatives from 1976 to 2005 and served as sheriff of Bolivar County for several years—revealed in an interview with historian Charles Bolton that segregation actually worked to maintain "wonderful" racial relations in the South:

> Race relations were wonderful from my standpoint. Everybody both black and white knew exactly what their place was, and nobody ever got out of their place. We all understood. The blacks understood. The whites understood. There was

a segregated system that was no problem. I say that from a plantation owner standpoint. I say that from a white heritage. You might find it different, but as far as arguments or any kind of contest or anything that would be problems we didn't have. (1999, n.p.)

These idealized versions of the past reflect both remembering and forgetting, deliberate or otherwise. Historian Paul Shackel argues that forgetting, more often than not, protects the powerful at the expense of subordinate groups (2001, p. 3). While some whites resist acknowledging the region's difficult and painful past, musicians like Willie King do not. Regardless of threats against his personal safety, King's message is one of defiance, a compelling counter-response to stories that deny the harsh realities and heinous acts of white terror. Not only does King expose the human rights abuses of the past, but he also insists that poor blacks and other minorities are still victimized by white privilege and power.

King's wholesale indictment of sharecropping, the most popular tenant-worker arrangement in the South (at least from the perspective of the white landowner) during much of the twentieth century, serves as his primary topic of concern. Repeated references to demanding and demeaning work, with images of work mules, cotton fields, stifling heat, empty stomachs, and mind-numbing exhaustion, command much of his attention in songs such as "You So Evil" and "Crawlin' Blues." The song "Twenty Long Years" is typical of the imagery often interwoven into many of his more politically-oriented songs: "Worked twenty years on the plantation/ All I got was a pat on my back/ Lord, they put me in a shack/ ... You know, I plowed the mules/ And, you know, I picked the cotton ...."

In another example, in the song "Ain't Gonna Work," King remembers plowing the fields with his mules and working his fingers "down to the bone" while picking cotton in Alabama. At the same time, he takes a swipe at the memory of the happy, contented worker by claiming that sharecropping was really slavery in disguise. Through an effective use of call and response, King and second vocalist Willie Lee Halbert repeatedly articulate a message of insubordination by announcing that "I ain't gonna work the plantation no more." By refusing to return to the plantation, King is hopeful that the oppressed will be freed from mental slavery because "we are justice-bound."

Yet, for King, the past is "not in the past," but very much in the present. In "Why the Good Lord Sent Us the Blues," a spoken word monologue that concludes *Freedom Creek*, King observes that blacks are still subjected to many of the same oppressive conditions he lived under as a sharecropper in the 1940s and 1950s. King echoes this sentiment in "Is It My Imagination" as he wonders whether it is even possible to escape a sociopolitical system that still upholds white privilege at the expense of full black emancipation. Although he no longer picks cotton under the suspicious eye of the "bossman," King laments that "no matter what I do I just can't win." The song's signature line, "Is it my imagination/ Look like I'm still living on the plantation," recognizes the plantation as both a physical site of labor and a highly charged symbol of domination that infects all social life. King's songs work effectively to remind listeners that while the power and influence of the sharecropping system has been blunted in the face of the successes of the civil rights movement, privilege and power still intersect with racism and oppression.

King convincingly links the past to the present with frightening efficiency in "Terrorized," written after the attacks of September 11, 2001. While obviously outraged by the sheer level of violence, destruction, and death associated with 9/11, King has argued that while the United States has spent billions of dollars on the "War on Terror," African Americans and other oppressed people are still living in a state of real terror on their native soil (*Willie King: Down in the Woods*). Propelled by a slow and ominous rhythm, King's uncompromising message is direct and forceful: "Talk about terror—people I've been terrorized all my days/ You took my name/ And you know you left me in chains .../ You know they turn around and hung me from the tallest oak tree .../ You know, I worked in the cotton fields .../ With no money and no shoes go on my feet ...."

In the first line of the song, King connects the outrage from the 9/11 attacks to his own personal drama, a familiar story to many African Americans and other oppressed, marginalized groups who are routinely subjected to discriminatory policies anathematic to the political ideals of justice and equality. King paints a grim picture of the life of a poor, dispossessed black sharecropper surviving in a world where one's basic human rights are subordinate to power and profit. Furthermore, the depressing effects of poverty are vividly noted as King decries a country that would allow its citizens of color to be devoid of food and clothes. Blacks who protest or violate the rigid code of racially prescribed behavior were subjected to fiendish tortures, an oak tree and a rope. While much of the song reflects King's own lived experiences, he also assumes the persona of the slave who was brought to the United States in "chains" and forced into assuming a new identity through the adoption of a European surname. From the beginning of the slave trade to the negative present, King chronicles numerous incidents of racism and brutality, all vivid examples of domestic terrorism that many Americans refuse to acknowledge. The song also implies that without some radical shift in human consciousness and political policy the future of poor African Americans will remain essentially unchanged. Ultimately, the song reminds us that domestic terrorism, which is similar in many respects to international terrorism, involving African Americans has existed in the United States since West Africans were kidnapped and shipped to Jamestown, Virginia in 1619.

The topic of slavery emerges in a richly provocative song, "Writing in the Sky (Katrina)." Yet, once again, the "dead" institution of slavery is contextualized in the present as the storm revealed the injustices of the present. In the song, his "mother" (Mother Nature, Hurricane Katrina) traveled from King's spiritual homeland, Africa, to inquire about his welfare. As the storm passed through the same geographical space that inhabited the slave world, it revealed the present-day misery and discontentment experienced by the poor. In other words, in the same place (land and sea) where slaves were transported, auctioned off to the highest bidder, and worked to exhaustion or an early death, live the descendents of these slaves who still sadly survive in a world marked by lack of opportunities, unemployment, and poverty. The storm revealed that, despite white perceptions to the contrary, racism still marks the American experience.

Meanwhile, King reserves some of his anger for Pickens County, Alabama where he has lived most of his life. In "Pickens County Payback," he enumerates a number of social evils, sharecropping, poverty, and hunger, as justification for impending revolution. He warns Pickens County (presumably city officials, law enforcement, and white landowners) that "you got to get ready for the big payback." Historically, African Americans living in the South who uttered such a threat would be severely punished, even murdered. Even today, King's words would not go unnoticed by the white power structure in Pickens County. As he announces in another song from *Freedom Creek*, "each and every day I put my life on the line." In the acoustic blues song called "Pickens County Blues," written by David Gespass, a lawyer who has worked with King on civil rights issues, King narrates the events surrounding the arrest and eventual imprisonment of two African American women who attempted to register black voters in Pickens County. At the end of the song, justice is eventually meted out as the sheriff and the district attorney are escorted to jail while the two African American prisoners are presumably freed.

Interestingly, King reserves some of his most stinging criticism for the black hypocrite. In "Uncle Tom," he spots black spies everywhere—at work, in church, and on the street—and announces that "Uncle Tom" must go. In "The Sell-Out," the Uncle Tom character reappears and haunts King on the plantation because "every time I try to make a move/ somebody watching me." Later, when King joined the civil rights movement, Uncle Tom "sold me out." To outwit his opponent, King announces that he "done made a change/ no more civil right/ From now on I'm talking about the human right." For example, when King was a teenager he defiantly told his plantation manager that he would not be returning to the fields to pick cotton. Rather than celebrating King's success, many of his fellow black workers were angry and resentful. As King tells his listeners in "Holding the Line," despite the fact that others will try to "wreck your life," it is important to remain defiant and steadfast, to keep on "holding the line."

While King is a fierce critic of social injustice, to stereotype him simply as an outspoken critic of injustice would trivialize and simplify both the person and the message. Blues scholar, John Sinclair, has observed that King tempers his protest songs with "tender pleas for love and compassion ..." (2002, n.p.). As King rejoiced in one of his songs, "when we start loving each other/ I like it like that." King's songs are similar to most protest music; his lyrics tend to avoid providing specific, concrete solutions to alter the undesirable present. He does believe, however, that empathy, compassion, love, unity, and peace are antidotes to many sociopolitical problems. It is only through love and compassion that individual human rights will be preserved. Thus, while critics have divided King's body of work into "love" and "political" songs, the distinction is illusory for both represent a single, consistent theme. Although he does not overtly attack the South's segregation policies, he implies in some of his songs that Jim Crow laws are responsible for much of the racial strife and division in the United States. To overcome decades of legal segregation, and its aftermath—self-segregation practices—King expresses an urgent need to bridge the racial divide in songs such as "America": "America, we've been separated too long/ We all need to come together/ ... with love like that/ You know, we can't go wrong." The black ghetto, a result—in part—of discriminatory US federal housing policies that helped construct white suburbia after World War II, leaving many African Americans and other minorities locked in public housing, is the topic of concern in "Clean Up the Ghetto." King encourages religious figures and even the President of the United States to "come on down from your high chair" and cure the dysfunction of the ghetto and unite warring gangbangers.

At the same time King discusses how love and compassion will inoculate the racial divide in the United States, he also reminds us of the global nature of human suffering and alienation, and thus calls on his audience to seek universal peace and love. In the title song to *One Love*, King recognizes that despite surface-level distinctions of race, income, country of origin (and other demographic variables), "we all look the same on the inside." In "Let's Come Together (as One Community)," King's words echo the voice of another champion of liberation, Bob Marley: "I'm calling all my brothers and sisters all over the world/ Don't make no difference who you are/ You may be black, you may be brown/ You may be red, and you might be white/ Let's come together as brothers and sisters." In "One Love (Monologue)," King tells his audience that despite the long-standing popular association, particularly in the African American community, between the blues and the occult (the blues is the "Devil's Music"), the blues has served as a healing agent to solve the world's problems: "The blues have helped heal the world. It's one of the solutions that the Great Spirit sent us. And we're thankful for not to abuse it, but to use it in a positive way to help spread love, bring peoples together from all over the world to sit down at the meeting table to have peace. ...."

As we have seen, Willie King's "struggling blues" recounts numerous human rights abuses visited upon Southern blacks by agents (e.g., the bossmen) who vigorously defended the virtues and values of white supremacy. Subjected to appalling working conditions with little or no financial compensation, African Americans were further traumatized by segregation laws that violated a basic right for freedom of movement. Pursued by lynch mobs, arrested and imprisoned on capricious laws, and often forced into labor camps (the convict-leasing system), African Americans were further terrorized by laws that denied them the opportunity to vote or hold political office. Yet, King's songs are not some spirited history lesson on human rights abuses of the past. He continually reminds listeners of the indivisible relationship between the past and present. The ugly residue of overt racism and discrimination, which characterized the "Old South," are manifested in present-day realities: poverty, illiteracy, inadequate housing, unemployment, and gang warfare. And it is important to remember that King lived in a poor black rural community in a region of the South that is still, in many ways, trapped in the

1950s. As a member of a vernacular community, King's words provide a strong "counter-memory" to some white Southerners who would prefer to "sugarcoat" or simply forget the past. Although he does not offer concrete solutions to eradicate the problems of hatred and division, King envisions in the title song for the album *Living in a New World*, a place where old lines of demarcation are replaced by love, unity, and peace. As a vehicle of social change, the blues is a powerful weapon of liberation, or in the words of Willie King, a "gift of God" for "anybody that's living under oppression" (Barretta, 2000, p. 25).

Acknowledgement

I would like to thank P. Renee Foster for her helpful and insightful suggestions and comments, which improved the overall direction and content of this chapter.

Chapter 6

The Aesthetic Dimension:
Cultural Politics, Human Rights, and *Hedwig*

Stefan Mattessich

Did you know that I am president because of you?—Vaclav Havel to Lou Reed (1990)[1]

The protagonist of the film musical *Hedwig and the Angry Inch* (2001) is an androgynous ex-philosophy student named Hansel Schmidt, who in the late 1980s emigrates from communist East Berlin to the United States, after a botched sex change operation, as the wife of an African American soldier, Luther Robinson. Hansel, now Hedwig, ends up living in a small Kansas town, where Luther, ironically on the same day as the fall of the Berlin Wall, leaves her for a young boy. Devastated on two fronts, Hedwig falls in love with a naive teenager, Tommy Speck, imparting to him a more cultivated sense of style as well as her own longstanding ambition to be a singer. Later Tommy, under the stage name Hedwig gives him, Tommy Gnosis, steals her songs and becomes a successful rock star. In protest Hedwig files a lawsuit and jealously dogs Tommy on a cross-country tour, playing outside each concert venue with a new band, the Angry Inch, at a chain of tacky seafood restaurants called Bilgewater.

Hedwig is more than a carefully plotted story of betrayed love and deflated dreams. It also provides an astute account of American cultural politics over the last 40 years, both because it fixes the trait of this politics in a transgendered subject for whom sexual identity is a malleable social property, something to be performatively achieved rather than presumed or given, and because it situates her in a consumer society seen from outside or as a whole, in its totality (since again Hedwig comes from the former East Berlin). All the film's various transvestic condensations—not only masculine and feminine or gay and straight but also music and narrative, text and image, live action and animation—evoke a fundamental aesthetic dimension of capitalist life that it critiques as much as it celebrates, in a spirit not far removed, we might say, from the German philosophy Hansel studied in his student days.[2]

---

[1]   Quoted without further attribution by Matt Welch (2003).

[2]   One thinks in particular of Critical Theory and the Frankfurt School. The term "aesthetic dimension" comes, of course, from Herbert Marcuse's 1978 book of the same name, aiming at a Marxist aesthetics, although the present essay takes its theoretical

The name for this aesthetic dimension, for the place in us of inherent malleability, is simply *human being* grasped as pure possibility without any content other than the capacity for normative negotiation of what one will be or how one will live.[3] It follows that this capacity by its very nature is indeterminate, felt in the resistance to being defined as one thing or another, and hence as a kind of *in*capacity at the same time.[4] We hear this paradox alluded to in the film, when Hedwig's East German mother tells him it's "better to be powerless." The boy s/he is at this time does a double take, puzzled by the statement, in which we also hear a clear allusion to the rhetoric of dissident movements in the former Soviet Union and Eastern Bloc countries, where resistance to totalitarian domination took an existential form derived in part from the experience of Western popular culture.

In his seminal essay from 1978, "The Power of the Powerless," Vaclav Havel linked the goals of these movements to an explicit rejection of "abstract projects for an ideal political or economic order" and the machinations of parties "on the level of real, institutional, quantifiable power." The locus of resistance lay rather in the negative space of this power, in withdrawal from it. Opposition implied potentialities carried over into the "singular, explosive, incalculable" contingencies of cultural life. No one person could master the situations in which these contingent forces circulated; the im-potence of the subject in culture was diffused rather into the underground scenes of decentered sociability that Havel witnessed in the Prague spring of 1968 and in later movements like Charter 77—especially the excitement generated around the rock band Plastic People of the Universe (and its famous Velvet Underground covers).

The spirit of the 1960s was palpable in these centrifugal social energies, although Havel would tease out in them a decidedly more centripetal counterpoint. For him the stake in the "Velvet Revolution" that eventually helped to terminate totalitarian rule in his country was an essential humanity felt in the opposition to

---

bearings elsewhere, essentially in deconstruction, since recent American cultural politics derives more directly from its skepticism about totalizing schemes and historicist accounts. For a measured sense of the limits of this skepticism from a "critical" perspective, see Fredric Jameson's "Marx and Postmodernism" (1989), an elaboration of the stakes in his seminal work on a late capitalist mode of production.

[3]   I echo legal theorist Drucilla Cornell's conception for the subject of an "original position" or a priori "imaginary domain" that, however ideal its status, she argues should be juridically guaranteed as a right for the subject to its own performative struggles with sex and gender norms (1996, p. 24 and *passim*).

[4]   In *The Coming Community*, Giorgio Agamben speaks of a "capacity to not-be" or an "existence in potentiality" as a "being that does not *presuppose* itself as a hidden essence that chance or destiny would then condemn to the torment of qualifications, but rather *exposes* itself in its qualifications ... such a being is neither accidental nor necessary, but is, so to speak, *continually engendered from its own manner*" (1993, p. 27). See also Werner Hamacher on the "happening of the existence without predicate" in a discussion of this temporal possibility as a distinctly human right (2004, p. 356).

power politics, determined as the substance of an unqualified social being that was disenfranchised but also dimensional, a "hidden sphere" coextensive with the subterranean cultures he so admired. "Individuals can be alienated from themselves only because there is *something* [italics mine] in them to alienate," he wrote, again in "The Power of the Powerless":

> The terrain of this violation is their authentic existence. Living the truth [presupposed in alienation] is thus woven directly into the texture of living a lie. It is the repressed alternative, the authentic aim to which living a lie is an inauthentic response. Only against this background does living a lie make any sense: it exists because of that background. In its excusatory, chimerical rootedness in the human order, it is a response to nothing other than the human predisposition to truth. Under the orderly surface of the life of lies, therefore, there slumbers the hidden sphere of life in its real aims, of its hidden openness to truth.

Havel's rhetoric is still persuasive where it points beyond an economy of repressive force by stressing the "textural" indistinction of truth and lies, authentic and inauthentic life. The individual's self-alienation is the sign of an irrepressible humanity. But just for this reason Havel also has to operate within that economy, unweaving in its texture "a repressed longing for dignity and fundamental rights" that will materialize, in its "hidden openness," as the "truth" of an aesthetic dimension.

The chord *Hedwig* strikes with this conceptualization of its own formal principle raises an interesting, and troubling, problem for us today. Cultural politics in the West consist in similar tactics of resistance to the hierarchies that govern parties or organized movements, at least in their revolutionary form (discredited after the fall of the Soviet Union). They have tended to be antinationalist on the one hand and committed to an ethical discourse of values (anti-authoritarian, feminist, anti-racist) on the other. But holding off from power politics, they also work within democratic parameters as single-issue movements based in a liberal contractarian order that, more recently, has turned sharply toward global policies of economic structural adjustment, war, and an oligarchic concentration of wealth and power. Hence the desired deconstruction of the self-identical political subject that Havel aims for in 1978 would produce in the post-Communist era its own "excusatory, chimerical" equivalent, since it is for the sake of the human's "hidden sphere" that Havel endorses the 1999 NATO bombing of Serbia and the 2003 invasion of Iraq. In both cases, state violence is deemed necessary to limit the power of rogue states that do not subscribe to or tolerate Havel's democratic "truth." He could thus assert, apropos the lack of a direct mandate for the attack on Serbia from the United Nations, that the spirit, if not the letter, of international law was upheld; the bombing campaign, he wrote then, happened "out of respect for the law, for a law that ranks higher than the law that protects the sovereignty of states" (1999, p. 53). This higher law, he goes on to add, is that of "human rights."[5]

The implication here is that the simple *human being* of the aesthetic dimension, linked to a concept of subjective autonomy understood as freedom from the political per se, is one of these human rights, and as such it lends itself to a legitimation strategy for a distinctly *neo*liberal political and economic order. The capacity that is also an incapacity, an "im-potence," becomes the qualification of people deprived of any other than their human rights, whether this means the immigrant, the refugee, the stateless prisoner, or finally the distracted consumer whose political being has been virtualized in a world marketplace. Whether human rights are violated or used ideologically to justify their violation, their *anti*-political character is *de*politicized. This implies in the discourse of human rights both a resistance to power on the model of a freedom from politics (what in classical liberal theory would be called negative liberty) and the rationalization of unfreedom (the negation of liberty). And the one doubles up on the other. Cultural anti-politics thus has to grapple with its own reflection in the anti-politics of the capitalist state.[6]

The Head as Wig

There are neither men nor women, Jews nor Greeks.—Saint Paul

The supposition of an aesthetic dimension need not, however, imply Havel's brand of metaphysical humanism, with its reliance on an alienable "something," a core subjectivity that precedes its performative expression. Thus *Hedwig* stages this supposition only on registers of social and sexual identity at which the "human" is more contested than given, more an historical product than an essential "truth." The symbol of this contestation in the film becomes the wig, or succession of wigs, Hedwig wears, both to catalyze her dreams of success and to denature gender categories.[7]

---

[5] He asserts in the same essay, "I always come to the conclusion that human rights, human freedoms, and human dignity have their deepest roots somewhere outside the perceptible world. These values are as powerful as they are because, under certain circumstances, people accept them without compulsion and are willing to die for them, and they make sense only in the perspective of the infinite and the eternal ..." (Havel, 1999, p. 24).

[6] Nancy Fraser sees this reflection as an "uncanny doubling" of cultural politics— second-wave feminism is her case in point—with the strategies and tactics of contemporary neoliberalism (2009, p. 115).

[7] In this *Hedwig* takes its cue from theories of cultural politics predicated on notions of discursively constituted subjectivity and normative resignification, whose most exemplary

But even when we keep this distinction in mind, the aesthetic dimension understood as a kind of pure possibility for the person to fashion his or her identity remains nonetheless a *universal*, and hence nourished by the same springs of philosophical thought about subjectivity as the liberal democratic tradition cultural politics tend to work both in and against. *Hedwig* acknowledges as much by building into its love story a reference to Aristophanes' origin myth as recounted in Plato's *Symposium*. The metaphysics of form in matter (*eidos, ratio, logos*) we sense in the symmetries of Aristophanes' round men, women, and hermaphrodites split in two by Zeus's thunderbolts—and split within themselves by a desire for the lost wholeness Plato will situate outside time or change, knowledge, language, or predication—glosses *Hedwig*'s various oppositional displacements in terms of an underlying commonality. Sexual difference in the myth, however originary it may have been, pointed for the Greeks to the subordination of biology in an eternalized hierarchy of values. Hedwig's transformation from man into woman, overlapping with her transition from East to West, thus centers attention on an aesthetic dimension where, as it were, sexual being takes place through a kind of erotic anamnesis Plato understood as a transcendence of the physical or an ascent to what he called the Universal Mind.[8] But the common element is more a modality or way of being that includes its own internal scission, its own missing half or other; this is how it remains undetermined, falling outside any logical scheme or category.

The price of Hedwig's emigration from East Berlin to the United States, once again, is a botched sex change operation. She has, as Luther puts it, to "leave something behind" (to leave as his wife), and this remainder (or trace) of her alienated manhood in the place where democracy was renounced (and Marxism tried) persists in her liberated womanhood as the possibility of cultural identity. Her "angry inch," what she "has to work with," she implies, in the capitalist society she has embraced, resolves the insufficiency of her being into the desire to emulate her childhood heroes (the "crypto-homo rockers" Lou Reed, Iggy Pop, and David Bowie). Expression is determined as castration, which underpins the controlled play on presence and absence we hear in dialogue—"how did a bare slip of a girly boy from Communist East Berlin become the internationally ignored song stylist barely standing before you?" Hedwig asks her Bilgewater audience at one point—and see in the film's mixed media displacements of past and present, realism and fantasy. For all its energy, *Hedwig* is static like collage, drawing what Freud said of the unconscious, that it has no time, into the dream-like stylization of a subjectivity turned, as it were, inside out, projected into the film's kitschy *mise-en-scène* as pop culture is internalized in (almost, if never quite, sentimental) songs, clichés, advertising slogans, the Cindy Sherman-esque imitations of different gender stereotypes.

---

adherent is Judith Butler. See her 1998 "Merely Cultural" for a rehearsal of the stakes in such theories. The essay is also a rejoinder to criticisms made in particular by Nancy Fraser.

  [8]   Agamben glosses this movement as a "transport [of] the object not toward another thing or another place, but towards its own taking-place—toward the Idea" (1993, p. 2).

And no matter how intense the frustrations become for Hedwig as the central narrative of Tommy's betrayal unfolds—no matter how much she is hurt by life or fails in expressing her identity as a singer—the dynamic remains one of the disavowals that engenders castration anxiety. The dissonance she experiences with others and inside herself dissimulates the deeper emptiness that virtualizes her every performative mode of being, and suggests a prior undifferentiated ground where Hedwig is finally neither man nor woman. Her "angry inch," in the song of the same name "Where my penis used to be/ Where my vagina never was," points to a desexualized stratum of the aesthetic dimension, and thus to a kind of *sameness* that gradually becomes, not so much what is celebrated as human, but the problem of Hedwig's implication in capitalist society. We may state the problem this way: castration anxiety doesn't just inaugurate sexual difference, it also produces the universal space of play where biology takes shape through the cognitive, perceptual, and even technological syntheses of our poetic self-fashioning. This universal, *coextensive with castration*, informs the right to cope with, resolve, or come to terms with sexual difference how we will. But the relation between this universal and the narcissistic unity that it takes within castration's logic of disavowal and denial remains undecidable. Is the right to an aesthetic dimension a right to this unity or to undoing the perverse structures of desire that constitute identity? And if it stops short of an answer to this question, that is if it only names the *pre*-political freedom to opt either for accommodation or resistance to consensus reality, does this not answer the question after all, by having nothing to say about why im-potent being, or non-coincident selfhood, would be right or just?

Hedwig grapples with this nonpolitical priority of a fundamentally transvestic identity through the love story it tells. Again because the aesthetic dimension, and the right that goes with it, results from the entry into culture (and history), desire emerges in the transcendent movement toward a Platonic Idea. When Hedwig falls in love with Tommy, she sees in him both her own possibility for cultural identity (they can collaborate, form a band, aspire for fame together) and the ideal wholeness toward which desire tends. This image of ideal wholeness materializes through her making Tommy over as the rock star who will eventually steal her songs. Tommy as the substance of this image, as the raw material for Hedwig's self-expression, literalizes the division (or lack) within desire by his betrayal, which is not simply a "forgetting," as Hedwig puts it, of what rock'n'roll truly means (nonconformist community, collaboration, trust) but also its constitutive contradiction. This is true even if we acknowledge that Hedwig needs Tommy for the recognition she cannot win on her own, given a social intolerance for her transsexual identity. The pathos of her thwarted right to self-representation thus does not preclude the resentment that implicates her in the desire of society (of the "Other")—we see this in her relationship to Angry Inch backup singer Yitzhak, who as her current boyfriend lives miserably in Tommy's shadow, and especially after she tears up Yitzhak's passport when he (but also she, since Yitzhak is played by a woman) threatens to leave the band. Both Tommy and Yitzhak turn back on

Hedwig the coercive dynamic that drives her aspirations to wholeness, the urge to control that only produces its own failure. The ideal, or Idea, *the norm*, we might say, necessarily undoes Hedwig, and makes of her performative negotiations a foreclosure of identity that is neither right nor just, only "what [she] has to work with" in capitalist society. Which entails that Hedwig is, ironically enough, only a kind of exemplary subject for such a society: her drama is what she has a *right to* in it.

The Right to Have Rights

> I ain't got the power anymore.—"Quicksand," David Bowie

The upshot is that cultural politics might not transcend the determination of the aesthetic dimension as autonomy in the classical liberal sense of a nonpolitical subjectivity. Whether we opt for anti-authoritarian dissent or authoritarian consent, the constitutive element of choice remains the aesthetic dimension's empty form, mirrored or doubled in a market-culture that remains intact through the struggle for self-representation. Cultural politics, at their best, engender the art of living in resistance to the subjective or discursive structures of social reality, and this resistance stops short of positing any particular program or system for how so to live.[9] Indeed on principle it can't, since what it posits are the conditions of possibility for the freedom of performance itself, which are also conditions for the unfreedom of conformity. The *decision* left up to the democratic subject thus stops short of the politics that would challenge the state.

None of this means we can't take anti-capitalist stands on the egalitarian grounds of culture, nor even that we can't sort human rights from their ideological manipulation and for the pragmatic end of an authentic justice. Cultural politics help us to switch off the light of consent, even as no one does it for us—except perhaps through the exemplification (Bowie would be a superlative case) of the "powerlessness" implied by a subjectivity felt only in relation to its potentiality, one moreover committed to its own undoing, or to letting itself be undone in its normative identifications. We might indeed reasonably enough wonder if this self-undoing is the same thing as autonomy for the private individual in civil society, since its displacement of subjective boundaries opens us up to a *social* implication that is immediate and determining. Critic Werner Hamacher glosses the mode of this more relational subjectivity as "prayer," the *euché*, "a wish," he writes, "that there may be less and more than politics ... something other than politics, that there

---

[9]   Recall Deleuze on revolutionary counterculture's "nomad" thought resisting serial codification. "We also know that the problem for revolutionaries today is to unite within the purpose of the particular struggle without falling into the despotic and bureaucratic organization of the party or state apparatus, a nomadic unit related to the outside that will not revive an internal despotic unity" (1984, p. 149).

may be a society and that this society *may* be that of the absolutely singular" (2004, p. 356). Hamacher goes on to link the subjunctive character of this sociability to a kind of *poeisis*, qualified by political philosopher Hannah Arendt's reading of St Augustine in her work *Origins of Totalitarianism*. "'The creation of man is not the beginning of something that, once created, exists in its essence'," he quotes, "'develops, remains or perishes, but rather the beginning of a being that itself has the ability to begin: it is the beginning of a beginning, the beginning of beginning itself'" (Hamacher, 2004, p. 356). The fundamental ground of this decision is its constitutive undecidability, its anticipatory openness to the future; as such it is a "parapolitical" right to what Marx called "species-being" and saw precluded in the civil society of a liberal democratic state (predicated on competition and mutual fear). Autonomy, Hamacher suggests, designates less the property of an individual than the inner life drawn forth in us by others as a shared recalcitrance to closed forms of identity. What shelters this "inside out" subjectivity is what he calls an undetermined "right to have [determined] rights."

The limits of this eucharism at the heart of what I am here calling cultural politics appear on the register of *desire*, where the recalcitrance to an identitarian (or authoritarian) being has to contend with its reduction in consumer society to little more than fantasies of rebellion. This is one reason why the mode of subjectivity sketched by Hamacher can only be that of the wish, of a "longing for fundamental rights" limited by the aggression that actually conditions the "citizen" as a consumer. Something of this double bind is legible in the conclusion of *Hedwig*, where Hedwig's contradictions become so intense that they break her apart. The wig comes off, the energy of self-representation turns not against identity per se but against its malleability, its transvestism. Stripped down, she hears Tommy sing her own song "Wicked Little Town" back to her, only this time he has changed the lyrics: the song is an apology but also a message, telling her from within the violence of her *poeisis* that "there's no mystical design/ no cosmic lover pre-assigned/ there's nothing you can't find/ that cannot be found ...." What Hedwig recognizes during this song is the desire that props up in her/ him the regulative idea (or norm) and hence her/his investment in the glamour that has replaced communal "species-being" with mere social emulation. Tommy brings this home to her/him, and to us, in the song when, on the words "my voice," offered to Hedwig as a sign of friendship, something s/he can "follow" and count on, he breaks off and the song goes on without him: recorded, reproduced, a copy of the originality that was never "his" to begin with. Expression discloses the void at its heart that ties it to the avoidance of disavowal (or castration anxiety), which in turn becomes the empty form of desire itself in consumer society.

Of course Hedwig changes with this revelation; it engenders in her/him the will to live more fully outside the embodied structures of consciousness posited by consensus reality as the condition for recognition in it. This change is coded as a reduction to the bareness of human being and a radical exposure to the world: a vulnerability, a passivity, that evokes the undetermined "someone" capable of "beginning" to live with finitude and for others. But the difference at issue here also conceals a repetition, since with it the aesthetic dimension of self-fashioning that *Hedwig* has all along been staging only crystallizes in its essential form. We sense this with the double S-shaped tattoo on Hedwig's ass, one of many similar symbols in the film, glimpsed in the final shot as s/he walks naked down the dark alley (a sort of social birth canal) toward milling passersby on the street. The tattoo's allusion to the metaphysics of sameness and difference, wholeness and fragmentation, goes as it were *with* her/him into the unconditioned future, and with the claim to a future that her/his final hesitation on the street suggests. We can thus say that nothing has changed at the end of *Hedwig*, or more precisely that the change has no content, since it lacks any programmatic dimension, and that it can only be taken up again or reiterated *like a program*, or as the program of her/his non-self-identity.

The deconstructive subtlety at stake in this paradox is quite controlled in the film; it knows very well its own cultural politics. But the clarity of this knowledge also underscores a problem present in the figure of the human, or rather in its "bare life" as a mode of resistance and freedom. Giorgio Agamben has glimpsed in the "sacredness" of this figure the anomalous category of the scapegoat, the outsider, the stigmatized other reduced to mere corporeal existence without any political qualification. *Homo sacer* is indeed for Agamben the subject of human rights whose destitution is elevated into a principle and a value—less for a society understood as symbolically unified than for the world marketplace envisioned for us by neoliberal policy-makers. And it is not merely the stateless person who embodies these "rights"; the citizen of liberal democratic society, borne up by an entire political tradition through which the figure of bare life runs for Agamben like a red thread, also carries within it the nonpolitical dispossession of an "essential humanity." The citizen "is a two-faced being," he writes, "the bearer both of subjection to sovereign power and of individual liberties" (1998, p. 125). To this extent the "rights" of the citizen become indicators of a merely nominal freedom.

Cultural Politics and Radical Democracy

> You have no power over me!—Sarah to the Goblin King (played by David Bowie), *Labyrinth* (1986)

Agamben has been criticized for an overly reductive conception of democratic space. For philosopher Jacques Rancière there is thus no room in his account for the contestation of what counts as politics, or as rational interaction in a communication scene. What we hear in this scene as an "animal" noise or nonsense (that is, the politically unqualified body) for Rancière is a claim on the arbitrary and historically contingent character of the rationality that holds social asymmetries of power in place. This claim is less interiorized as human and set off from power (in its negative liberty and via its metamorphosis through the Christian-metaphysical tradition) than power's human expression, taken on as one's own and *aware of itself* in the fields of force we commonly inhabit. "Bare life" is not for Rancière incapable of politics but, on the contrary, politics itself as what he calls the "absent foundation" of all decision, all expression, indeed all forms of power. "Strictly speaking, democracy is not a form of State," he writes. "It is always beneath and beyond these forms. Beneath, insofar as it is the necessarily egalitarian, and necessarily forgotten, foundation of the oligarchic state. Beyond, insofar as it is the public activity that counteracts the tendency of every State to monopolize and depoliticize the public sphere" (Rancière, 2006, p. 71).

We sense in rhetoric like this the antinationalism of cultural politics wrested from the determination of its aesthetic dimension in the *privatized* possibility for recognition, rights, or "happiness" permitted by the state (always for Rancière a police state). The stress is placed on what identities (of every kind, on every level) *don't know*, or have "forgotten," about themselves: that anti-authoritarian desire is bound up simultaneously with a capacity for authoritarian closure, and thus enacted, exercised, through the reflection on this fact, through its becoming conscious of its own inherent structure of disavowal where a social and political implication is concerned. This does not come down to the same thing as avowing what is denied; it points to a knowledge centered on a constitutive "forgetting" and thus willing to enter a democratic space in all its inherent risk.

By re-centering cultural politics in a properly self-critical dimension, Rancière opens them up to what they do tend to equivocate: the kind of politics that can oppose the oligarchic constitution of the state and on its terrain, which is to say all the way down to its foundation in our own freedom and decision. Rancière calls attention to the closed totality of the (neoliberal) state in social life; indeed he sees it in the state's projection of its own totalitarian tendencies into this life and as a justification for its biopolitical management of an unruly or ungovernable populace.[10] If in this process he rejects the antidemocratic stigmatization of the person (and the populace) that operates in the legitimation strategies of today's neoliberal order, he also sets the person off from its "human" passivity or passion, which for him is only another version of its stigmatization.[11] Democracy for Rancière is not the "society" generated within the purview of state control qua consumerism, possessive individualism, representational or electoral politics, or even social movements that stop short of contesting the discursive field in which politics is effectively neutralized. Or rather, democracy is all these when, fissured

---

[10]   *Hatred of Democracy* (2006) focuses on the ideological link forged in contemporary French political discourse between democracy and totalitarianism, based generally in equivocations about the *need* for elite classes to mediate reason (or logos) for people incapable on their own of exercising it. The actual agenda that reduces the democratic subject to the narcissistic consumer whose desire is essentially authoritarian, for Rancière, is conditioned by the perceived anachronism of democratic politics for oligarchies composed of capitalists and their technocratic experts.

[11]   See also *Disagreement* (1999, p. 124) and "Who Is the Subject of the Rights of Man?" (2004, p. 306); the latter also succinctly lays out Rancière's critique of Agamben.

in their an-archic ground and turned, as it were, against themselves, resistance is volatilized by the question of its own complicity—the question, that is, *of resistance as the form of authoritarian investment.*

The nuance in Rancière's thought appears with the shift of what is universal or "true" onto the fulcrum of this question, or this resistance, which is quite literally *yours* and *mine*, everybody's or "just anybody's" relation to power. In this sense the aesthetic dimension is always already political (and not pre-, non-, or anti-political); it exists only insofar as we unweave the spell of power in ourselves, and constitutes a right only to this unweaving activity or auto-deconstructive practice. Indeed anything not practical in this way misses the peculiar positivity that Rancière ascribes to our negative liberty. It misses the "egalitarian contingency" that he says underpins the "inegalitarian contingency" (2006, p. 94) of all social structures, and hence the lie of every hierarchy, every vertical structure of identification when it mystifies or naturalizes the inevitable differences between people, between who we are, where in social space we come from, and what we know. By making these differences the signs of a fundamental equality, Rancière foregrounds the most important political question today: what are the modes, conservative or liberal, fundamentalist or secular, conformist or nonconformist, of *our own* equivocation where the "nature" of authority is concerned? Rancière further suggests that it is only by enacting the answer to this question at the level of subjective identity—his term is "subjectification"—that we participate in the universality, or the rationality, of the aesthetic dimension that we claim as a human right.

Of course cultural politics have always moved on this practical terrain, and Rancière is accordingly only one of their best theoreticians. What he doesn't speak to is how this auto-deconstructive politics can become an interest for those who consciously or unconsciously believe in authority. No one once again does it for you; the mode at issue is one of singular modifications, precarious acts, uncertain epiphanies. The double bind legible at the conclusion of *Hedwig* thus remains for Rancière in the attenuation of any programmatic view of politics that would force a change of belief in others: "forgetting" as the right mode of political being does not mean that the "consensual forgetting of democracy" (2006, p. 92) that Rancière himself observes to be happening in our midst is any less likely. As much as he can re-term what Hamacher, for instance, calls a "wish … for something other than politics" (2004, p. 356) as a political event, he can only fall back within its subjunctive or singular "plea" for the sort of rationality he affirms as politics in those who in effect do not, and maybe cannot, feel it.

It might be too much to ask of *Hedwig*, and the cultural politics it reflects, or refracts, in (what is for Rancière an oxymoronic) "democratic society," that it do more than symptomatize this double bind in the same manner. We can say that the film tests the limits of its own principles—its commitments to an aesthetic dimension—where for Hedwig possible or malleable identity *fails*, and something else—finitude, facticity, exception—must be faced in its intractable otherness. The risk is that Hedwig's willingness at the end to come into an embodied relation to the world falls back upon some kind of human *nature* that feels itself as the depoliticized abjection of Agamben's "bare life," and so figures the exhaustion of our performative resignifications in the social entropy of today's antidemocratic capitalism. What's left, on this account, would be the sort of sentimentalized community Hedwig praises near the end in the song "Midnight Radio," which again stops short of the engagement with capitalist power that we clearly need of politics today. But I think another reading is also possible: one that sees in Hedwig's final nakedness, in his/her reduction to the fleshy "nature" beneath and beyond her masquerades, what literary critic Susan Maslan calls "the locus of sensibility, of feeling, and consequently of sympathy" (2004, p. 362). The human, in this light, would be what the subject or citizen represses in order to be a universalized member of a politically qualified state. As the residual *sign* of what has been lost through this repression, "included in the *polis* only as an exclusion," (2004, p. 362) Maslan writes, the human becomes a name for the recognition of what we have in common, and for the equality that Rancière asserts as the foundation of any political order. Hedwig signifies in this way at the end of the film because s/he has cut the knot of suffering and aggression that constitutes identity and understood the "truth" of her own worldly implication. With this knowledge of what we are indeed capable of, the "power of the powerless" becomes not just a prayer but also an objection, drawing forth from the very dehiscence of the ground on which we stand the perhaps unsuspected strength for true protest.

Chapter 7

The Evolution of the Political Benefit Rock Album

Neil Nehring

In 2002 Jon Langford, leader of both the Chicago-based alt.country band the Waco Brothers and the still-extant British punk band the Mekons, produced a musical collection entitled *Executioner's Last Songs*, attributed to the Pine Valley Cosmonauts. The album consisted mainly of cover versions of ballads about executions, murder, and vigilantism sung by notable indie-rock musicians such as Neko Case and Steve Earle, as well as lesser known performers including the duo Tim Kelley and Christa Meyer. *Executioner's Last Songs* had the dual intention that typifies the political benefit album: raising funds, for the Illinois Coalition Against the Death Penalty, and raising consciousness, by promoting opposition to capital punishment. Although the album actually appeared shortly *after* Governor George H. Ryan of Illinois issued a moratorium on executions in the state because a number of death-row inmates had been proven innocent, Ryan faced a firestorm of criticism for his decision, and the resumption of executions remained a distinct possibility.

Executioner's Last Songs proved not merely a small success of the "act locally, think globally" sort in raising over $40,000, a considerable windfall for a small nonprofit group. The album was featured in *Rolling Stone*, and even sparked a contretemps between two of the best-known American rock critics, Greil Marcus and Robert Christgau, over the very concept of the benefit compilation. "Aren't tribute albums terrible?" Marcus observed in *Salon*, in a review of the compilation in his "Real Life Rock Top 10" column (2002). (The tribute album—usually a tribute to a musical performer or group, occasionally to a political figure such as Nelson Mandela—is a "closely related subgenre" also typically "threatened by piety and inconsistency," as Christgau puts it in his response to Marcus; *benefit* and *tribute* are often used interchangeably by others besides Marcus.) Why is it, he asked, "that the finer the cause, ... the worse the tribute album?" Only the inherently flawed nature of the benefit/tribute album, apparently—no exact problem is mentioned—can explain "why such imaginative and inventive performers fall so short of ... songs that are in their blood" (Marcus, 2002). The actual musical performance is somehow necessarily vitiated by the concept behind it.

Addressing Marcus's "low sanctimony tolerance" in the *Village Voice*, Christgau conceded that political benefit compilations typically "are doomed at conception" (2002). Beyond the piety or leaden seriousness, the musicians seemingly feel compelled to adopt, the organizers have to "make the inevitable mishmash cohere," the problem of consistency shared with the tribute album. But Langford's project is actually an exception, in Christgau's view, because it "beats the odds [in an] unexpected way," thanks to the collection being "populated by working professionals outdoing themselves rather than luminaries exercising their *droit de signeur*" (or literally "the lord's right"). Relative anonymity—the likes of Case and Earle do have substantial followings—"is a virtue," Christgau concludes (2002). "I'm not Bono, you know," Langford joked in an interview (quoted in Perry, 2002), when Bono had recently denounced rock music as a political force and began jetting to high-profile United Nations conferences merely to lend the aura of his presumably inspirational celebrity to the cause of erasing Third World debt.

Marcus would appear to have no truck with such distinctions between degrees of celebrity. But his withering essentialism, in attributing a seemingly universal musical futility to the political benefit album, is intriguing because I have the highest respect for his critical acumen, even if the absolutist claim that such a well-intentioned genre inevitably results in irredeemably lackluster music seems dubious. The logical way to determine whether such a sweeping judgment seems warranted is to survey the major markers in the history of the political benefit album in rock and roll, from its origin with *The Concert for Bangladesh* in 1971 to *War Child Presents Heroes: An Album to Benefit Children Affected by War* in 2009. (War Child assists young war refugees around the world.) One finds, in fact, a number of enthusiastically received recordings, some of which actually raised significant sums of money. To emphasize the latter achievement, Jon Landau's review of *The Concert for Bangladesh* in *Rolling Stone* was accompanied by a blown-up copy of a check, featured in the album's artwork, made out to the United Nations Children's Fund for Relief to Refugee Children of Bangladesh by Madison Square Garden, the concert's host venue. Only $2 million made it to UNICEF, unfortunately, before an Internal Revenue Service audit of Apple Records held up a further $8.8 million until 1981 (Romanowski and George-Warren, 1995, p. 419). The first major musical benefit for groups combating AIDS, and the album Christgau considers the "greatest tribute or benefit comp ever," the Red Hot Organization (RHO) compilation *Red Hot + Blue: A Tribute to Cole Porter* (1990), sold a million copies, and RHO has raised millions of dollars through its succeeding series of releases. (Given the continual controversies over AIDS, such benefits are ineluctably political; some of the finest benefit albums in general, such as *The Bridge: A Tribute to Neil Young, Sweet Relief: A Benefit for Victoria Williams*, and *Light of Day: A Tribute to Bruce Springsteen*, have involved noncontroversial health issues, so I will only note them in passing.) But I remain unmoved by *Red Hot + Blue*, and in the course of listening to the collections discussed here, I came to the conclusion that Marcus is right when it comes to aesthetics.

The financial achievement in some cases is unquestionable, and in tracing briefly the evolution of the political benefit album in rock and roll it is clear that the artistic achievement has hardly been entirely disparaged. The most recent stage in that evolution presents an odd if not disquieting situation, however, involving simply the sheer plethora of political benefit albums nowadays—for the year 2009, above, I could have included *Dark Was the Night* (the latest RHO release), *Rhythms del Mundo Classics* (an Artists Project Earth benefit for climate crisis projects and natural disaster relief), and *The Sun Came Out* (credited to 7 Worlds Collide and benefiting Oxfam International). The political benefit album is now so commonplace as to constitute a genre in its own right; not *droit de signeur*, but *de rigeur* ("necessary according to fashion," that is) strikes me as the operative Francophone expression. A mild controversy erupted in the summer of 2009, for instance, over whether Radiohead would appear on a David Bowie tribute being released by War Child in 2010. There were no politics at issue, only simple questions regarding Radiohead's presence gracing the collection and which Bowie song the group would perform—"China Girl"? "Kooks"? "Life on Mars?"? wondered eager fans. Because of the participation of Joss Stone, the Hard Rock Cafe collection *Serve3: The Hard Rock Benefit Album*, released in support of World Hunger Year, was featured on the *Celebrity Gossip* website in 2008.

Better there are benefit albums for worthy causes than not, certainly, and perhaps it is a sign of a better world being born, having reached the readers of *Celebrity Gossip*, that the benefit album is so commonplace nowadays. But in the very recent past, in the sudden efflorescence documented here, they have also threatened to become trivial, merely another part of the scenery in contemporary rock music. The political benefit album is as common as dirt, "a dubious staple of the music industry":

> the onslaught of benefit albums has so ingrained the concept in the popular mindset that they're now being satirized (South Park—Chef Aid). But because the field is so overcrowded, they've also become less effective. Nowadays, for a benefit album to receive any substantive media attention, the titular "cause" must either be politically poignant or command sought-after entertainers to have the kind of galvanizing effect organizers aim for. (Green, 1999)

Seen in the worst possible light, the political benefit album has conceivably become increasingly popular with musicians as a form of compensation for the political cowardice of their work released under their own names. A number of American critics have damned rock music over the last three decades for its unwillingness to confront the atrocities perpetrated by neoconservatives ranging from Reaganites to the Bush-Cheney mob, a problem that reached critical mass with the beginning of the first Persian Gulf War conducted by the United States, which coincided with the Grammy Awards in 1991. While the ceremony took place, a number of musicians backstage, led by Steven Tyler of Aerosmith, cheered television images of the initial bombing. (Bob Dylan at least performed an indecipherable "Masters of War" to no discernible end.) David Crosby may have been a fatuous hippie when, legend has it, he announced in the heyday of the counterculture that the first supergroup Crosby, Stills, & Nash, was "the voice of the revolution, man," but at least hippies never cheered for war. That the finest anti-Reagan song, "Bonzo Goes to Bitburg" by the Ramones, emerged from a group who were ordinarily Reagan *admirers*, and a muddled Green Day album, *American Idiot*, could be considered daring, even radical, by many in the new millennium, indicates that something has been wrong for some time now.

The political benefit album could represent only a safe demonstration of social conscience, given the cover provided by the safety-in-numbers approach of appearing with a horde of other performers, supplanting riskier direct personal statements that might alienate fans and/or the authorities, whether record companies or the state apparatus. The former executive director of Amnesty International, Jack Healey, who organized the *Conspiracy of Hope* concerts in 1986 and the *Human Rights Now!* tour in 1988, once observed that by the mid-1990s, rock stars had "forgot[ten] that music is to be a weapon against oppression and injustice" (Wilonsky, 2001). His view would seem to be confirmed, in particular, by the fact there is a notable dearth of political benefit albums after *Help: A Charity Project for the Children of Bosnia*, organized by War Child in 1995, until the appearance in 2001 of a collection Healey organized, *Groundwork: Act to Reduce Hunger*. The one rock benefit released between 1995 and 2001, *No Boundaries: A Benefit for the Kosovar Refugees* (1999), is such an irredeemably haphazard, uninspired collection, widely considered a disgrace, that it hardly merits mention.

Worthy causes are hardly necessarily risky ones either; who would condemn an artist for supporting World Hunger Year? *Rock the Net: Musicians for Network Neutrality*, organized by Jeff Tweedy of Wilco in 2008, promoted the prosaic cause of preventing telecommunications companies from increasing fees for bandwidth use. It is tempting to observe that a number of benefit albums involving more combustible causes, such as *East Timor Benefit Album* and *Indie Aid Abroad*, released in 2000 in support of the victims of Indonesian repression in East Timor—brutalized by an overt attempt to destroy an entire society—feature only obscure indie bands. *For the Lady*, on the other hand, produced on behalf of the internationally admired Burmese human-rights activist Aung San Suu Kyi in 2004, featured major artists including Coldplay, Eric Clapton, Paul McCartney, Pearl Jam, R.E.M., Sting, and U2, surely a sign that taking up her cause posed no hazards, whether commercial or political. The album appeared a full 13 years after she received the Nobel Peace Prize, moreover, making rock stars essentially the last people on the planet to take up her cause.

Two other collections from 2004 devoted to the victims of the appalling violence in Darfur, on the other hand, were hardly star-studded, although R.E.M. does appear on *Songs for Sudan* (obscured, though, by being available only through Oxfam International's music website, and now long gone). The more provocatively titled *Genocide in Sudan* features Danger Mouse, DJ Spooky, and System of a Down—not unknowns to music fans, but hardly celebrities on the scale of the luminaries on *For the Lady*. And while *Genocide* does include white indie rockers such as Tortoise, the other genres represented—hip-hop, house, reggae, trip-hop—are almost entirely rooted in black culture tangential to rock. The live album *Wed-Rock*, recorded in 2004 and released in 2006 to support the group Freedom to Marry in the heated battle over gay marriage, features indie-rock groups such as Le Tigre and Sleater-Kinney, whose fans already knew the groups included gay and bisexual members. They are certainly well known, but hardly have an audience so broad that their appearance on the album would prompt a backlash by marginal, less committed fans, like that experienced by the Dixie Chicks after Natalie Maines made disparaging comments about George Bush at a British concert in 2003. Even the marginally popular artists on *Executioner's Last Songs* experienced some backlash from ostensible fans for coming out against capital punishment.

The original political benefit rock album, *The Concert for Bangladesh*, was recorded in August of 1971 while war still raged between India and Pakistan, although the war had ended by the time the recording appeared. Organized with unquestionable nobility by George Harrison, at the behest of Ravi Shankar, what was really most sensational about the concert and succeeding album was the two-fold treat of Bob Dylan's emergence from hibernation and half a Beatles reunion, with Ringo Starr's participation. Landau greeted the album as an unmitigated success: "[P]art of the record's beauty is that Harrison staged a concert worthy of his purpose in every respect. ... [H]elp has been given, people have been reached, an effort has been made and results will be felt. The total effect was that the event did justice to everyone connected with it" (1972, p. 42). In producing the album, though, Harrison decided to present the concert without any editing or enhancement of the performances, one reason Christgau, for instance, was less than impressed in his contemporaneous review of the record, which he assigned only a "B-": it offered "exactly what I heard at the Garden. ... [M]ail your check [and] avoid the middleman" (1981, p. 89). Retrospective accounts of the musical achievement tend to be kinder, but the historical memory is also tainted by the commercial manipulation behind the scenes, with Columbia demanding the rights to the tape version in return for allowing Dylan's appearance, and Harrison's manager Allen Klein (I am gritting my teeth and speaking no ill of the dead) refusing to allow retail discounting of the album's list price. This last move might seem to maximize the return for the beneficiaries, but questions have lingered ever since concerning whether the entirety of the profits reached UNICEF, which in fairness seems inevitable given the delay of a decade occasioned by the IRS.

The Concert for Bangladesh remained unique for what, in retrospect, seems a surprisingly long time. One can find descriptions of the album as the inspiration for the surge of musical political benefits in the *mid-1980s*, which says something about the actual extent of the political engagement in rock and roll. The only political benefit album to emerge from the rock world between 1971 and 1985 was *Concerts for the People of Kampuchea*, which presented the highlights of a week-long series of shows at London's Hammersmith Odeon in 1979, orchestrated by another ex-Beatle, Paul McCartney, on behalf of the victims of the Pol Pot regime. The album did not actually appear until 1981, so it hardly bore the sense of urgency of *The Concert for Bangladesh*. The delay is likely due in no small part to its generally uninspiring performances; I have never seen a more ubiquitous album in used record stores. That it appeared at all has a good deal to do with McCartney astutely including punk and new wave acts such as The Clash, Elvis Costello, and The Pretenders that were just breaking through to a larger audience—by 1981 The Clash were bankable.

In the watershed year of 1985, the all-star Band Aid single "Do They Know It's Christmas?," organized by Bob Geldof and Midge Ure in an effort to raise funds to combat famine in Ethiopia, continued an astonishing success dating to its release in December, 1984, resulting in the historic *Live Aid* concert broadcast around the world. Some accounts assume that the notoriety of the Band Aid recording led to actor Harry Belafonte finally succeeding in his efforts to enlist pop stars to create a benefit single likewise intended to combat famine in Africa, but in fact Michael Jackson and Lionel Ritchie had begun work on the song "We Are the World" before the end of 1984, with the recording session taking place shortly after the beginning of the new year; after the single's success, an album of the same name appeared. Later in 1985, Steven Van Zandt put together the "Sun City" single and *Sun City* album to support the anti-apartheid charity group Africa Fund. The first two songs were extraordinary financial successes: "Do They Know It's Christmas?" became the biggest-selling single in British history; the Band Aid trust, which also includes funds from the *Live Aid* concerts, had as of 2004 raised almost $150 million. "We Are the World," which eventually raised around $50 million, became the biggest seller in history in the United States and on the international market. (Internationally it was eclipsed by Elton John's tribute to Princess Diana, "Candle in the Wind," in 1997, which may indicate, distressingly, that it is schmaltz, not empathy, that drives such massive successes.)

Artistically, both leave much to be desired. The recording of "Do They Know It's Christmas?" was fairly chaotic, and the line-up of groups and singers—e.g., Duran Duran and Spandau Ballet—encapsulates the dreary "haircut band" phase that dominated British pop music after punk. While "We Are the World" features more enduring performers such as Ray Charles, Bob Dylan, and Neil Young, it has from the start been denounced for the imperial first-person of Michael Jackson's lyrics; the punk rock band the Dickies released an album entitled *We Aren't the World!* a year later. Greil Marcus denounced the song's first-person rhetoric about making choices as an unconscious channeling of sentiments akin to a jingle for Pepsi (quoted in Garofalo, 1992b, p. 29), to which both Jackson and Ritchie were contracted, a point echoed by none other than Geldof, who also, like Marcus, dislikes virtually all subsequent benefit albums. (Although he didn't write the song, Jackson would go on to grace the world just two years later with "Man in the Mirror," yet another, even more narcissistic paean to simply changing oneself—whether politically as well as cosmetically seems uncertain, with hindsight—in order to change the world.) Though scarcely approaching the other songs' commercial success, "Sun City" is far superior in this regard because it is clearly an *angry* song, with a specific point of attack in supporting the cultural boycott of South Africa, which had recently been willfully violated by cranks such as The Kinks and Linda Ronstadt. "Sun City" has been credited, in fact, with doing a good deal to raise awareness of the boycott, of which Paul Simon, for example, subsequently and very publicly ran afoul while making the well-intentioned 1986 album *Graceland*. (It seems to be almost lost to historical memory that Simon was hardly blameless; see Denselow, 1989, pp. 194-8.) As on "Do They Know It's Christmas?," each line of the verses is sung by a different singer, but "Sun City" draws from an unusual amalgamation of genres—one verse alone features George Clinton, Joey Ramone, Jimmy Cliff, and Darlene Love—and the effect is a powerful sense of widespread solidarity. Given a brief instant to take a stand, most of the performers (why Hall & Oates were there I don't know) put a stamp on it that embodies their entire career and personae. I still occasionally play "Sun City" with pleasure, even excitement.

Whatever the relative value of their artistic achievements, the political benefit recordings of 1985 now seem like an extraordinary, long-lost model of commitment, for the simple, obvious reason that musicians actually gathered together to perform. This has continued to occur in sporadic live events, but subsequent political benefit albums, with the potential to reach a much wider audience than a live event, evolved very quickly away from the model of direct participation in the studio by an array of musicians represented by Band Aid, USA for Africa, and *Sun City*, to the now-common, "practically effortless" practice of collecting donated songs on samplers (Green, 1999). Outside of the most repressive dictatorships, it does not take much commitment or risk to mail a tape to someone. Interestingly, the benefit album that Robert Christgau considers far and away the best ever recorded, *Red Hot + Blue*, released in 1990, is also a stepping-stone in this direction. Because the collection consists of covers of Cole Porter, the artists necessarily had to record their contributions specifically for the occasion. At the same time, the recordings were all done independently, so there was no full-scale collective creation involved. The tension between the artists' idiosyncratic choices and the mild constraint of Porter's songbook does result in an unusual range of moods—as a punk fan I prefer Debbie Harry and Iggy Pop's uptempo "Well Did You Evah," which ranks with Pop's better-known duet from the same year with Kate Pierson of the B-52s on "Candy"—but this disparateness has invited the same charge of unevenness that Christgau levels at other benefit compilations.

Three years later, in 1993, the Red Hot Organization played a major role in the second watershed year in the evolution of the political benefit album into a motley sampler, with the release of *No Alternative*, a collection of cutting-edge "alternative" groups (hence the title) and performers (on the major label Arista, in fact), also in the service of AIDS education. The compilation, including Pavement, Smashing Pumpkins, Soundgarden, Matthew Sweet, and Uncle Tupelo, was astutely selected enough that to some extent it helped define the canon of alternative or indie rock in the 1990s, thanks especially to an accompanying television special broadcast on MTV with the intention of reaching a younger audience with little exposure to the work of AIDS organizations. While *No Alternative* had the greatest commercial success of any benefit released in 1993, and is worthwhile musically as well, its influence in the long term has proven a liability. In retrospect the album's primary accomplishment was to establish the template for a political benefit album: a collection of mild rarities, whether top-drawer unreleased songs, live recordings, or hard-to-find B-sides from singles. It is no wonder the benefit album has acquired a reputation for incoherence, or that *No Alternative* now haunts used-CD stores the same way *The Concerts for Kampuchea* litters used-record bins. Christgau recently observed that "none of the dozen-plus subsequent Red Hot albums has matched th[e] standard" (2009) of *Red Hot + Blue*, including *No Alternative*.

I also refer to 1993 as a watershed because of another indie-rock-based benefit, *Born to Choose*, which took much the same approach as *No Alternative* in lining up heavyweights (relatively speaking) such as Natalie Merchant, Pavement (again), R.E.M., Soundgarden (again), Matthew Sweet (again) and Lucinda Williams in support of abortion rights. Although it coheres less satisfactorily than *No Alternative*, *Born to Choose* has its virtues: for one thing, there is a single purpose-written song, entitled "Born to Choose," one of the finest performances by the Mekons, including Jon Langford, from the late stage in their work as a full-time band. The CD artwork has a great deal of information, including essays by the National Abortion Rights Action League (NARAL) and the first female rock critic and noted feminist Ellen Willis, contact information for a variety of reproductive-rights and women's health groups, and statistics on teen pregnancy and abortion. *No Alternative*, in contrast, essentially hides its purpose in a few lines of fine print regarding AIDS awareness, although the TV special was certainly open enough about its subject matter.

The liabilities of *No Alternative*'s grab-bag approach were sufficiently evident that a challenge appeared in fairly short order, in 1995, in the organization of War Child's aforementioned *Help: A Charity Project for the Children of Bosnia*, which was recorded in exactly one day, September 3, 1995, and released within a week, following the model of John Lennon's attempt at a newspaper-like record, "Instant Karma." The 18 artists included on *Help* did not work as a single collective, as did the assemblages on "Do They Know It's Christmas?," "Sun City," and "We Are the World," although Noel Gallagher of Oasis recorded the first song with Johnny Depp, and then returned to collaborate on the last song, a cover of the Beatles' "Come Together," with Paul McCartney and Paul Weller. Instead, the songs were recorded in quick succession, with necessarily mixed but sometimes fairly inspired results, the latter including an early version of Radiohead's "Lucky," a song that would later stand out on the epochal album *OK Computer* (1997), and a cover of Elvis Costello's Thatcherphobic "Shipbuilding" by Suede. The admirably intentioned Lennonesque spontaneity of *Help*, however, has in the long run remained a complete anomaly, and the mailed-in assortment of ostensible goodies on *No Alternative* much more the norm—"big names fobbing off outtakes" as Christgau (2009) sums it up.

When the subsequent hiatus in political benefit albums by rock performers was finally broken in 2001 by *Groundwork: Act to Reduce Hunger*, a previously unforeseen liability of the tribute album, the possibility of horrendous mistiming, effectively obliterated a promising effort: another "cause" emerged unexpectedly with the events of September 11, 2001. Despite having rare unreleased songs by notables such as Sheryl Crow, Madonna, and Moby—collected by Madonna's sister Melanie Ciccone, a former music executive at Warner Brothers—*Groundwork* was eclipsed by compilations such as *America: A Tribute to Heroes*, the even more super patriotic *God Bless America*, which immediately went to the top of the charts, and *The Concert for New York City*. Jack Healey, the liaison with the United Nations Food and Agriculture Organization's Groundwork project, which had benefited from TeleFood concerts featuring world music since 1996, lamented that "We would have been like Live Aid if the attacks hadn't happened" (quoted in Wilonsky, 2001). Ciccone "had hoped to get a little more network time, but it's hard to compete" since, as she notes with acid understatement, September 11 "caused a certain amount of myopia" (quoted in Wilonsky, 2001), as evidenced by the wild popularity of uncritical patriotism in popular music. The consignment of *Groundwork* to virtual nonexistence is the strangest saga in the history of the political benefit rock album.

In general, though, that history has been a checkered one because the genre, far from strange, has been so mundane and predictable. And yet there may be hope in the thing yet: *War Child Presents Heroes* and *Dark Was the Night* received high praise from Christgau (2009) for aptly summing up the state of indie music in 2009, in the contrast between the former album's energetic dissent and devotion to traditional song form and the way the latter, however amelodic, makes poetry out of a youthful defeatism bred by the Bush II era. The best that can safely be said is that political benefit albums have become increasingly common in the rock world because money matters, as even a relatively small-scale bohemian such as Jon Langford could repeatedly point out—and they do raise money. Whether they raise consciousness as well, or simply preach to the choir, is another matter, albeit one that is essentially indeterminable anyway except by an impossibly extensive ethnography. We will not know about the latter issue unless and (un)'*Til Things are Brighter*, the title of a combined AIDS benefit (for the Terrence Higgins Trust)/Johnny Cash tribute helmed by none other than Langford, who deserves his reputation as the most indefatigable radical in show business.

Chapter 8

Which Music for Which Catastrophe?
The Functions of Popular Music
Twenty-first Century Benefit Concerts

Sam O'Connell

Often, the entertainment industries' first responses to join relief efforts following contemporary catastrophes continue to follow in the tradition of the television-broadcast benefit concert model first established in its modern form with the 1985 concert event *Live Aid*. Though the reasons for which benefit concerts are produced in the twenty-first century are varied—terrorist attacks, natural disasters, etc.—little has changed in their formatting; they are still star-studded entertainment events that provide a forum through which popular music and celebrity appearances help shape public response to catastrophe. Whether they model appropriate social behavior or enable social change, though, depends on how their response to the specific catastrophe for which they are produced is scripted. To investigate the functions of contemporary benefit concerts, I compare *America: A Tribute to Heroes*, performed in the immediate wake of 9/11, and *A Concert for Hurricane Relief*, performed after Hurricane Katrina, just days after the levees broke and flooded New Orleans. Structurally, these two events are very similar. They were both designed as *Live Aid*-style benefit concerts to raise money for the victims of each catastrophe. Each featured musical performances and celebrity appearances by top-name musicians with either a musical or biographical connection to the location of each event (New York City or the New Orleans-Mississippi Delta Region respectively). Despite their similarities, though, the two events provide a fertile comparison for understanding and interpreting the ways that benefit concerts attempt to script an appropriate, collective response to catastrophes as well as what happens when that script is not executed as planned.

Typically, benefit concerts present important contexts for "collective mourning and patriotic nationalist celebration" (Forman, 2002, p. 196). For exactly this purpose, *America: A Tribute to Heroes* was produced and performed just ten days after the events of 9/11. This concert represents the epitome of what Murray Forman considers to be essential for popular music during the context of a crisis: "a critical awareness of which songs and genres are deemed most appropriate under the circumstances and, by extensions, which are largely excused from public debate and excluded in the process of defining appropriate public sentiment" (2002, p. 191). Following Forman, a few key moments demonstrate how *America:*

A Tribute to Heroes enacted its script of national unity and patriotism: Bruce Springsteen's "My City of Ruins," Tom Hanks's introduction, Clint Eastwood's concluding remarks, and Willie Nelson's rendition of "America the Beautiful." Taken together, these bookends are indicative markers of the event's success at creating a bridge both from the local focus on New York City, Washington, DC, and Somerset County, PA to the call for a nationalist project of post-9/11 patriotism.

Performed on September 21, 2001, *America: A Tribute to Heroes* opened with Bruce Springsteen, strumming an acoustic guitar and playing the harmonica, performing "My City of Ruins," introduced in its new context as "a prayer for our fallen brothers and sisters" (*America*). As the concert's opening number, "My City of Ruins" effectively set the tone for the evening of music, testimony, and prayer to come. In this single moment, with his simple, understated musical performance, Springsteen established the concert's objectives of defining the new role of popular music, forging a collective "American" community, transitioning from mourning to renewed patriotism and offering a tribute to those "fallen brothers and sisters." Commenting on the changing role of popular music after 9/11, Jon Pareles of *The New York Times*, writes "music has now enlisted in a role that has been unfamiliar for as long as most of its stars have lived: providing not just solace, but solidarity" (2001, p. E3). As this benefit's first song, "My City of Ruins" provides an example of how popular music was employed and restructured for *America: A Tribute to Heroes*. As has been noted, though, "My City of Ruins" was not written for the broadcast; nor was it written about New York City. According to Bryan Garman, "The song had been written prior to 9/11; Springsteen had performed it during his 2000 tour, and its lyrics originally referred to the dilapidated state of his former stomping grounds, Asbury Park, New Jersey" (2007, p. 78). Adding to the song's genealogy, Pareles writes that despite being "written before the attacks about a decrepit New Jersey seaside town," it "suddenly seems to depict ground zero" (2001, p. E3). Certainly with Springsteen's introduction of the song as a prayer in the wake of 9/11 and lyrics like its simple, unanswerable question, "How do I begin again?/ My city's in ruins," the song makes for an easy transposition from the reality of Asbury Park to the symbolic New York City (*America*). By repositioning his "city," Springsteen's performance represents the first step in charting the benefit concert's role as a eulogy for the fallen men and women now remembered as "heroes" in a script that transitions from the localized relief effort to a national, political project.

Following Springsteen's command to "Rise up!," the concert makes a seamless transition to Tom Hanks, the evening's first non-musical performer. Performing not as the host of the evening but as the first celebrity presenter, he asserts, "We're going to try and do something" (*America*). Opening his comments with the rhetoric of "we," Hanks highlights the collective effort of the evening's concert. Quickly, though, Hanks provides some context for his use of "we":

That was the message sent by some very American heroes ... They found themselves aboard the hijacked Flight 93 that went down in Somerset County,

Pennsylvania on September 11, 2001. They witnessed the brutality on board and somehow summoned the strength to warn us and take action. United they stood and likely saved our world from an even darker day of perhaps even more unthinkable horror. (*America*)

Here, Hanks makes the point to draw a distinction between those in whose honor the benefit has been produced and those performing as a part of its entertainment. As Phil Gallo notes, throughout the concert "The focus stayed squarely on the intent of the evening, and at the best moments, the music served as an emotional coda to a particularly touching anecdote" (2001, p. 2). In the transition from Springsteen's musical introduction to Hanks's spoken-word tribute to the actions of those aboard Flight 93, *America: A Tribute to Heroes* quickly identified the eponymous heroes, the "real" heroes, as those who were directly involved in the events of 9/11 and its aftermath.

Switching his focus from those to whom the concert and its fundraising effort were dedicated, Hanks then poses the question that "millions of us everywhere have asked ourselves, 'What are we to do?'" and offers one answer: "In their undying spirit, we all feel the need to do something, however small, symbolic, to honor these remarkable heroes among us" (*America*). At this point, Hanks contextualizes for the audience exactly who he and his fellow performers are in relation to the "heroes" of 9/11 before explicitly stating why they have gathered to perform on this evening. He says:

Those of us here tonight are not heroes ... We are merely artists, entertainers here to raise spirits and we hope a great deal of money. We appear tonight as a simple show of unity to honor the real heroes and to do whatever we can to ensure that all their families are supported by our larger American family. (*America*)

In this rhetorical move, Hanks suggests that he and his fellow performers occupy a similar position to the audience watching at home. They, too, suggest to the event's television audience that they are asking questions like "What are we to do?," though the performers' questions arguably assume a didactic function through the platform of the benefit concert performance. Thus, in answering their call to service, the performers use their celebrity to help model and shape a new, authorized, American identity for the re-imagined community of post-9/11 America.

In describing the benefit, Lynn Spigel argues "the program appealed to a desire to see Hollywood stars, singers, and sports heroes reduced to 'real' people, unadorned, unrehearsed ... and literally unnamed and unannounced" (2005, p. 134). The reduction of these performers to "real" people, however, was merely part of the evening's subtle, muted theatricality. Taking Tom Hanks's introduction as a perfect example of this scenario, we can see that his performance in the concert's opening moments cannot help but recall some of his more famous characters: the astronaut Jim Lovell, who famously uttered, "Houston, we have a problem," while remaining calm in crisis; and Capt. John Miller who stormed the beaches of Normandy and died fighting for his country. These characters each represent both Hanks's version of the "ordinary man made good" and his own version of "heroic" American identity. Despite his claim of being merely an artist, his presence in the concert models one version of American heroism. Lastly, Hanks concludes with the recognition that this concert is a liminal moment in the public sphere of broadcast television. He reminds us, "This is a moment to pause and reflect, to heal, and to rededicate ourselves to the American spirit of one nation, indivisible" (*America*). On that note, the evening continues to fulfill the goals he outlines with musical performances, testimonies of named heroes and their acts of heroism, and passages from historical leaders on various definitions of heroism and, importantly, patriotism.

Charting the subsequent performances and celebrity appearances, Spigel argues that the concert was "a stunning example of how post-9/11 television has created not a public sphere per se, but rather a self-referential Hollywood public sphere of celebrities who stand in for real citizens, and who somehow make us feel connected to a wider social fabric" (2005, p. 135). In creating the portrait of this wider social fabric, the collection of actors and musicians pushed several different, yet still related, agendas in terms of advocating for a united and tolerant American community. Among the other performances from the concert worth noting are the appearances of such figures as Will Smith and Muhammad Ali who spoke together following a pre-recorded segment entitled, "Muslim Kids." The partnership of the two men, one the cinematic Ali and one the actual, advocated for a tolerant acceptance of American's Muslim population as distinct from the terrorists of 9/11. Promoting the event's unity project, in a less than subtle way, George Clooney appeared to remind us "that the money would be administered by United Way and gave the phone number which spelled TO-UNITE" (James, 2001, p. B1). Similarly, reviews of the concert's other performances discuss the ways in which the music served to highlight the program's overall agenda. Pareles offers a brief account of some of the more noticeable and obvious statements made by the evening's musical choices. He writes, "Tom Petty glared into the camera and calmly vows, 'I won't back down'; Sting denounces violence in 'Fragile.' Neil Young sings John Lennon's 'Imagine,' dreaming of an end to nationalism and religion; U2 in 'Walk On,' sings 'Alleluia'" (Pareles, 2001, p. E3). Adding to Pareles's commentary, Garofalo writes, "If Tom Petty's toned down, but still somewhat aggressive, rendition of 'I Won't Back Down' was a call to arms for the nationalist project that was about to get underway, it was offset by Neil Young's stirring performance of John Lennon's 'Imagine,' which conjured up visions of a world with neither religions nor countries and 'nothing to fight or die for'" (2007, p. 7). The distinct tonal differences of these two songs, as well as their repeated citation in review after review of the concert, demonstrate how successfully scripted the event was and how well the selected music fit the multiple agendas of the overall program. Songs that were reflective and asked questions like "My

City of Ruins" and "Imagine" were answered with assuredness in declarations such as Petty's "I Won't Back Down" as the benefit concert enacted its nationalist agenda.

Following Celine Dion's soaring performance of "God Bless America," the evening's penultimate musical number, Clint Eastwood appeared for the final spoken remarks of the event. If Hanks set the contemplative tone of the concert in calling this a moment to pause and reflect, Eastwood's remarks took the necessary step of heralding the difficult journey to come: "Tonight we've paid tribute to those who were lost and those who survived the fire and the fate that rained down upon them and the heroes at ground zero who in life and death were an indelible badge of honor" (*America*). Speaking here in the past tense of the evening's entertainment, Eastwood signals to the viewing audience that the time to reflect was over and a new phase both for the concert and the nation was about to begin. Opening his prepared statement with a description of 9/11 as "the twenty-first century's day of infamy," an explicit allusion to President Roosevelt's reaction to the bombing of Pearl Harbor, Eastwood prepares the audience for the conflict to come. After recalling the nation's most famous historical attack, he continues:

> The terrorists wanted 300 million victims; instead they are going to get 300 million heroes. 300 million Americans with broken hearts, unbreakable hopes for our country and our future. In the conflict that's come upon us, we're determined as our parents were before us to win through the ultimate triumph, so help us God. (*America*)

In this final moment of Eastwood's remarks, before the introduction of "America the Beautiful," Eastwood stands before the event's attentive audience, and like Hanks before him, becomes the embodied representation of the cinematic characters for which he is best known: a symbolic amalgamation of his cowboys such as *Unforgiven*'s Bill Munny and Josey Wales and his renegade lawman Dirty Harry. Implicitly recalling these cinematic visions of his celebrity persona—all men that seek to enact revenge no matter the legality, cost, or collateral damage— Eastwood prepares both the American and the global audiences for the likely military response to come.

With this image of the heroic American male, *America: A Tribute to Heroes* continues utilizing the celebrity presence of the event to model a unified, national audience and community. As Kip Pegley and Susan Fast have argued, "this celebrity-filled event was an opportune occasion for social modeling" (2007, p. 29). According to their argument, and certainly embodied in the examples of both Tom Hanks and Clint Eastwood, "Even when conditions are stable, stars function in part to construct a notion of what people are 'supposed' to be like, contributing in particular to the definition of social roles" (Pegley and Fast, 2007, p. 29). Over the course of the entire event's narrative, then, Hanks and Springsteen, in the beginning, modeled for the audience the appropriate tone and necessary stage of reflection. By the end of the evening's performance, though,

Eastwood-as-celebrity modeled the social role of avenger, defending and restoring the honor of America, the beautiful.

Fittingly then, the concert concluded with the icon of the American heartland Willie Nelson performing "America the Beautiful," introduced by Eastwood as a song that "celebrates America and beckons us to what we can become." Nelson's performance embodied one final definition of the social roles required by the audience in the wake of 9/11: that of unity and community borne out of what Eastwood refers to as the American spirit. As Pegley and Fast point out, "the opening of 'America the Beautiful' began behind Eastwood, marking the first time in the concert that an introducer's words became conflated with music, increasing the emotional potency of the message" (2007, p. 40). Nelson, notably, was not performing a solo rendition of the folk standard; he was backed by a chorus of every celebrity present for the evening's event. As Pegley and Fast point out, "The image of a unified American community was built through a number of means, including the use of backup singers or the presence of ... vocal choirs" (2007, p. 35). In this final moment of the performance, then, the concert combined the power of celebrity as a tool for social modeling with the idea of the vocal chorus which "not only represent the extended community (including the viewing audience) but, importantly, *sanction* the soloist's sentiments," which in this case revolve around Nelson's rendition of "America the Beautiful" repurposed to represent a post-9/11 vision of America (Pegley and Fast, 2007, p. 35). *America: A Tribute to Heroes* ends with one final visual reminder of the catastrophe of 9/11 as a way to conclude its scripted agenda of unity and patriotism: a backlit image of "Old Glory" flying at full mast high over the rubble and remains left behind by the fallen towers at Ground Zero, at once invoking the visual symbolism of memories such as the American military at Iwo Jima, which, we now know, was also staged, and the national anthem's optimistic and defiant vision of the flag, still there.

While *America: A Tribute to Heroes* seamlessly executed its script for national unity through popular music and celebrity appearances, *A Concert for Hurricane Relief* was affected by the competing narratives surrounding Hurricane Katrina that ultimately resulted in the very breakdown of the benefit concert model. If *America: A Tribute to Heroes* demonstrates how a concert can successfully advocate for a united, authorized public, *A Concert for Hurricane Relief* reveals what can happen when a benefit concert is usurped by the performers for the purpose of creating an unauthorized counter narrative. The potential for a counter narrative to emerge during a benefit concert is best seen in Kanye West's performance which caused the concert's breakdown and represented the tensions between the public and counter-public narratives of Hurricane Katrina's relief effort. In the end, *A Concert for Hurricane Relief* when compared to *America: A Tribute to Heroes* helps us understand and interpret the cultural roles of benefit concerts: whether those roles are to serve the hegemonic power structure of a society or to offer a vocal protest against them.

In the annual year-in-review issue of *Rolling Stone* for 2005, noted documentary provocateur Michael Moore recapped the year's noteworthy moments of subversive popular culture in an article entitled, "Mavericks, Renegades and Troublemakers." In this piece, Moore offers an updated list of "the seven words you can't say on television" (2005, p. 65). He writes, "In a time of carefully managed information dissemination and a media afraid to veer from the Official Story, it was, perhaps, the pivotal moment of the year, the instant when culture and politics collided, and the apple cart of a president who once had a ninety percent approval rating was turned upside down" (Moore, 2005, p. 65). The seven little words that inspired such praise from Moore were Kanye West's unscripted comments during the *A Concert for Hurricane Relief*, which was produced by NBC and aired on the broadcast network and its affiliates in the days after Hurricane Katrina in a relief effort to once again use a gathering of musicians and celebrities to raise money following yet another twenty-first-century catastrophe. Enlisted for his celebrity rather than as a musical performer, West, presenting alongside comedian Mike Myers, went off script. Instead of discussing the breaching of the levees around New Orleans, West uttered, to parrot Tom Hanks from four years earlier, the thought so many of millions of Americans were thinking: "George Bush doesn't care about black people" (quoted in de Moraes, 2005, p. C01). In this one statement, Kanye West derailed the event, drawing attention away from the official, scripted narrative of a New Orleans-style funeral to the unofficial, re-scripted counter narrative of a government's failed response to help its citizens in large part because of the race and class of those victims. West's improvisation not only hijacked the live concert from the event's producers but also shed light on the conflicting narratives of Hurricane Katrina, the failed relief effort and its real victims.

While *A Concert for Hurricane Relief* has come to be remembered culturally in terms of West's performance, it was in actuality intended to follow very much in the footsteps of successful benefit concerts like *America: A Tribute to Heroes* and other *Live Aid*-style concerts. However, given the performance's external context of the fractured, failed response to Hurricane Katrina as opposed to that which followed 9/11, *A Concert for Hurricane Relief* lacked the unified symbolism of its predecessor on the narrative level of its performance and on the symbolic level of its reception. In 2001, *America: A Tribute to Heroes* was heralded for, among other things, the unprecedented industrial cooperation between various media industries. *A Concert for Hurricane Relief* was just one among many concerts produced after Katrina, the variety of which has been cited as representative of the fractured response to Katrina, its depiction in the media and its reception by multiple audiences.

Writing on the entertainment industry's revival of the trend of benefit concerts, which proved so successful after 9/11, as a way to help in the relief effort for the victims of Hurricane Katrina, Michael Brick argues that the cultural divisions in the emerging debate "about the poor and black residents being left to drown while the well off and white escaped ... are showing up in divergent charity efforts being organized by the music industry" (Brick, 2005, p. 7). Situating this debate largely in terms of race, continues quoting sociologist David Wellman: "The fact that we have different charities raising money reflects that we have different ways, different-colored people experienced the tragedy" (2005, p. 7). In covering the entertainment industry's fractured response to Katrina, Brick and Wellman recall the way in which Katrina had from the very beginning of its coverage teetered between competing narratives in the news media, particularly in terms of race and class. According to Carol Stabile, the racial identity of the victims of Katrina, "those left behind," affected the coverage of the catastrophe from the outset, because, as she notes: "the victims of Hurricane Katrina were different in one important regard: they were predominantly African American" (2007, pp. 688, 689). As a result of this difference, the social drama that followed Hurricane Katrina and the breeched levees of New Orleans "involved a conflict between a disaster story entailing the victimization of African Americans and a crime story centering on white fear of black criminals" (Stabile, 2007, p. 690). Thus, given the conflicting social dramas that began to be written after Katrina, Brick concludes, "the competition that has emerged among fund-raising efforts reflects cultural lines that were already drawn" (2005, p. 7).

In addition to *A Concert for Hurricane Relief*, Hurricane Katrina and its aftermath inspired *Shelter from the Storm: A Concert for the Gulf Coast* and a concert produced and sponsored by BET (Black Entertainment Television). Of these, *Shelter from the Storm* was designed to replicate most explicitly the success and format of *America: A Tribute to Heroes*. At one end of the spectrum it was intended as another simulcast relief effort to foster a collective, communal response to help rebuild the Gulf Region and New Orleans after Katrina. At the other end of the spectrum, though, BET's concert was produced specifically in response to the racial undertones of the catastrophe because, as told by one network representative to *The Washington Post*, "BET places special priority around the needs of African Americans" (de Moraes, 2005, p. C1). Implicit in this statement, of course, is the argument that not only do other networks not care about the needs of African Americans but also neither does the news media or the federal government. Situated somewhere between these two ends of the relief effort's spectrum of responses, then, can be found *A Concert for Hurricane Relief*. Citing network insiders, Lisa de Moraes continues: "NBC rushed its special onto the air in response to a call from Harry Connick, Jr. to NBC chief Bob Wright and/ or NBC Universal president Jeff Zucker, asking the network what could be done to help hurricane victims" (2005, p. C1). Musically, then, *A Concert for Hurricane Relief*, buoyed by Connick's involvement as one of New Orleans' favorite sons, was shaped by the symbolic sound and spirit of a New Orleans funeral.

According to Murray Forman, "New Orleans brass bands simultaneously— and without contradiction—capture funeral sorrow in recognition of a life ended and wildly spontaneous sensuality in celebration of lives being lived" (2002, p. 192). Similarly, as performance scholar Paige McGinley reminds us, "Due in part to New Orleans' heritage as a musical city, musical performance became a primary means by which the tragedy was commemorated, represented, reckoned with" (2007, p. 59). It therefore makes sense that the concert began with jazz music performed by New Orleans natives Harry Connick, Jr. and Wynton

Marsalis. As two of the heirs apparent and contemporary advocates of New Orleans jazz, Marsalis's and Connick's musical appearance contributed to the soundtrack of post-Katrina New Orleans by recalling its musical legacy during an elegiac benefit concert which was intended in part to serve as a funeral, "mourning a 'lost' New Orleans that could never return" (McGinley, 2007, p. 59). The soundtrack that came to accompany Hurricane Katrina and its aftermath was compiled from the musical legacy of this "lost" New Orleans and included among its representative genres ballads, jazz, blues, ragtime, and zydeco tunes describing floods, disaster, Mardi Gras, and life in Louisiana (McGinley, 2007, p. 57). Thus, *A Concert for Hurricane Relief* was, in its conception, trying to invoke the spirit and music of a New Orleans funeral for the lost city through jazz performances by the likes of Connick and Marsalis, while also including more neutral pop performances by other natives of the Gulf Coast region like Tim McGraw and his wife Faith Hill. Originally, then, the concert was scripted to celebrate the city and its musical legacy as a way to inspire donations from viewers in the relief effort while avoiding any politicized content. Ignoring that script, though, was Kanye West who hijacked the concert.

Rather than following the teleprompter's pre-written message about the breeched levees and flooding of New Orleans, Kanye West seized the moment and the media and turned the national attention on what he and many others contend was the true story of Hurricane Katrina and the poorly executed relief efforts. West's interruption began before the now infamous seven words about George Bush's concern for black people. Immediately following Myers's scripted line, "The landscape of the city has changed dramatically, tragically and perhaps irreversibly. There is now 25 feet of water where there was once city streets and thriving neighborhoods" (quoted in de Moraes, 2005, p. C01), West deviated from his script. His first comments offered a lengthy condemnation of the media's portrayal of Hurricane Katrina and its multiple victims:

> I hate the way they portray us in the media. You see a black family, it says, "They're looting." You see a white family, it says, "They're looking for food." And, you know, it's been five days [waiting for federal help] because most of the people are black. … America is set up to help the poor, the black people, the less well-off, as slow as possible. … We already realize a lot of people that could help are at war right now, fighting another way—and they've given them permission to go down and shoot us! (quoted in de Moraes, 2005, p. C01)

Excerpted here, West's comments cite several storylines circulating in the media in the wake of Hurricane Katrina. First, his response to the portrayal of African Americans in the media directly calls attention to a scandal in which Yahoo News posted two photos: one of a white family and one of an African American family. As West notes, the captions in these photos referred to the subjects as "looking for food" and "looting" respectively, thereby marking the differently coded behaviors of the victims of Katrina as a result of their racial profile, "which to many indicated a double standard at work" (Ralli, 2005, p. C1). Second, West calls attention to the lack of efficiency and urgency in the response based on the victim's race. Setting the foundation for his next comment, West lambastes the federal government for being set up to help poor and black citizens as slowly as possible. West then "throws back to Myers, who is looking like a guy who stopped on the tarmac to tie his shoe and got hit in the back with the 8:30 to La Guardia" (de Moraes, 2005, p. C01). Myers returns to the scripted speech on the teleprompter before West deviates one final time to say: "George Bush doesn't care about black people" (quoted in de Moraes, 2005, p. C01). Following this last statement, the broadcast feed of the event is immediately and obviously interrupted by a jumpcut to an unprepared Chris Tucker, the next speaker "who started right on script" after a brief delay to realize he was now live on camera (de Moraes, 2005, p. C01).

Focusing on this moment, we can perhaps best understand West's performance as a hijacking. In their research on media events, Dayan and Katz argue "the scripts proposed by the organizers of an event do not necessarily coincide with the enacted event" (1992, p. 63). Additionally, they argue that there is "a desire to control the definitions and the character of an event, and to maximize the profit (or minimize the loss) of association with it" (Dayan and Katz, 1992, p. 73). For *A Concert for Hurricane Relief* the proposed script was that of a respectful, spirited funeral buoyed by the traditional and festive music associated with New Orleans. West, though, appeared as a hijacker, who Dayan and Katz describe as a performer that wishes to protest the proposed script and "explode the myth of value consensus implied by the event" (1992, p. 74). Following Katrina and the news scandals like that of the distinctly different racial undertones of the photographic captions mentioned above, questions were raised over both the media's coverage of the event and the government's response to it. Importantly, as Neal Ullestad argues, "When questions are raised and previously concealed aspects of reality are exposed, people tend to look for answers" (1992, p. 48). Continuing, he writes "Such answers needn't come from within the hegemonic system, but someone must be available with radical answers when they are being sought" (Ullestad, 1992, p. 48). For many in the audience, then, Kanye West provided a direct, clear-cut answer to questions over the relief effort for victims of Hurricane Katrina: that President George Bush did not care. This radical, unplanned answer left the event's producers struggling with the editorial choice of "whether to transmit an aberration or 'hijacking' of an event" by removing West's comments from the broadcast (Dayan and Katz, 1992, p. 78).

As described from the live feed above, the event stayed with Kanye West for the duration of his comments before awkwardly cutting to the evening's next celebrity Chris Tucker. Since the concert was broadcast as a live event, West's comments were able to go out uncensored, because "the person in charge 'was instructed to listen for a curse word, and didn't realize [West] had gone off-script'" ("Stars Offer Heartfelt Performances in Benefit," 2005). Because of this oversight, the audience for the live East Coast feed of the broadcast was able to see West's statement performed uncensored. The West Coast audience, however, got a different performance. For them, West's second statement about President Bush was cut from the broadcast, which McGinley cites as "[exploiting] the parameters of the increasingly rare live broadcast, setting off a firestorm of debate in the press" (2007, p. 59). In other words, the live broadcast of the event was not only revealed by West's comments but also it was then violated by the event's producers who edited the broadcast when it was re-aired, as seemingly "live," to its second audience. In making that edit, though, the producers wound up drawing even more attention to the perceived truth of West's statement. The event concluded with one last attempt to restore the consensus viewpoint of the evening's producers before the final musical number, "When the Saints Go Marching In": Matt Lauer's remarking upon and explaining the evening's performance, and particularly those opinions expressed by some of the performers that may not align with the party line of the intended, scripted, official broadcast. Translating the event for the viewing audience, Lauer explained that "emotions in this country are running very high. Sometimes that emotion is translated into inspiration, sometimes into criticism. We've heard some of that tonight. But it's still part of the American way of life" (quoted in de Moraes, 2005, p. C01). Then, shortly after the event ended, NBC worked to rearticulate its official position and distance itself from West's criticisms by issuing a statement:

> Tonight's telecast was a live television event wrought with emotion. Kanye West departed from the scripted comments that were prepared for him, and his opinions in no way represent the views of the network. It would be most unfortunate if the efforts of the artists who participated tonight and the generosity of millions of Americans who are helping those in need are overshadowed by one person's opinion. (quoted in de Moraes, 2005, p. C01)

Despite the efforts of NBC's executives, however, West's words have come to define both the concert and the failed relief effort of Katrina.

While Dayan and Katz argue that "It is correct to regard most media events … as 'reinforcing' or 'hegemonic,' in the sense that they remind societies to renew their commitments to established values, offices, and persons," Kanye West's performance in *A Concert for Hurricane Relief* serves as a reminder of the fact that "some people enter a narrative, but with a different orientation, an alternative, even a hostile, role" (1992, pp. 147, 141). As a benefit concert, *A Concert for Hurricane Relief* was configured in relation to the conflicting narrative frameworks for its audiences. According to Stabile, the primary frameworks affecting the context within which the concert was performed and against which West was responding alternated "between a narrative framework that criminalized displaced people, thereby blaming them for the horrific situations in the Superdome and the convention center, and a frame that understood the government's inability to act—and the racism that underlay that inability—as criminal" (2007, p. 701). Thus, these frameworks can be understood as the preconditions of the event that shaped the reception of West's performance, as well as the lasting potential for social change as a result of the popular music concert.

Writing on the mega-events of the 1980s Media Aid phenomenon, Garofalo argues, "it is important to critically evaluate the potential of these events for social change" (1992a, p. 55). Taking up that charge, Michael Moore suggests that West's comments made possible social change after Katrina by bringing light to the unwritten, and previously unspoken, story about the real victims of Hurricane Katrina. He writes, "Spoken with simple sincerity by Kanye West ... [his words] shout out of the nation's flat screens like a laser beam of truth" (Moore, 2005, p. 65). Further, he adds that "stunned viewers could not believe that someone had said what many had been thinking—but no one was saying" (Moore, 2005, p. 65). With his so-called laser beams of truth, West was heralded as a hero throughout both the black press and many sectors of the entertainment industry, most notably the hip-hop sector. *The New York Amsterdam News*, for example, entered the dialogue writing "it's our view that rapper Kanye West's unexpected, from-the-heart condemnation of Bush during the NBC televised *A Concert for Hurricane Relief* was not only appropriate, it was necessary" (Rogers, 2005, p. 21). As a result of their necessity, West's comments moved him "into a pantheon of African American musicians who have seized the public platform to speak truth—at least their sense of it—to power" (Mitchell and Werde, 2005, p. 5). Responding to the comments, rapper and Def Jam Recordings' president/CEO Jay-Z said, "I'm backing Kanye 100% ... This is America: freedom of speech" (quoted in Mitchell and Werde, 2005, p. 5). Further praising West's performance, rapper and political activist Chuck D adds "This industry is run by a bunch of grown white men who have benefitted off rap being infantile. ... But Kanye West is 28 years old. It's commendable when a cat realizes, 'I'm a grown man and I have to speak on a situation'" (quoted in Mitchell and Werde, 2005, p. 21).

West entered the discourse himself both in answering the media's questions about what prompted the comments and in recalling the moment in subsequent performances. In an interview with *Rolling Stone* in which Austin Scaggs asked West about when he came up with his comments about Katrina and Bush, West explained:

> I knew I wasn't going to read the whole [scripted] levee thing, because we'd practiced that earlier. I didn't think about Bush until the telethon. I saw him [on TV]—I'm like, "Wait a second, dude, that guy over there, he doesn't care." But America was already headed that way. I think it was a common opinion. (Scaggs, 2005, p. 72)

Adding to this explanation, Moore quotes West's thoughts from his conversation with the rapper, "How can I read these words when the truth needs to be said?" (2005, p. 66). In addition to publicly discussing his inspiration and his opinion on the truth of the situation surrounding Katrina, West also recalled his appearance on *A Concert for Hurricane Relief* in later performances that in turn help us to decode the original concert. For example, in his self-centered performance during the following week's concert *Shelter from the Storm* West, according to Paige McGinley, the artist "composed an alternative soundtrack that countered musical performances of passive mourning of the 'disappearance' of New Orleans" (2007, pp. 57-8). On this performance, McGinley argues "West's musical performance enabled him to do something he could not do in a speech to the camera—rebuke those who criticized him for 'politicizing' the 2 September event" (2007, p. 60). Looking back to the initial concert, then, we can decode the impact of West's performance as a hijacker of the broadcast as a moment in which popular music and the benefit concert model enabled a counter-public to resist the social, cultural, and political norms proposed by the public response to the social drama of Hurricane Katrina.

As a way of concluding, it is important to note in both cases that the immediate response to 9/11 and Hurricane Katrina was to put on a massive, musical event as a way to model the appropriate social response. Though West's performance prevented *A Concert for Hurricane Relief* from being the intended funeral service for Katrina that it set out to be, that concert and *America: A Tribute to Heroes* both used pared down celebrity performances, thematically and textually relevant, appropriate music, and the technologies of the mass media to create culturally and socially meaningful concerts. In the end, despite Susan Fast's worry over "whether anyone else feels a sense of fatigue around benefit concerts and whether they have become less powerful mechanisms for raising awareness and perhaps also money" (quoted in Garofalo, 2005, p. 339), the concerts analyzed here demonstrate the many potential functions that benefit concerts can serve in the twenty-first century.

Chapter 9
From Midnight Music to Civil Rights, from Bluesology to Human Rights: Gil Scott-Heron, American Griot

Ian Peddie

In an address given to the first conference of Negro writers in New York in 1959, the playwright Lorraine Hansberry spoke passionately about the pressing need for a writer able to address the experiences of African Americans. The task at hand, Hansberry asserted, was one of "cultural and historical reclamation—to reclaim the past [and] the future" (1993, p. 136). This undertaking, rendered still more taxing by the presence of "villainous and often ridiculous money values that spill over from the dominant culture" (Hansberry, 1993, p. 137), necessitated what the author called "a new Romanticism" able to examine in every detail aspects of American culture. Like a good number of artists and writers at the time, Hansberry was, in fact, mining a seam that drew inspiration from the massive global, anticolonial movements that gained momentum after World War II, when according to Penny Von Eschen, "eight hundred million people—more than a quarter of the earth's population at the time—revolted against colonialism and won their independence" (1997, p. 125). Reconceptualizing the African American struggle for rights within a framework of such seismic changes abroad necessitated the deployment of appropriate narratives through which calls for rights and self-determination could be organized. Africa and Asia, where developing ideologies of freedom and equality were the means through which former colonies asserted their right to emancipation, supplied African Americans with a burgeoning nationalism they could adapt to their own situation; in developing countries this sense of nationalism manifested itself as anticolonialism and decolonization; in the United States, where independence movements exerted a significant influence, it emerged as the struggle for civil rights.[1] Inevitably, among a beleaguered ethnic community denied equal rights, as black Americans were, independence movements struck a particularly profound chord. In this climate, it should scarcely need saying, then, that the culture of conformity, the lens through which so much postwar culture has been critically filtered, is wholly inadequate to explain not only African American resistance but also analogous forms of opposition and

---

[1] For a discussion of the influences independence movements in Africa exerted on the United States see Medevoi (2002) and Von Eschen (1997).

revolt that appeared with more and more frequency. Crucial in this respect is the overt rebelliousness of figures such as James Dean and Marlon Brando in film, the antithetical stance of the Beats in literature, assertions of homosexuality by authors such as James Baldwin and Gore Vidal, and the inexorable rise of rock and roll, with its anti-authority, parental-defying message (Medevoi, 2002, pp. 170-71). The presence of such a critical mass of evidence suggests that a more fitting title for the 1950s might, then, be "the illusion of assent," an aphorism certainly applicable to reality as many African Americans understood it. Certainly, and very much in contrast to the "team player" consensus of the time, African American experience was predicated on opposition to the prevailing social order. This was yet another example in which African Americans had much in common with those decolonized people with whom they increasingly exhibited a reciprocity of interests. In fact, the possibility of forging a diasporic identity around a correlation between black America and recently emancipated peoples in Asia and especially in Africa became a key feature of the African American quest for rights.

The reversion of so many sovereign nations to indigenous control intensified and deepened African American agitation for equality in various ways. At its core what the unraveling of empire actually revealed was the weakening and diminishing of forms of hierarchy that had previously appeared unbreakable. That the old order could be challenged, that it could in fact be overthrown, and that these possibilities nourished the undermining of established ways of conceiving of power and governance provided a vital sense of impetus that breathed new life into oppositional consciousness. "The end of deference," that guilty euphemism coined by the British as their empire crumbled, and which unsuccessfully attempts to attribute imperial demise to a loss of faith in institutions, echoes throughout these debates. For, in reality, to end deference is to disavow authority, which is, of course, a fundamental aspect of breaking the psychology of dominance and oppression. One of the most articulate observers of the damage deference inflicted on his race was Malcolm X, who in a speech delivered in Detroit in November, 1963, made the end of deference the mainstay in the struggle for emancipation. During slavery, Malcolm X asserted,

> The house Negroes—they lived in the house with master, they dressed pretty good, they ate good 'cause they ate his food—what he left. They lived in the attic or the basement, but still they lived near the master; and they loved their master more than the master loved himself. They would give their life to save the master's house quicker than the master would. The house Negro, if the master said, "We got a good house here," the house Negro would say, "Yeah, we got a good house here." Whenever the master said "we," he said "we." ("Message to the Grassroots," 1963)

Malcolm X saw the conflation of interests slaves made between themselves and their masters as a profoundly inhibiting psychological barrier, one that militated against the struggle for equality long after slavery had ended. In the challenging and inflammatory rhetoric for which Malcolm X became famous, the equation was simple enough: black nationalism would pave the way for revolution, just as it had, he felt, throughout Africa. In Malcolm X's pan-Africanist vision, so evident were the similarities between nationalist movements in developing countries and the situation of African Americans that merely to suggest an analogy was enough.

Whether others found Malcolm X's chronology of progression, from Bandung to Kenya's Mau Mau insurgents, to the revolutionary movement in Algeria, an accurate vision of progressive self-definition that could be domesticated and presented to would-be American revolutionaries is a moot point.[2] What is significant is that along with Malcolm X, a good number of influential African Americans also envisaged common cause between themselves and those committed to self-determination in former colonies. Former Ghanaian leader Kwame Nkrumah's conclusion that "the flowing tide of African nationalism sweeps everything before it" (1961, p. 262) ensured that unlike some of their white counterparts, perhaps, these rebels had found their cause, and they imagined the domestication of anticolonialism in a variety of ways. Cultural commentators such as Eldridge Cleaver suggested that African American consciousness was undergoing a form of awakening: "prior to 1954," he asserted, African American experience was tantamount to living "in an atmosphere of Novocain" (1999, p. 22); to others, such as Harold Isaacs, there was a palpable "loss of fear ... the fear posture of the Negro has changed very markedly" (1963, p. 52). The cultural changes these influences effected took on many forms. The arrival of soul, for instance, with its emphasis on black consciousness and pride, and its afrocentric leanings, was in many ways a benchmark of black self-definition. But these are only the most conspicuous examples of the narrative tropes through which African Americans began to align their position with that of emerging peoples in the process of throwing off the yoke of imperialism. Indeed, the social vision such thinking inspired produced some of the most stimulating literature of the period, as recourse to the work of James Baldwin, Lorraine Hansberry, Ralph Ellison et al. will testify.

But the seismic changes that wrought the continents of Africa and Asia exerted a profound influence on American music too. If we accept critic and musician Archie Shepp's contention—and we should—that "Black music has transmitted the seeds of Black experience far more effectively than mere words acquired second hand" (1981, p. xii), then it is that medium that provides the most illuminating record of African American self-determination. References to the struggle for decolonizaton and self-definition, it is worth reiterating, were almost always more than mere gestures of assent; so high were the stakes that contemporary musicians were in no doubt that a defining moment was at hand. As jazz saxophonist Sonny Rollins explained in the liner notes to his portentous 1958 album *Freedom Suite*, "how

---

[2] The 1955 Asian-African Conference at Bandung, Indonesia was convened to promote Asian-African economic and cultural cooperation and to oppose imperialism and colonialism. Significantly, neither the United States nor the Soviet Union was invited to the conference.

ironic that the Negro, who more than any other people can claim America's culture as his own, is being persecuted and repressed; that the Negro, who has exemplified the humanities in his very existence, is being rewarded with inhumanity." *Freedom Suite* (1958), the full version of Charles Mingus's *Mingus Ah Um* (1959), and Max Roach's *We Insist: Freedom Now* (1960), the latter with songs titled "All Africa" and "Tears for Johannesburg," suggested a similarity of interests between the growing US civil rights movement and newly freed Third World countries. Further implied similarities between the struggles of black Americans and newly decolonized countries are coded throughout music from the mid-1950s onward. Notable in this respect is John Coltrane's "Kulu Se Mama" (1965), a sophisticated composition replete with African percussion that produced a sound one critic described as "like a man strapped down and screaming to be free" (Sidran, 1981, p. 142). Such meditations on Africa helped foster a myriad of compositions calling for equality, of which perhaps the most notable include Sam Cooke's Dylanesque "A Change is Gonna Come" (1964) and The Impressions' "Keep on Pushing" (1964) and "We're a Winner" (1968), both written by Curtis Mayfield.

These and other similar compositions articulated a disturbing vision of inequality and oppression in a society riven along racial lines. Growing exasperation over the continued absence of black self-definition was always liable to crystallize at any moment and did, in fact, as war broke out in Vietnam. In 1966, world heavyweight boxing champion Cassius Clay refused to answer the draft call, countering instead that armed conflict was contrary to the teachings of the *Koran*. More controversially, Clay added the rejoinder that "No Viet Cong ever called me Nigger," a comment that soon adorned many a banner at Civil Rights and antiwar demonstrations. Not only did the pointed allusion to the illegitimacy of imperialism implicit in Clay's comment allude to the prevailing North American embracing of newly emancipated states, it also suggested that the ideology of rebellion could be figured in racial terms, indeed as African American.[3] In ways reminiscent of how the colonized's exclusion from the public sphere encouraged a "reactive vocabulary of violence and retributive justice" (Bhabha, 2004, p. xx), the rhetoric of rebellion among African Americans frequently embraced anticolonialist terms in ways that implied frustration over their own absence of real power. The provocative Last Poets, a largely black nationalist group of writers and musicians who emerged in the late 1960s, adopted a hard-edged approach to the quest for equality that indicted African Americans over their own alleged reluctance to embrace significant change. As aggressive as their notorious single "Niggers Are Scared of Revolution" (1970) is, it also incorporates a *carpe diem* immediacy that, given their relatively high profile, no doubt exerted influence on those already inclined to view independence movements in developing countries as synonymous

---

[3]   As Medevoi points out, in his inaugural address President John F. Kennedy offered "those new states whom we welcome to the ranks of the free ... our word that one form of colonial control shall not have passed away merely to be replaced by a far more iron tyranny" (2002, p. 167).

with their own plight. Tactics of the kind used by The Last Poets, where African Americans were indicted for their absence of revolutionary fervor at the same time as they were baited into acting, were familiar motifs aimed more at keeping the quest for equality in the forefront of public vision than anything else. Yet they were a form of cultural witnessing, too, that like every account we have considered so far, crystallized as a history of struggle, a chronicle of emancipation, and one of many narratives of self-definition that remain an essential part of American society. There is no artist whose vision provides a more emphatic glimpse into the extent to which independence movements influenced African American music than Gil Scott-Heron.

Born in Chicago in 1949, but raised in the segregated world of Jackson, Tennessee, Gil Scott-Heron, a published author by the age of 19, has written poetry, fiction, and music of great distinction for over four decades. After writing the thriller *The Vulture* (1970), which he followed with *The Nigger Factory* (1972), a novel that examined contemporary America through the topical issues of stasis and change, his debut volume of poetry, published under the same title as his first album, *Small Talk at 125th and Lenox*, appeared in 1970, while later volumes included *So Far, So Good* (1990) and *Now and Then: The Poems of Gil Scott-Heron* (2000). But it is for his music that Scott-Heron is most famous; by his own admission, music is the medium in which his most socially committed work can be found. "My song writing is different from the fiction and poetry," he explained in the liner notes to *Small Talk at 125th and Lenox*. "It's more explicitly political. And so a vital influence on me as a songwriter, was Malcolm X, because he was such a force in the lives of black people" (Liner notes, n.p.). Scott-Heron was too intelligent a writer not to appreciate the implications of the connection between Malcolm X and "the lives of black people," for as we have seen, the latter brought with him a firm conviction that "the same rebellion, the same impatience, the same anger that exists in the hearts of the dark people in Africa and Asia is existing in the hearts and minds of 20 million black people in this country who have been just as thoroughly colonized as the people in Africa and Asia" (quoted in Golden and Rieke, 1971, p. 431). Along with the ideologies and goals they inspired, these and other polemical sentiments, which, depending on one's viewpoint, ensured that Malcolm X was either a hero or a fifth columnist, were of fundamental importance to artists like Gil Scott-Heron.

As one might expect, then, in an artist whose formative years were influenced by Malcolm X and left-wing Black Panther founder Huey Newton, Scott-Heron's work carried a revolutionary charge, notably in his most famous song, "The Revolution Will Not Be Televised," whose evocative title has not surprisingly been bandied about rather indiscriminately. Read in the context of its time, however, this ostensibly stirring call to action was more of a warning against the dilution of revolutionary spirit via the distorting affects of media than it was a simple call to arms. A quarter of a century later, in "Message to the Messengers," a song in which Scott-Heron drew rappers' attention to the precedent his earlier work had set, the artist confirmed what he had in mind: "We was talkin' about television and doin' it on the radio,/ What we did was to help our generation realize,/ They had to get out there and get busy cause it wasn't gonna be televised." What was televised were some of the more demonstrative examples of social unrest that were part of the US fabric in the late 1960s, and as Craig Werner and others have pointed out, such broadcasts had a "disastrous effect on the movement for racial justice" (1998, p. 158). Riots and looting, for instance, were relatively minor aspects of the protests, though they were issues which suspiciously seemed to dominate the news bulletins. Ironically, then, from a completely different perspective to what Scott-Heron had in mind when he wrote such antagonistic lyrics, the media also appeared to confirm his warning that "the revolution will not be brought to you by Xerox in four equal parts." Hence what "The Revolution Will Not be Televised" reveals is that Gil Scott-Heron was beginning to understand the rage of the oppressed just as he seemed to grasp the importance of the struggle for consciousness that is central to freedom and equality.

As early as 1971, however, in his debut album, *Small Talk at 125th and Lenox*, the song "Brother," for all its familiar connotations, sounded a note of caution: "We deal in too many externals, brother," Scott-Heron sang, "Always afros, handshakes, and dashikis/ Never can a man build a working structure for black capitalism/ Always does a man read Mao or Fanon." As Scott-Heron knew, visible demonstrations of self-determinism were one thing; changing established thinking about oppression was altogether another. Significantly in this respect, one of the key aspects of the work of Martinique-born theorist Frantz Fanon (1925-61) was his emphasis on the "colonized mind," a condition wherein the oppressed internalize the dominant ideologies of the oppressor. In turn, this leads to the perpetuation of inequality and inegalitarian power relations inherited from imperialism and colonialism. Like "The Revolution Will Not Be Televised," "Brother" suggests that it is incumbent upon blacks to experience the realities of social agitation rather than having them filtered through television or the exertions of their fellow "brothers." Because there is no "working structure for black capitalism," "Brother" intimates that calls for African Americans to display "traditional" attire and appearance, manifestations of which appeared throughout the 1950s and 1960s, could be invoked as a form of social discrimination, as the following lyrics suggest: "Calling this man an Uncle Tom/ And telling this woman to get an afro,/ But you won't speak to her if she looks like hell, will you, brother? …/ You need to get your memory banks organized, brother./ Show that man you call an Uncle Tom just where he is wrong./ Show that woman that you are a sincere black man." The song closes by reminding would-be revolutionaries that they have an obligation toward their own community because, "That's what brothers are for, brother."

Reminders of social responsibility are scattered throughout Scott-Heron's work. Amid the post-industrial terrain wherein he set so many of his narratives, emotionally charged stories such as "No Knock," "Inner-City Blues," and "Billy Green Is Dead" are three songs typical of the theme and direction Scott-Heron's protest invariably took. Equally, in one way or another, they are all concerned with rights. "No Knock," which first appeared on the 1972 album *Free Will*, is a response to former attorney general John Mitchell's attempts to grant the police the right to enter a private dwelling without knocking; "Inner-City Blues," inspired by Marvin Gaye's song of the same name, examines a ghetto islanded from the rest of society: "So you say you never heard of the 'Inner City Blues'/ And what's more you don't understand at all/ What the ghetto people mean when they say 'living behind walls'." In "Billy Green Is Dead," the focus lay with the dearth of political consciousness and the preoccupation with frivolous trivialities: "Yeah, I heard when you tol' me,/ You said Billy Green is dead./ But let me tell you about these hotpants ...."

The tactical immediacy of such songs—and there were many of this nature—served multiple purposes; they raised consciousness, they illuminated the social inequality and continuing segregation that blighted America, and they encouraged Scott-Heron to consider the underlying causes that condemned so many black Americans to poverty. Recourse to the black diaspora revealed depressingly familiar patterns of global racial oppression that Scott-Heron thought were replicated in the United States too. In song after song, the poet invited parallels between the black American experience and the dream of emancipation he saw embodied in the global struggle for freedom. In "The Liberation Song (Red, Black and Green)," Scott-Heron invoked a narrative around the three colors of the Pan-African Flag, the banner of African American unity which was adopted as article 39 of the Declaration of Rights of the Negro Peoples of the World on August 13, 1920.[4] Using the imagery of changing seasons imbues the flag with a natural resonance allowing the singer to employ a figurative mode that also summons the timelessness of past struggles for freedom. Having established a sense of metaphorical legitimacy, the singer concludes that "And all you got to do,/ Brothers and sisters, reach out your hands,/ We're gonna take you there/ Black stands for liberation, yeah." The closing "yeah" here is no verbal affectation; rather it is an affirmation that confirms the legitimacy of the sentiments expressed in the song. As each verse makes clear, the refrain of "freedom everywhere" is contingent upon reaching out in terms of both action and thought. Scott-Heron is clearly aware, however, of the difficulty involved in recognizing the shared possibility of emancipation, especially when it was asking people to consider their own position in relation to those of other apparently distant places and cultures. As if to assist in this process, the song closes with a series of declarations where the flag "stands for liberation/ It stands for a brand new nation/ It stands for liberation/ It stands for a brand new nation/ Yeah." In a similar confirmatory way that the poet Langston Hughes—a great hero of Scott-Heron's—concluded a number of

---

[4] The creation of the flag was a response to the song "Every Race Has a Flag but the Coon," which was wildly popular at the turn of the century. The Pan-Africanist Marcus Garvey, a key figure in the adoption of the flag, saw it as a unifying banner designed to oppose the racism prevalent at the time.

his "blues" poems, the final closing "Yeah" here is an affirmation that confirms the accuracy of the entire narrative.

"Liberation Song" first appeared in 1975, on the singer's powerful *The First Minute of a New Day*, and it was one of a raft of songs that harnessed the consciousness of self-definition inspired by several high-profile struggles for state independence from the mid-1960s onwards.[5] On that same album, the portentous "Winter in America" saw the artist consider the implications of an absence of any clear social vision during the contentious domestic period that marked the beginning of the end of the Vietnam War: there "ain't nobody fighting," he suggested, "'cause nobody knows what to save." For those who "never had a chance to grow," he went on, the "con-stitution was a noble piece of paper;/ With free society they struggled but they died in vain/ and now democracy is ragtime on the corner/ hoping that it rains." The implication of a nation sundered between the powerful and the powerless is exactly what Scott-Heron had in mind when he articulated this Manichean contrast. There was nothing wrong with this vision, of course, and in many ways it was an accurate articulation of society. But as the artist knew, the issues his work examined were always more complex than this; by implication, for instance, in the context of the influences anticolonial movements were having on Scott-Heron's music, "Winter in America" (summer is elsewhere) is more of a nod to freedom movements around the world than it is a comment on the country's demise.

Three years after Scott-Heron had made a foray into the politics of Vietnam through the song "Did You Hear What They Said?," a painful lament about a mother crying after her son had been "shot in the head to save his country," the artist's exploration of the consequences of alienation and disaffection in America moved him in his notes, included in *Now and Then: The Poems of Gil Scott-Heron* (2000), to remind others of a diaspora from which African Americans could take inspiration. "In our hearts," he wrote, "we feel ... a Spring of brotherhood and united spirit among people of colour," that "there is a restlessness within our souls that keeps us questioning, discovering, struggling against a system that will not allow us space and time for fresh expression" (2000, p. 63). The similarities between these sentiments and much anticolonial consciousness require no rehearsal; of fundamental importance to Scott-Heron, of course, is that such intimations toward cultural self-determination were a step on the road to the attainment of collective rights which were fundamental to the independence struggles and from which his work took encouragement.

As Gil Scott-Heron's career progressed, allusions toward anticolonial struggles and the parallels they suggested with domestic issues grew more sophisticated. The youthful outrage of his earlier albums gave way to a more reflective response,

---

[5]   Often as a result of decades of struggle, many former colonies secured independence during this time. Some of the more high-profile examples include Zambia (1964), Gambia (1965), Botswana (1966), Guinea-Bissau (1973), Mozambique (1975), and Angola (1975). Independence in the latter trio was achieved only after bloody armed conflict.

one no less strident, however. A useful example in this respect is "Delta Man (Where I'm Coming From)," a song which first appeared on the album *Bridges* (1977). What is striking in this song is the calmness through which the call to revolution is delivered. In a song that declares its subject as "change," the manner in which Scott-Heron is able to usher in revolution as an inevitable consequence of the poor treatment afforded blacks in post-Civil War America is compelling. Inspired by the "brothers in the Caribbean and Africa," the song is a historical panorama of oppression, with reference to the black diaspora represented by slavery in the Mississippi Delta, sharecropping in Nebraska, expansion into the West and the carceral reality of urban, inner-city life. The song closes with the poet's declaration that "the point I'm trying to make, movin' from place to place and time to time" is that not only that "change is surely bound to come" but that people should not fear revolutionary change. In fact, as Scott-Heron advises, "Put a little revolution in your life/ and you'll understand where I'm comin' from." This is an invocation delivered replete with the assumption that the call for revolution is itself nothing outlandish, that it is almost a part of an action currently in progress and that if it is not already a shared aspiration then it soon will be. In that sense, the song echoes the conclusions Frantz Fanon made regarding the revolutionary importance of the griot as an opponent of colonial rule. That is, under colonial conditions, and particularly in reference to the oral tradition, the griot was a key figure in modernizing traditional stories which could be subsequently melded with contemporary struggles and thus charged with new political significance. As Fanon asserts, this fosters a new way of thinking, one in which "the present is no longer turned in upon itself but spread out for all to see," wherein "the formula 'this all happened long ago' is substituted by that of 'What we are going to speak of happened somewhere else, but it might well have happened here today, and it might happen tomorrow'" (2006. p. 182). To this we might add, in the descriptive vocabulary of "Delta Man," that the drama of inequality as quotidian fact encourages the conclusion that Scott-Heron's historical allusions are in part synonymous with thought and deed that drove the quest for self-governance across the globe after World War II.

"Delta Man" calibrates the familiar, "you see," "you'll understand" with a desire to "direct the change," all of which indicates a more nuanced grasp of the potential for amelioration than some of the artist's earlier work. Weighed against songs such as the aggressively confrontational "Comment #1," where, amid some very explicit language, the poet concluded that "The time is in the street you know … And the new word to have is revolution. People don't even want to hear the preacher spill or spiel because God's whole card has been thoroughly piqued. And America is now blood and tears instead of milk and honey," "Delta Man" assumes a calm air borne of an assurance that the coming liberty has traversed the plain of protest and has now progressed to the point of moral appeal. Orchestrated to the soul/funk accompaniment of a wailing guitar, with audible sighs and breaths and affirmative "yeahs," the most prominent motif in "Delta Man" is the collective experience the song fosters. Using successive accretions, not least the often added and frequently repeated "it'll all be better if we get together" along with the song's central refrain, "oughta be where I'm comin' from," is a communal technique that echoes tactics commonly employed by colonized peoples as they progress toward opposition. In fact, at this point Scott-Heron's work typifies the trajectory of development Fanon ascribes to colonial writers: "While at the beginning the native intellectual used to produce his work to be read exclusively by the oppressor," Fanon notes, "whether with the intention of charming him or of denouncing him through ethnical or subjectivist means, now the native writer progressively takes on the habit of addressing his own people" (2006, p. 181). Not only does this insightful comment illuminate a typical trajectory common to much postcolonial writing, it suggests the levels of sophistication at work among opponents of imperialism. Significantly, for the purposes of this chapter, it is also approximates to the evolution Gil Scott-Heron's work has undergone.

With this proviso in mind, and as an exercise in the development of a musician, it is worth contrasting Scott-Heron at the beginning of his career with his position in the mid-1970s. By then, as a mature writer of growing distinction, Scott-Heron was comfortable enough to address "his own people" in the kind of calm and measured tone largely absent in some of his more shrill earlier pronouncements. While such sophisticated sentiments would soon become standard operating procedure for the man one critic later described as "a poetic conscience for America" (Geesling, 2007, n.p.), from whatever approach one cares to adopt, Scott-Heron's journey from rebellion to resistance in one way or another invariably crystallizes around the issue of human rights. Illustrative in this respect is the artist's responses to the 1981 election of Ronald Reagan. In a 1985 interview, Scott-Heron expressed his concern that Reagan's approach to discussing social security gave the indication that "only black folks are on welfare." Responding to such perceptions, Scott-Heron saw his own role very much in social terms; he was, he offered, "trying to help people to be more vocal in their objections to what's happening—every citizen has a voice, has a potential, and we are trying to encourage people to use it" (quoted in Ellison, 1989, p. 71). These sentiments informed his deeply ironic song "B-Movie," which was also written in response to Reagan's succession to office. The song explores the illusionary desire for "simpler times" that invariably underpins nostalgia, a theme the song suggests that Reagan exploited in order to gain office. For Scott-Heron this was tantamount to an evasion of political and social responsibility; clichés about standing "tall in the saddle" and how we "gave them hell" which Reagan used and which the song openly mocks, only made it worse. Scott-Heron's answer was a kind of didactic irony that mocked contemporary news bulletins: "... and here's a look at the closing stocks," he sings, "Racism is up. Human Rights are down. Peace is shaky. War items are hot ... Jobs are down, money is scarce and Common Sense is at an all-time low." Nevertheless, caricatures of this nature had more than a grain of truth to them: during the Reagan era, as Scott-Heron warned, the idea of rights as he and many of his fellow Americans understood it differed widely from the beliefs of the Reagan administration. In "B Movie" he mocks, "Civil Rights, Gay Rights. Women's Rights. They're all wrong! Call in the cavalry to disrupt this perception of freedom gone wild. First one of them wants freedom and then the whole damn world wants freedom!"

For Scott-Heron, circumscribed notions of freedom were nothing but a contradiction. To governments, however, freedom and its accoutrements are as often as not construed as a threat. In 1976, long before the apartheid movement in South Africa became a *cause célèbre* among musicians, Scott-Heron's *From South Africa to South Carolina* included a number of protest songs that deepened the artist's belief in a reciprocity of interests between African Americans and those he called "our brothers over there." "Over there" in this case referred to Johannesburg, the city from which his song took its title, though it is clearly meant to be explicative of Africa writ large. "Johannesburg's" function is, if not didactic, then certainly inspirational; the idea that despite overwhelming odds against them black South Africans were resisting apartheid, or "defyin' the Man," the singer finds exalting. Although he concludes that "their strugglin' over there ain't gonna free me," it is the denouement, that "we all need to be strugglin' if we're gonna be free," that sanctions the closing line, "Don't you wanna be free?," and establishes the sentiment as an affirmation rather than a question.

As these lyrics imply, Scott-Heron envisioned African movements toward self-definition as politically and ethically inevitable—and such thinking influenced his view of the possibility of change for African Americans. Many of his compositions on African struggle and liberation cohere as reminders of communal obligations, as exhortative calls to struggle, or as means of encouraging collectivist notions of a diasporic identity. The song "Third World Revolution," issued on the 1978 album *Secrets*, offers a combination of all three of these approaches: "It will hit you without warning/ and simply carry you away./ It's gonna be so doggone easy,/ you'll know you knew about it all the time./ It will answer all the questions/ that were playing with your mind./ It's the Third World Revolution/ and we're standing at the gate,/ You can make your contribution/ while the world is changing shape." All the familiar tropes appear in this song: the inevitability of change, the consequential sense of awakening, and the obligation to participate in social amelioration for the common good. It bears repeating, however, as Scott-Heron does several times in the song, that it is the Third World that is leading this revolution. Legitimating such seismic changes involved an ideological shift if only because for many people, as "Third World" implies, the "Third World revolution," would come as a surprise—albeit a pleasant one. For others it would be the arrival of agency potentially momentous enough to alter the world order, as the last verse makes clear: "We're gonna take this world through changes,/ not the other way around./ See the world is slowly rearranging/ can't nobody stop us now./ It's the Third World Revolution/ and we're standing at the gate." Powerful rhetoric of this nature came to a head in Scott-Heron's work of the late 1970s. In his notes to "Beginnings (First Minute of a New Day)," collected in his slim volume of poetry *Now and Then* (2000), the poet felt sure that there was "a revolution going on in America/ the world ... as disruptive as an actual earth-tremor, but it is happening in our hearts" (Scott-Heron, 2000, p. 69). The conviction that "revolution" comes from the heart recalls Malcolm X's contention that real change is possible only when those who have unwittingly internalized forces of domination are weaned of such adherence.

In his insightful study, *Black Music*, LeRoi Jones claimed that "Negro music is essentially an expression of an attitude, or a collection of attitudes, about the world" (1967, p. 13). This was true for Gil Scott-Heron just as it was for another of his great heroes, John Coltrane: African American music was synonymous with black consciousness. At the same time as it articulated black experience and reflected black social visions, Coltrane felt that music was capable of capturing "the whole of human experience at the particular time that it is being expressed" (quoted in Kofsky, 1970, p. 209), and it is in this sense that we must see Gil Scott-Heron's music. Thus in addition to providing a significant chronicle of postwar American cultural politics, Scott-Heron's music functions as a conscience, one that reminds America that the nation that first set foot on the moon also created the military-industrial complex, which, in his song of the same name, the artist memorably— and perhaps more accurately—called the "military and the monetary." Implicit in such aphorisms—and Scott-Heron coined many such prescient phrases—was the artist's refusal to accept a world, a society, based on superiority and subordination. As we have seen, postwar struggles for independence in Africa and Asia provided the ideological framework through which Scott-Heron formulated a body of music that celebrates the incipient power of the black diaspora, especially its ability to affect change, both internationally and domestically. In the hands of Gil Scott-Heron, these issues resonated in terms of the struggle for equality and rights, and much of the singer's lyrical content was articulated in the language of rights. In the poem "Bridging" he spoke of "Africa! From the continent" to "Afro-Americans! From the discontent" (Scott-Heron, 2000, p. 72); in "95 South (All of the Places We've Been)" he sang of towns "where there was no freedom or future around"; in "Beginnings: The First Minute of a New Day," a gorgeously melancholic ballad, the artist lamented, "We want to be free/ Yet we have no idea/ Why we are struggling here/ Faced with our every fear/ Just to survive." Examples such as these underscore the contention that Scott-Heron's music serves as a bridge between narratives of rights, civil and human. For all these reasons, in the search to discover, as Marvin Gaye famously put it, "what's going on," the novelist/poet/ singer Gil Scott-Heron, the "Godfather of Rap" and the "Minister of information," as he has been called, emerges as the one of the most important griots of the American urban experience.

Chapter 10

Plight of the Redman:
XIT, Red Power, and the Refashioning of American Indian Ethnicity

Christopher A. Scales

In 1972 XIT, a group of young American Indian musicians from Albuquerque, New Mexico, gathered together in Motown Record's legendary Hitsville recording studio in Detroit and began cutting the tracks for what would become their first LP, the politically incendiary *Plight of the Redman*. Released that same year on Rare Earth Records, a subsidiary of Motown that featured non-African American musical acts, the recording was one of the first overtly political albums to be released by the label. As such, according to Tom Bee, the group's leader, Motown didn't know how to market it and the recording met with some resistance from radio stations and retail chains. In an interview done years later with the newspaper *Indian Country Today*, Bee claimed:

> As soon as they heard "Go away White man, this is our land," they said "We don't want the record." They heard it as a slap against America. The album was never meant to be militant or radical, it came from the heart and told a story, but unfortunately the truth hurts and cuts deep. The press called us "the musical ambassadors of the American Indian Movement [AIM]." We believed in their platform, we did a lot of benefits in conjunction with AIM, and the message in our music basically was their platform, so it was a perfect combination. (quoted in Murg, 2008)

Inspired by Bee's statement, in this chapter I contend that XIT's music was an important and influential musical expression of a larger cultural transformation that was taking place across Indian country in the late 1960s and early 1970s. In making this argument I will outline explicit links between XIT's music and the ascendant Red Power movement, a politically radical social movement that sought greater public recognition for the political and social issues facing Native Americans in the 1960s and 1970s.

Red Power and XIT were both products of the same historical, structural, and ideological forces; both pursued similar goals of forging intertribal links among Native Americans and, in doing so, both participated in the construction of a new supratribal "American Indian" *ethnic* identity. The rise of Red Power marked a significant historical shift in Native Americans' political relationships with each other and their collective relationship to the US state, as for the first time in American history a demographically significant number of Native Americans began to think of themselves as politically and, perhaps more importantly, culturally united as "American Indians." I am very purposefully highlighting American Indian *ethnic* identity as a new and historically unique kind of identity formation because it signals the distinctive position of Native Americans within the US state in the latter half of the twentieth century.[1] The purpose of examining XIT and their music through the historical lens of Red Power is to illuminate the roles that both political activism and music play in the process of ethnogenesis, tracing out specifically the social work carried out by each of these practices in the ongoing construction of American Indian ethnic identity.

Throughout this argument I treat American Indian "ethnicity" as a new and distinct social formation both with its own boundaries and with a unique set of semiotic practices used for maintaining those boundaries.[2] Fredrik Barth rather famously described ethnicity as "a process that is self-perpetuating with shared fundamental cultural values expressed in a united way by members who identify themselves, and are identified by others, as constituting a distinct category" (1969, pp. 10-11). Barth's work stressed the "maintenance" of "ethnic boundaries," suggesting that, "the critical focus of investigation ... [is] the ethnic boundary that defines the group, not the cultural stuff that encloses it" (1969, p. 15). In insisting on the importance of boundaries—a system of classification that defines members and non-members of the in-group—the central contribution of Barth's work is that it served to de-emphasize the role of "culture" as a defining feature of ethnic identity (Fenton 2004, p. 109). Barth insisted that rather than emerging organically from primordial social groupings, cultural practices and artifacts were important only in so much as they were consciously and strategically *selected* and subsequently *understood* as markers of difference by insiders and/or outsiders. Furthermore, while cultural practices and artifacts are consistently and persistently used to construct and defend ethnic boundaries, they can change over time, sometimes quite rapidly. Thus, there are no *specific* cultural practices (for example, language or religion are often thought to be defining characteristics for many ethnic groups) that are necessary for ethnic group formation; rather it is

---

[1] Throughout this chapter I use the terms "Native," "Native American," and "indigenous" interchangeably to refer to the indigenous peoples of North America. The term "American Indian" is used with greater specificity and is intended to denote the historically particular supratribal *ethnic* identity that emerged during this period.

[2] Steve Fenton suggests that "a theory of ethnicity has to be a theory of the contexts under which ethnicity becomes 'activated'" (2004, p. 2). I argue that during the ascendency of Red Power American Indian political and social public discourse took on unique ethnic dimensions, as historically specific social, political, and cultural conditions emerged that created a context for the emergence of American Indian ethnic identity.

simply the process of selection for the purposes of boundary maintenance that is critical for group cohesion.

During the process of ethnogenesis, ethnic boundaries and the cultural "stuff" that is selected and deployed to maintain these boundaries are constantly negotiated and contested by insiders and outsiders. Ethnogenesis, which may tersely be defined as "the development and public presentation of a self-conscious ethnic group" (Roosens, 1989, p. 141), is a term that is evocative of precisely this kind of negotiation. In writing about ethnogenesis among indigenous peoples in particular, Nagel and Snipp have suggested that "ethnic reorganization" is "characteristic of all minority groups but is particularly important in understanding the ethnic survival of indigenous peoples in colonized societies" (2001, p. 488). Ethnic reorganization refers to a fundamental reorganization of a group's social structure, a redefinition of group boundaries, and creative transformations of cultural practices, ideologies, and material culture. In particular, they suggest that "cultural reorganization" involves processes of "cultural revision," "cultural blending," and "cultural revitalization." Cultural revision is a process whereby "Indian communities, confronting powerful external forces, respond in a variety of ways by sometimes resisting, sometimes participating, sometimes adapting" (Nagel and Snipp, 2001, p. 499). Cultural blending "can range from cultural 'borrowing' where non-indigenous celebrations (e.g. holidays) or practices (e.g. circumcision) are adopted into a culture, to a more equal mixing of two cultural streams" (Nagel and Snipp, 2001, p. 501). Cultural revitalization "can be built on the back of prior institutions and practices that have slipped into disuse, or can involve the creation of entirely new cultural forms" (Nagel and Snipp, 2001, p. 502). In examining XIT's music I want to pay particular attention to these processes of revision, blending, and revitalization, noting how aspects of the lyrics, the musical style, and aesthetic decisions about record production all serve as examples of the kind of larger "cultural reorganization" that was taking place across Indian country in the early 1970s, fueled, in large part, by Red Power activists.

The Rise of Red Power

Red Power ideology and activism developed in response to a series of American government policies enacted in the 1950s that fundamentally altered the social conditions of countless Native communities and individuals. Fuelled by a desire for the rapid assimilation of Indians into mainstream North American society, post-World War II federal Indian policy in the United States featured a strong push toward the urbanization of the Native population. Lured by government programs and the promise of funding, job training and placement, close to 100,000 Native Americans relocated to certain targeted cities in the US. The percentage of the Native population living in urban areas rose from 13 percent in 1950 to 44.5 percent in 1970 (Sorkin, 1978), signifying a major demographic shift. This new urban Indian population began to participate in mainstream North American popular culture and activist politics.

New urban Natives began to form their own organizations, both social and formal. Relocation funds provided the means for the creation and operation of a number of Indian centers as well as many intertribal social clubs, athletic leagues, powwow dance groups, Indian newspapers and newsletters, and political organizations.[3] The growth in both the number and sophistication of these organizations was linked directly to government funding. Funds made available through the Great Society programs of the 1960s (and other minority/urban development programs) provided urban Indian communities with important non-BIA (Bureau of Indian Affairs) funding sources, radically changing the social and political structure of the larger Indian population (Nagel, 1996, p. 128). According to Straus and Valentino,

> One result of increased federal funding and related organizational growth in urban areas is that urban Indians became conscious of themselves as such ... Community came, in some sense, to replace tribe in individual orientation and motivation. "The Community" became personified and spoken of as if it had thoughts and desires, likes and dislikes, preferences and sensibilities ... Tribal enrollment was irrelevant to community membership, and, indeed, many in the community were not enrolled and/or had not enrolled their children. Tribal affiliation was assumed and understood to enhance the urban community, but common history, culture, and concerns were emphasized. (2001, p. 88)

The shift in focus from "tribal" identity to a more generalized "Indian" identity had two significant effects. First, it signaled a growing social and cultural difference between reservation and urban communities,[4] and second, this kind of cultural and organizational development became a launching pad for activism, ethnic pride, collective purpose, and political unity (Nagel, 1996, p. 124).

On November 20, 1969, a group of 89 Indians calling themselves the Indians of All Tribes landed on Alcatraz Island and laid claim to the land under the terms of the 1868 Treaty of Fort Laramie, which granted the signatories (the Lakota nation, Yanktonai and Santee Sioux, and the Arapaho) the rights to all unused

---

[3]   During the course of this research I spent time locating numerous Native-run newspapers, finding an incredible boom of new Native presses from around 1969 to 1973.

[4]   Vine Deloria has suggested that the cultural uniqueness of urban communities was also tied to the large number of intertribal marriages that took place in the cities. Caught between two or more tribally specific cultural traditions, individuals began to improvise new behaviors that then became habitualized as "pan-Indian" behaviors (i.e. behavior that is uniquely hybrid and not part of any one particular tribal cultural practice or custom). He writes, "By the 1970s, it was possible to find wholly new kinds of behavior generally accepted as being Indian, when in fact they represented changes that had occurred within the previous generation" (Deloria, 2005, p. 30).

federal property that had previously been Indian land. The group issued a press release that rhetorically reflected their supratribal roots and agenda:

> ... We the Native Americans, re-claim the land known as Alcatraz island in the name of all American Indians ... We feel this claim is just and proper, and that this land should rightfully be granted to us for as long as the rivers shall run and the sun shall shine. Signed INDIANS OF ALL TRIBES. (Johnson et al., 1997, pp. 27-8)

It is telling to note that such a diverse and intertribal group of Native Americans felt the right to lay claim to the island on the basis of a treaty negotiated and signed principally by Sioux communities. This kind of symbolic maneuvering was typical of the supratribal refiguring of Indian identity, as specific *tribal* rights were claimed to be the concern and right of *all* Native Americans.

The occupation grabbed national headlines and sparked nationwide interest on the part of both Indians and non-Indians. Native Americans from all over the country traveled to San Francisco to join the protesters on Alcatraz. Lasting a total of 19 months, the population of protestors ranged from close to one thousand in June of 1970 to the 15 that were finally removed by US marshals on June 11, 1971. The occupation became a symbolic cornerstone for the political and ethnic reawakening of American Indians. The Alcatraz takeover had been engineered by young, urban Natives (70 members of the original group were students from UCLA) who were not afraid to be unlawful and who courted the media as a powerful ally. Lakota scholar Vine Deloria Jr., the foremost chronicler of the ascendency of Red Power and whose seminal book from 1969 *Custer Died for Your Sins* stands as a milestone in the intellectual crystallization of Red Power ideology, has written that the occupation was "the master stroke of Indian activism" (1996, p. 184). He further notes that,

> Alcatraz inspired young Indians everywhere and its organization, Indians of All Tribes, was quickly copied all over the country. Almost instantaneously the nation was blanketed with groups calling themselves Indians of All Tribes and they meant business. An activist roll call comparable to the Civil Rights roll call of Selma, Birmingham, and Memphis was quickly made up. (Deloria, 1996, p. 184)

The success Alcatraz had in garnering media attention did not go unnoticed by members of the recently formed American Indian Movement (AIM). AIM, founded in 1968 in Minneapolis by a group of urban Ojibwas including Dennis Banks, George Mitchell, and Vernon and Clyde Bellecourt, began as an organization concerned with urban Indian incarceration rates (Johnson, 1996, p. 128). However, following the example of Alcatraz, the organization undertook a new multifaceted political strategy engaging in a series of land occupations intentionally designed to focus media attention on Indian rights issues. These occupations functioned both symbolically *and* as a concrete way of confirming Indian claims to land. AIM also began to reiterate the importance of Native American cultural and spiritual traditions (Deloria, 1974, p. 186).

AIM went on to become the most radical and notorious political wing of Red Power, and was at the center of a number of public protests and occupations throughout the 1970s. The media coverage of the Civil Rights and Black Power movements also served as examples for AIM, and these parallel movements provided a model for the rhetorical strategies of Red Power. "Black Power" became "Red Power"; instead of "sit-ins," Natives of the Pacific Northwest held "fish-ins"; "uncle toms" became "uncle tomahawks"; and perhaps most obscure, "oreos" (black on the outside, white on the inside) became "apples" (Nagel, 1996, p. 130). However despite the rhetorical similarities there was little direct co-operation (and sometimes there was outright tension) between the two movements (Deloria, 1969, pp. 179-80). They were fighting for different goals. Civil Rights activists wanted social justice, to change the system to allow for equal rights regardless of race or ethnicity. American Indian activists were more aligned with Black Power nationalists who wanted out of the system entirely. Red Power activists weren't looking for equal rights, but instead stressed cultural sovereignty and treaty rights.

AIM's focus on treaty rights was part of their larger agenda of trying to establish ties with reservation Indians, especially traditionalists and other tribal leaders who were becoming increasingly uncomfortable with the radicalism of AIM and with their growing importance as spokespersons for *all* Native Americans. With all of its main chapters existing in urban centers, AIM's membership was largely urban, and the reservation was important to AIM as a cultural touchstone. In this way the emerging American Indian ethnic identity being constructed by Red Power was very much concerned with the symbolic cache of cultural authenticity embedded in reservation-based tribal identity. However, while Red Power activists borrowed many of the signs of cultural authenticity from reservation traditionalists, their meanings were reworked to fit a more supratribal agenda. Concern over "tribal sovereignty" was transformed to become a call for sovereignty for *all* American Indians. For urban American Indians, tribal affiliation became a marker not of a specific tribal heritage, but of pan-Indian inclusivity (all tribal Natives are "American Indians") and exclusivity (red versus white).

AIM's involvement with the Pine Ridge reservation in South Dakota, and the town of Wounded Knee in particular, is perhaps the most well-known and widely publicized attempt by the organization to forge ties to a reservation community. The occupation of Wounded Knee in 1973 marked a significant shift in Red Power activities away from high-profile occupations like Alcatraz, Fort Lawton, or the BIA building, toward more participation in local, reservation-based political struggles. The 1972 Trail of Broken Treaties and the subsequent occupation of the BIA buildings magnified strains between the Red Power organizations like AIM, who were framing Indian political struggles within a national framework, and reservation people, whose political concerns tended to reflect more local and immediate struggles with BIA and state officials (Nagel, 1996, p. 170).

The conflict at Wounded Knee developed from a dispute between some members of the Oglala Sioux Tribe and the tribal administration headed by Richard Wilson, who was accused of being both corrupt and a puppet of the BIA. In response to Wilson's assembly of the "Guardians of the Oglala Nation" (GOONs), a paramilitary group created to quell anti-Wilson resistance, traditional tribal leaders contacted AIM for help. A 71-day armed standoff ensued between over 200 AIM supporters (led by Dennis Banks and Russell Means), and the Wilson government and its supporters. The siege began on February 27, 1973, and when it ended on May 9, two Indians were dead and an unknown number wounded, including casualties among federal forces.[5]

Wounded Knee, and the years of conflict and political turmoil at Pine Ridge that followed, exemplifies both the loyalty, and also sometimes the factionalism, that AIM, and the Red Power movement in general, inspired. AIM's activism provided a means to arouse ethnic pride, frame Indian grievances, and reaffirm Native cultural traditions. In other words, activism legitimated a supratribal Indianness—an "American Indian" identity—as an ethnic identity.[6]

Plight of the Redman

It is within this social and political context that XIT emerged, releasing two politically charged LPs in the early 1970s, *Plight of the Redman* in 1972, and *Silent Warrior* in 1973. XIT was the brainchild of Tom Bee, a Dakota Sioux adopted off reservation at birth who grew up in Gallup, New Mexico. Bee had been involved in the local music business in Gallup and Albuquerque since the age of 15, working as a singer, songwriter, and later as a band manager. Three of the members of the group that eventually became XIT, guitarist and lead singer A. Michael Martin, bassist Mac Suazo, and drummer Lee Herrera, began their musical collaboration in the acid-rock "garage" band Lincoln Street Exit, who were performing in and around Albuquerque in the mid-1960s. The band was eventually "discovered" and signed to the small local Albuquerque record label Lance Records by Tom Bee, who was a co-owner of the label at that time. Bee became their manager, producer, and co-wrote a number of songs with Martin. Eventually the band drew the attention of Bobby Shad, who signed the group to

---

[5]   See Matthiessen (1983) for a definitive discussion of the Pine Ridge standoff.

[6]   This is not to suggest that there was not opposition to the movement and the new ethnic boundaries it was constructing. Many Christian Natives and BIA supporters were quite hostile to AIM and what it represented. The FBI used the factionalism that AIM inspired as justification for launching a covert Counter Intelligence Program against the movement accusing AIM of not actually speaking for the American Indians but of being a revolutionary organization with possible Marxist and extremist ties.

his own label, Mainstream Records.[7] In 1970 the band released their only LP, *Drive It*, on Mainstream; a collection of mainly psychedelic blues-rock numbers, the album was a showcase for the songwriting talents of Martin and Bee. In that same year, in support of the LP, the band traveled to Bakersfield, California to perform as part of a fundraising event for a radio station. While in California Bee drove to Los Angeles and made the rounds to a number of record label offices, dropping off "demo tapes" of his own compositions, hoping to score a publishing deal with a major label. Soon afterwards Motown Records contacted Bee to purchase his composition "We've Got Blue Skies," a song The Jackson Five eventually recorded on their 1971 album, *Maybe Tomorrow*. At that time Motown had recently started Rare Earth Records, a subsidiary label dedicated to producing and promoting rock acts. Looking for new talent, they asked Bee if he was involved with any rock groups. Thus, Bee secured a recording contract for Lincoln Street Exit, who by this point had added rhythm guitarist R.C. Gariss and had become known in and around Albuquerque simply as Exit. Bee kept the name but changed the spelling to XIT, an acronym that represented the "Crossing [X] of Indian Tribes." While this new name was an accurate reflection of the intertribal roots of the group—Mac Suazo and Lee Hererra were both of Pueblo decent, Bee was Dakota, and R.C. Gariss was a mixed-blood Cherokee—it was also, and perhaps more importantly, very much in keeping with the supratribal spirit of Red Power activists and of the "ethnic" identification of many urban dwelling American Indians.[8] In an interview with *Indian Country Today*, Bee suggested that he was very aware of the politics involved in naming the group. He stated, "Motown wanted us to change our name to something stereotypical, like Yellow Horse. That was around the time the American Indian Movement was representing Native Americans in a contemporary fashion without stereotypes. We came up with XIT" (quoted in Murg, 2008).

Tom Bee wrote all of the lyrics for the *Plight of the Redman* LP and was the driving force behind its political message. The album was almost certainly the first Native American "concept album"; the entire LP was organized as a retelling of American history from a Native American perspective, a musical analogue to Dee Brown's classic text *Bury My Heart at Wounded Knee* (1970). The two-part thematic organization of the recording utilizes the natural grouping of a two-sided LP record. The songs on side one depict a pre-contact indigenous utopia: "At Peace" describes Native Americans as "A proud happy people/ [who] were here

---

[7] Among record collectors Mainstream is well known as the label responsible for releasing the first recordings of Ted Nugent (as a member of the Amboy Dukes) and Janis Joplin (as a member of Big Brother and the Holding Company).

[8] A. Michael Martin was the only non-Native in the group. Shortly after the release of *Plight of the Redman*, which signaled a new politically radical direction for the group, Martin left the band. Tom Bee suggested to me in a personal interview that he thought Martin, as a non-Native, was simply uncomfortable singing Bee's politically charged lyrics. As a result, on their second LP, *Silent Warrior*, Tom Bee took over as the lead singer and frontman of the band.

long before the Whiteman came," living in perfect harmony with nature and each other. "I Was Raised," extols the virtues of a "traditional" Indian upbringing; Martin sings: "As a young Indian boy/ I was raised/ the true Indian way. Free as the wind/ on wings of white clouds/ those were happy days." Side one ends with "Nihaa Shil Hozho (I Am Happy About You)," an acoustic love song that mixes lyrics in both Navajo and English. Side two opens with "The Coming of the Whiteman" and "War Cry," which chronicle colonial conquest and the Indian wars respectively, while the song "Someday" describes the reservation era of the late nineteenth and early twentieth centuries. This history is bookended by the songs "Beginning" (the first track of side one) and "End?" (the last track on side two), both of which reference the contemporary concerns of the Red Power movement, thereby literally framing American Indian history within the context of Red Power.

Lindstrom has suggested that ethnogenesis is a process that attempts "to read the present in terms of the past by writing the past in terms of the present" (1982, p. 317). History is a particularly fertile site for the creation of shared ethnic alliances and allegiances. *Plight of the Redman*, and XIT more generally, was very much concerned with historical continuity and with linking tribal pasts to contemporary realities. I interpret Tom Bee's and XIT's construction of history as part of a larger strategy on the part of American Indians to create what Yamasee scholar and historian Donald Grinde Jr. has called a "usable past." Grinde has written:

> ... until American Indian scholars develop an independent voice and discourse, [the] separate and adjacent reality created by Western thought to comprehend the "other" will keep Native American historical identity in thraldom. It is not that the dominant societies discourse is "wrong," but rather it is decidedly "incomplete" when compared to the historical discourses of the dominant colonial powers. In essence, until there are more Native voices involved in the process of creating and inventing a usable past for American Indian people, there will not be sufficient and appropriate historical discourse that can be internalized and utilized by America's native peoples. (Grinde, 1995, p. 211)

The key point here is that Native American history must be internalized to be usable and must have the potential to be usable before it can be internalized. I would add to this assertion that "usability" is, in part, predicated upon widespread dissemination. As such, XIT's album, released by a major US label with international distribution, was an important vehicle for this reimagined Native history.[9]

---

[9]   Since the 1980s these kinds of "decentered" social histories have become far more frequent in Native American studies. But at the time the album was released, the idea that Native people could tell their *own* version of American history, a history that replaced the standard grade school textbook narratives of western "expansion" and "manifest destiny" with descriptions of colonial domination and genocide, was radical indeed.

Apart from the overall concept of the album, the lyrics of XIT's songs are overtly political and reflect a commitment to the values and ideology of Red Power as well as a noticeable concern for the cultural and social interests of specifically urban Indians. The first song on the album, "Beginning," with lyrics by Tom Bee, is striking in its use of rhetorical strategies and language, which mirrors that of Red Power leaders:

> Hey ya heh
> akodaani
> Dii nihi keyah ho
>   akonisin
> Little is really known about the American Indian
> Or what links the human soul with the earth
> The Indians believed that this land was created for us by the Great Spirit
> And that it would be theirs ... forever
> The New World
> This is what the whiteman called our land
> But it was not new at all
> The redman
> Inhabitants of America for centuries

In drawing a distinction between "the whiteman" and "the redman," this race-based rhetorical strategy is, intentionally divisive and essentializing. In referencing the discourse of race—the tacit assumption that "racial" difference (meaning phenotypic traits) equals "cultural" difference (meaning ideology and behavior)—the argument is structured in such a way that bloodline carries with it a certain guarantee of shared cultural history and heritage, a brand of essentialism that was used quite effectively by Red Power activists to build consensus between American Indians across the country. American Indian *ethnic* identity was understood as a birthright and thus something that was in many ways "beyond culture," which is to say beyond the very real cultural differences that persisted between urban and reservation communities, to say nothing of the social and cultural differences that have existed throughout American history between different tribal communities.

This kind of ethnic construction is a complex mix of both the internalization and the contestation of the dominant society's configuration of Indian ethnicity. On the one hand the racial essentialism of "redmen" and "whitemen" is a reflection of the "blood quantum" policies employed by many tribal governments for policing tribal or band enrollments. On the other hand, Euro-American constructions of Indian ethnicity are often based not on bloodline, as is the case with African Americans for example, but rather on stereotyped and often fuzzy notions of "authentic" Indian culture.[10] When bassist Mac Suazo pensively states in the song that, "little is really known about the American Indian," he is speaking directly

---

[10]   See for example, Deloria (1998) and Clifford (1988) among others.

to non-Natives and to Euro-American stereotypes of Indian identity that inform not only popular culture mythologies but also the history of American federal Indian policy.

Musically, *Plight of the Redman* displays the kind of stylistic blending and creative indexing that is now a common occurrence in much contemporary Native popular music, with uniquely "American Indian" musical elements embedded within a rock writing and production style very typical of the time period. Unique indigenous instruments (the drums and bells), sung vocables, and fragments of untranslated Native language texts all serve to indexically link the music, and thus the members of XIT themselves, to more "traditional" Native musical culture; however, with the exception of the use of Native language, no *specific* tribal musical tradition is referenced.

The song "Beginning" opens with a slowly rising bowed string bass melody accompanied by the sound of wind, abruptly interrupted by a thunderclap. A single large bass drum begins beating, followed by the sounds of multiple jingling bells (similar to those that might be found on a powwow dancer's regalia) and other, higher pitched "indigenous sounding" drums. Several short melodic phrases, sung using vocables typically found in many Native American "traditional" intertribal songs (perhaps the most well know being intertribal powwow songs and the peyote songs of the Native American Church), enter at different times and at different places across the stereo field. An acoustic guitar enters and is almost immediately followed by a chorus of voices singing four lines of text, the first line consisting of vocables followed by three lines that use the Navajo language. This lyrical and melodic refrain is used as the central theme for both the songs "Beginning" and "End" (giving a cyclic thematic unity to the album): "Hey ya heh/ akodaani/ Dii nihi keyah ho/ akonisin," which loosely translates as "That's what they say/ This is our country/ That's what I think" (McAllester and Mitchell, 1983, p. 621). These four lines, sung with hymn-like solemnity are repeated throughout the rest of the song, and they form the central melodic figure over which Mac Suazo delivers the rest of the lyrics in a dispassionate but determined speaking voice.

It is worth noting that Bee chose to write some lyrics for the LP in Navajo, despite the fact that none of the band members (at that time) were of Navajo decent. Apart from the four-line refrain of "Beginning" and "End," the acoustic ballad "Nihaa Shil Hozho (I Am Happy About You)" also makes extensive use of Navajo, featuring lyrics that alternate between verses written in Navajo and English. In a personal interview Bee commented on the use of language on the album, claiming,

> I wrote those [lyrics] in Navajo, having grown up in Gallup, right near the Navajo reservation there. That's a border town, I spent a lot of time on the Navajo Nation, Window Rock, St. Michaels, all those areas. ... See, when I was writing those poems [that would eventually become the lyrics for the songs on *Plight of the Redman*], I didn't think that they'd ever be heard. I thought that it was just going to be a regional thing. So obviously, because I was living in that

region, I wrote them regionally, you know what I'm saying. So I just basically used the language of the area. (Tom Bee, phone interview with author, July 28, 2009)

While the Navajo language lyrics may have been inspired by local concerns, they nonetheless constitute a powerful symbol of cultural difference, marking XIT's music as uniquely "American Indian" and as fundamentally different from the many other kinds of protest music being recorded and performed in the 1970s. Even for American Indians who did not speak or understand Navajo, the presence of a Native language in the music was both a powerful reminder of their own cultural difference from the American mainstream as well as a marker of XIT's cultural authenticity as American Indians with urban roots who are still connected to reservation languages and lifeways.

In the spoken lyrics of the song "End?" XIT explicitly aligns itself with Red Power by conjuring the symbols of the Alcatraz and Fort Lawton occupations at the end of the text:

"End" (Lyrics by Tom Bee)
Hey ya heh
akodaani
Dii nihi keyah ho
    akonisin
The Indian has been out there on the ghetto of the reservation for a long, long time
We have existed without adequate food, clothing, shelter, or medicine, to name but a few
In their place we have been given malnutrition, poverty, disease, suicide, and bureaucratic promises of a better tomorrow
Your America has not been a land of your proclaimed equality, and justice for all
May your God forgive you
The treatment of our people has been a national tragedy and disgrace
The time has come to put an end to that disgrace
Alcatraz, Fort Lawton,[11] whatever necessary

---

[11]   Interestingly, on a reissued version of the album, the text of "End" in the liner notes replaces "Fort Lawton" with "Wounded Knee." Of course, when the album was originally issued, the 1973 Wounded Knee confrontation had yet to take place. At that time, apart from the takeover of Alcatraz by Indians of All Tribes, the occupation in 1970 of Fort Lawton, a recently decommissioned US Army installation in Seattle, by a group calling itself the United Indians of All Tribes Foundation was the most highly visible and widely publicized act of civil disobedience on the part of Red Power activists. In 1989, after Tom Bee acquired the publishing rights to the album from Motown, Sound of America Records (SOAR), a Native American music label founded by Bee, reissued the recording on CD. The insertion of "Wounded Knee" as a replacement for "Fort Lawton" into the re-released liner notes, despite the fact that the recording itself still included the original "Fort Lawton" lyric is a

We must manage our own affairs and control our own lives
And through it all
Remain to be
The True Americans!

The inclusion in the lyrics of these important sites of Red Power activism support Vine Deloria's claim regarding the importance of Red Power activists in defining American Indian ethnic identity. He suggests that at that time, "'Indianness' was judged on whether or not one was present at Alcatraz, Fort Lawton, Mount Rushmore, Detroit, Sheep Mountain, Plymouth Rock, or Pitt River. The activists took over and controlled the language, the issues, and the attention that other Indians had worked patiently and quietly to build" (Deloria, 1996, p. 185). The song "End" also features a gospel-inspired choir of back-up singers, which serves to link XIT's music to the musico-rhetorical strategies of many African American performers who were themselves connected to the Civil Rights and Black Power movements (perhaps providing more evidence of the re-signification of some of the signs of African American political protest, connecting these musical stylistic practices with the ideology of Red Power supratribalism). This kind of cultural and semiotic blending was structurally iconic with urban American Indian ethnic identity, which was necessarily musically and culturally cosmopolitan and hybrid.

Conclusions

Returning to some of the theoretical arguments laid out at the beginning of this chapter, I suggest that XIT's music exhibits many of the typical characteristics of cultural reorganization described by Nagel and Snipp, including cultural revision, blending, and revitalization. Cultural revision is exhibited in XIT's use and playful manipulation of the recording industry and the structural conventions of Euro- and Afro-American popular music. In a sense, XIT adopted the dominant society's construction of Indian ethnic boundaries (Indians as "culturally Other") while reorganizing and reconstructing the *content* within those boundaries. XIT represented the new "American Indians" who proudly wore their indigenous identity on their sleeves but who also played rock music and engaged in activist politics. Cultural blending is seen in XIT's creative use of several different indigenous and non-indigenous musical styles, a blending structurally homologous with the members of XIT themselves, and no doubt many of the fans of the group, who were urban-dwelling Natives familiar with a wide range of American popular musical styles and genres. Cultural revitalization is exhibited in the textual construction of a "usable past" constituted in and through Tom Bee's powerful lyrics

---

testament to the importance of Wounded Knee as a central and powerful symbol of Red Power activism and, more specifically, AIM activism.

In examining the music of XIT, I hope to have shown not only that popular music is an important historical record of Red Power activism, but that this music was a significant *catalyst* for American Indian ethnic identification and participation in much the same way that Red Power activists used strategically organized acts of civil disobedience to court media attention as a way of broadcasting and disseminating the political concerns and ideological orientation of the movement. A key project of Red Power was to reconcile the hopes and aspirations of urban and reservation dwellers, progressives and traditionalists, and people of many different tribal communities and cultural backgrounds. As such, Barth's emphasis on borders rather than the stuff within borders is essential to understanding how American Indian ethnic identity solidified. The "cultural content" within those borders was under constant negotiation as internal discussions between different Native American communities continued. Bee suggested to me in a personal interview that XIT's music was particularly important in this ongoing negotiation, particularly in bridging divides between urban activists and reservation communities:

> A lot of the AIM people and the reservation people have said [to me] that XIT's music brought about a lot of unity between both the urban AIM people and the reservation people. Because basically it inspired a certain amount of pride in who they were, pride in the culture, the heritage, all these thing that, I think sometimes, with all the oppression, you forget who you are as a people, you know what I mean. And so I think that without a doubt [the music was helpful], because many, many people during that time would tell us how we inspired the whole area and how we helped to promote unity with the music, and how it was all about just being Native and not being an individual tribe, or not being from an individual reservation. Or even if you were an urban Indian, you know, you were still Indian and you were still "one of us," so to speak. (Tom Bee, phone interview with author, July 28, 2009)

Of course, Bee is basing these assertions on what is no doubt a wealth of anecdotal evidence and it is doubtful that accurate sales statistics that speak to the music purchasing habits of urban and reservation dwelling Indians in the early 1970s exist in any form. But what is of interest to me, in the context of this chapter, is his investment in linking XIT's popularity to reservation communities and to the music's ability to bridge the cultural gap between the urban and reservation dwellers. This kind of investment is an explicit acknowledgement of both cultural and social tensions that existed between the two larger Indian constituencies at that time as well as the perceived importance of reconciling these two communities for the greater political and social good of *all* American Indians.

I have classified Red Power as an example of ethnogenesis because the conscious mobilization of cultural difference constructed within the discourse of the movement and actualized in the music of XIT was key to the spread of Red Power ideology across American urban centers and onto the reservations. The importance of XIT's music lies in its effectiveness in creating positive change in the individual lives of American Indians both in urban and on reservation communities. American Indian ethnicity was based on a re-imagined American Indian common historical and cultural heritage. This common heritage was uniquely constructed by mainly urban Natives and was put into artistic practice in syncretic cultural forms like the music of XIT. XIT's music became the perfect cultural expression of this emergent supratribal ethnicity: urban, culturally hybrid, and revolutionary. A group of Dakota, Pueblo, Cherokee (and later Creek and Navajo) Indians, singing songs with lyrics in both English and Navajo, performing and recording rock music and signed to the iconic Black music record label Motown records, working with veteran Motown staff record producer Michael Valvano, who no doubt had a large part in the liberal use of string arrangements (part of the signature "Motown Sound") in the music, this heady eclectic mix of cultural and social signs and subject positions that came together on *Plight of the Redman* was iconic of American Indian ethnic identity in the early 1970s.

Finally, throughout this chapter, I have attempted to read the ideologies and practices of Red Power semiotically. Semiotic discourse involves both a struggle over the means of signification as well as a struggle for resignification. The Red Power movement struggled to control both the production of new signs as well as the rearticulation of old signs with new ideological meanings. American Indian ethnic identity was constructed from a collage of signs and practices—traditional and contemporary, indigenous and non-indigenous, Euro-American, African American, urban, reservation-based, national, international—each coded and recoded to align with a supratribal ideology. *Plight of the Redman* is a powerful example of this kind of semiotic recoding and rearticulation, the kind of creative cultural response that has become a regular feature of a great deal of postcolonial artistic practice.

Acknowledgments

I would like to thank Tom Bee for generously giving his energy and attention to this project and for finding the time to give a lengthy phone interview, and providing me with a wealth of stories, historical details, photographs, and invaluable insights about the ideologies and practices of the Red Power movement in the 1960s and 1970s.

Chapter 11

"The Country We Carry in Our Hearts is Waiting": Bruce Springsteen, Franklin Delano Roosevelt, and the Search for Human Rights in America

David Thurmaier

In his 1941 State of the Union address, known as the "Four Freedoms" speech, President Franklin D. Roosevelt envisioned what kind of nation the United States would be as it watched world events unfolding in World War II. The first two "essential human freedoms," speech and religion, were drawn from the First Amendment to the Constitution, to which he added two additional freedoms to his list—freedom from want and from fear. Roosevelt ended his speech with a firm declaration about these freedoms: "Freedom means the supremacy of human rights everywhere ... Our support goes to those who struggle to gain those rights or keep them" ([1941] 1968, p. 449).

At the height of World War II on January 11, 1944, Roosevelt again presented his State of the Union address to Congress. This time, he spoke more pointedly and directly to citizens of his own country and elucidated some of the themes from his "Four Freedoms" speech in more detail. His message was serious and reflective. He was not worried about whether the United States would win the war militarily, but rather his concern was to begin shaping the way Americans re-imagined the country in the coming peacetime. In order to accomplish a "new basis of security and prosperity [which] can be established for all, regardless of station, race or creed" ([1944] 1968, p. 484), Roosevelt presented his "Second Bill of Rights" that focused on economic fairness, equality, and opportunity.

In 2004, 60 years after the "Second Bill of Rights," Bruce Springsteen wrote an opinion piece for *The New York Times* endorsing John Kerry for president. This essay was notable because it marked the first time Springsteen explicitly endorsed a candidate and addressed politics in print instead of music, and what he wrote serves as an encapsulation of his political and social beliefs forged over nearly 40 years of creative output. In the piece, he emphasizes themes that fans of his songs will recognize: American identity, racial conflict, war and peace, class distinctions, and the prospect for better human relations based on "respect for others, honesty about ourselves, faith in our ideals" (Springsteen, 2004). While Springsteen is a hugely successful rock musician, his finest songs have examined these issues with a sensitive eye and presented them to the public in unvarnished ways that challenge the views of his listeners.

Interestingly, too, though Springsteen makes no reference to Roosevelt, there is a clear thematic connection between the two in their writings. This chapter examines Springsteen's journey toward becoming a strong supporter of human rights through lyrical and musical analysis of songs that specifically engage issues of freedom and liberty, as well as those with a subtler approach to human rights. Analysis of Springsteen's music has often been overlooked in favor of a close reading of the lyrics, thus I devote more attention to the musical elements here in an effort to expand scholarly understanding of Springsteen's musical contributions. I will also show how Roosevelt's progressive politics of social justice has been imaginatively and creatively expressed in Springsteen's music.

The "Second Bill of Rights" and "Human Rights"

Cass Sunstein describes Roosevelt's 1944 speech as follows: It "wasn't elegant ... It was messy, sprawling, unruly, a bit of a pastiche, and not at all literary. ... But because of what it said it has a strong claim to being the greatest speech of the twentieth century" (2004, p. 10). The speech is significant and meaningful because it articulates an economic and social fairness for all people, not just the ruling elite or wealthy. It is even more notable that this document was written four years before the United Nations Universal Declaration of Human Rights of 1948, which spells out some of the same concerns. Roosevelt proposed a set of eight "rights" that in his eyes would "spell security" for the United States:

> The right to a useful and remunerative job in the industries or shops or farms or mines of the nation;

> The right to earn enough to provide adequate food and clothing and recreation;

> The right of every farmer to raise and sell his products at a return which will give him and his family a decent living;

> The right of every business man, large and small, to trade in an atmosphere of freedom from unfair competition and domination by monopolies at home or abroad;

> The right of every family to a decent home;

The right to adequate medical care and the opportunity to achieve and enjoy good health;

The right to adequate protection from the economic fears of old age, sickness, accident, and unemployment;

The right to a good education.

([1944] 1968, pp. 484-5)

Sunstein notes that the impetus for this speech was the Great Depression, "as inadequate education, hunger, and unemployment emerged not as inevitable features of free market societies but as *human rights violations*" (2004, p. 36, emphasis mine). Thus, in Roosevelt's mind the government should intervene and promote fairer policies that benefit all citizens.

According to Michael Freeman, "'Human rights' is a concept ... for thinking about the real, and expressing our thoughts" (2002, p. 2). Moreover, he asserts that human rights only become "relevant to ordinary people when the relative security of everyday life is absent or snatched away ... Human rights are most needed when they are most violated" (Freeman, 2002, p. 3). Clearly, in the aftermath of the Great Depression, and in the midst of a world war, Roosevelt believed that strong declarations of human rights were extremely important. Thus, human rights must be "equal ... inalienable ... and universal" (Donnelly, 2003, p. 10).

Born to Run

Bruce Springsteen's life and career are marked by numerous paradoxes. He is one of the most famous rock musicians in the world, yet lives what most would admit is a "normal" life.[1] He holds many awards and honors, and continues to sell out concerts every time he tours, but after immediate successes he often withdraws and changes his musical path. He is an energetic performer who plays the largest arenas, yet is equally captivating and sometimes even nervous playing in smaller venues. And most relevant to this chapter, he frequently tackles political and sociological themes in his music, though in interviews he has stated that he "never start[s] with a political point of view" and did not grow up in a "political house" (Springsteen, 1996).

Springsteen exemplifies the many paradoxical aspects of being a modern American in a variety of ways. It is rare for most rock musicians to appeal to people of all political stripes, which Springsteen does. A famous example is the misinterpretation of his hit "Born in the U.S.A." by conservative politicians and commentators including Ronald Reagan and George Will.[2] Even a cursory glance

---

[1] For a description of his "normal life," see DeCurtis (1998).

[2] For a good summary of these events, see Gilmore (2004, pp. 273-6).

at the song's verses reveals a decidedly less patriotic and even depressing story about a Vietnam veteran's struggles to re-assimilate into society upon returning home from the war. Yet despite the occasional misreading, Springsteen's songs appeal to his listeners—those who are political and apolitical—because of their honest portrayal of hard-working, earnest people who often struggle in their pursuit of the elusive American dream.

He started out as a so-called "New Dylan," signed in 1972 by John Hammond, the producer who also signed Bob Dylan. His early songs and albums contained Dylanesque lyrics, fast and furious in their stories and characters, barely allowing the music to breathe.[3] After a series of favorable reviews and a growing fan base, he achieved his first significant success with *Born to Run* in 1975. The songs still dealt with most of the same issues as in his earlier work, but this later music was more sophisticated and the lyrics more profound. Yet after this huge leap forward commercially and artistically, he seems to have wanted to write more meaningful songs that told stories about the plight and struggles of the "common man." June Skinner Sawyers explains that "darkness, alienation, isolation, and a healthy dose of cynicism" entered Springsteen's lyrics, but the songs were always "leavened with a smidgen of hope" (2004, p. 9). This blend of hope and despair becomes a recurring theme in nearly all of his music post-1975. *Born to Run* also works as a metaphor to describe Springsteen's career, depicting the journey of a young musician striving and searching—running—toward a place where his music "would resonate down the road ... to have value and a sense of place" (Sawyers, 2004, p. 9).

Getting Involved

Springsteen's new lyrical focus arose out of his own research. In the late 1970s, his manager, Jon Landau, suggested that he read writings by John Steinbeck and Flannery O'Connor, to name two, as well as watch films by John Ford, who directed the film adaptation of Steinbeck's *The Grapes of Wrath*. Additionally, while on tour in 1978-79, he read *A Pocket History of the United States of America* by Henry Steele Commager and Allan Nevins, which in Bryan K. Garman's opinion, "enabled Springsteen to examine the social and economic forces that had shaped his life" (2000, p. 197). This book also showed Springsteen how the "American dream" could get corrupted by "forces that controlled" average people's lives (Marsh, 1979, p. 57). Of course, those "forces" refer to the disparities created between economic classes. Similar to Roosevelt in his speeches, Springsteen's music began to examine the inequities between people, and propose more equitable solutions to bridge this divide.

---

[3]   The song "Blinded by the Light" from 1973's *Greetings from Asbury Park, NJ* is an illustrative example.

On the cusp of the 1980s, Springsteen took a more active role in political and human rights events. His first significant foray into this world was participation in a series of 1979 concerts for the organization Musicians United for Safe Energy, also known as the *No Nukes* concerts. While none of Springsteen's performances or comments directly addressed the antinuclear theme of the concert, it is notable that he performed his seminal song "The River" live for the first time at this event. "The River," one of Springsteen's earliest human "story" songs, tells a bleak tale about an unemployed young man struggling to survive in a depressed economy and trying to provide for his wife (and baby on the way). Whether intentional or not, Springsteen's performance of "The River" at an explicitly political rally highlighting the exploitation of people for the sake of global industry proved to be an excellent arena to test his politically-conscious music in front of his fans. As the video of the performance shows, his audience reacted favorably.

Following the *No Nukes* concerts, and after reading Ron Kovic's *Born on the Fourth of July*, Springsteen organized a benefit concert for the Vietnam Veterans' Association, where he "felt as though his music had served a 'useful' purpose" (Garman, 2000, p. 202). In particular, the latter event inspired songs on his album *Nebraska*, including "Born in the U.S.A.," which was later re-recorded and rearranged for his 1984 album of the same name.

Springsteen's growing dedication to human rights culminated in performances on the *Human Rights Now!* tour of 1988 which benefitted Amnesty International. The tour's dates coincided with the 40th anniversary of the United Nations Universal Declaration of Human Rights, and featured a number of socially conscious performers including Sting, Peter Gabriel, and Tracy Chapman. At the time Springsteen said, "I think that Amnesty makes the world a less oppressive, less brutal place to live, and I want to help Amnesty do its job" (quoted in Garofalo, 1992b, p. 50). He performed a wide variety of music on the tour, ranging from his hits to the Bob Dylan song "Chimes of Freedom." In addition to his musical performances, Springsteen was particularly outspoken in his on-stage comments, discussing the "systematic apartheid of South Africa and the economic apartheid of my own country" (O'Connor, 1988). This event was highly significant, because as Reebee Garofalo points out, "These artists would seem to have put a great deal 'on the line' since Amnesty International is not a 'safe' organization ... [and] many of the artists were radicalized even more by their interaction with stalwart human rights activists" (1992b, p. 50). This experience provided Springsteen with an opportunity to showcase some of his more politically inspired music, and reach an international audience in venues outside of the traditional rock tour. Most importantly, it set him on a course to explore human rights issues in his subsequent music.

Springsteen's Musical Aesthetic

I would argue that Springsteen's music and approach to songwriting is largely responsible for the clarity and potency of his lyrical messages. Far from his image as a guitar-slinging rock star on display throughout the mid-1980s, his songs that focus on human rights and social issues feature a different type of musical presentation altogether. In this sense, they are closer to the type of folk music (or what we might call "singer-songwriter" music today) Springsteen started out performing as a "New Dylan."

A summary of salient musical characteristics found in these songs can be constructed by analyzing how Springsteen treats common parameters: chord structure, harmony, melody, rhythm, and instrumentation:

- *chord structure*: simple, repetitive, direct, limited
- *harmony*: usually major keys, several songs in minor keys or modes
- *melody*: small vocal range, often incorporates drones or one-note melodies for effect
- *rhythm*: straightforward meters, occasional mixed meters particularly around choruses, syncopation used to emphasize the text
- *instrumentation*: built around acoustic guitar, early verses often unaccompanied, instruments are added to each verse and chorus, prominent use of keyboards for fills or to enrich the sound, simple background that never obscures the text

Anyone familiar with folk music, especially the work of Springsteen's predecessors Woody Guthrie, Pete Seeger, and Bob Dylan, will notice at least three similarities in musical materials. First, the chord structure of most songs is simple, containing only a few chords repeated frequently. Second, their songs are built around the softer timbres of the acoustic guitar, which allows the words to remain prominently in the musical texture. Finally, the composers craft the music *around* the words so that they can bring out the meaning of the text more convincingly. For instance, it would be rare for a song about despair to be written in an upbeat tempo in a major key. In Springsteen's case, the songs I will analyze retain a general similarity to Dylan and Guthrie in their musical materials, but he updates the instrumentation and sound to reflect a more modern sensibility.

I have chosen to examine five post-1975 songs divided into four categories, and these songs illustrate and address common themes found in Springsteen's work. They also correlate to subjects and goals presented by Roosevelt in his speeches, thus tying together history and music. I have selected a mixture of well-known and lesser known songs, trying to avoid those already studied in depth and shedding light on those gems often overlooked in Springsteen's catalog:

- "human rights" songs: "Streets of Philadelphia" and "Dead Man Walkin'"
- war song: "Shut Out the Light"
- fear song: "The Ghost of Tom Joad"
- hope song: "Livin' in the Future"

"Human Rights" Songs

The two songs listed in this category address human rights in the sense explained by Freeman, where "human rights become relevant to ordinary people when the relative security of everyday life is absent or snatched away" (2002, p. 3). Roosevelt captures similar sentiments in his "Second Bill of Rights" when he asserts that "a new basis of security and prosperity can be established for all, regardless of station, race or creed" ([1944] 1968, p. 484). Of course, in 1944 protections for minority groups were some years off, but Roosevelt's inclusion of race and class made an important statement at the time.

In Springsteen's case, the two groups of "ordinary people" are homosexuals in "Streets of Philadelphia" and death-row prisoners in "Dead Man Walkin'." The two groups are different in about every way except for how society in general treats them when it comes to human rights. While America's treatment of gays and lesbians has come a long way in the past 40 years, Springsteen wrote "Streets of Philadelphia" in 1993 in the midst of the AIDS epidemic when there was still much confusion and misunderstanding among the general public about the disease and those afflicted. Similarly, America's use of the death penalty has waned in recent years, as inequities have been exposed and prisoners have been exonerated by improved evidential techniques. Like "Streets of Philadelphia," Springsteen wrote "Dead Man Walkin'" in 1995 before many of these changes occurred. Another tie binding the two songs together is their origin, both written for films designed for the mainstream public. This allowed Springsteen's burgeoning political commentary to reach a wider audience, and interestingly revived his own career, which was moribund by the early 1990s. Both songs were also highly successful: "Streets of Philadelphia" won a Golden Globe and Academy Award for Best Song, and a Grammy award for Song of the Year; "Dead Man Walkin'" was nominated for an Oscar as well.

In his usual way, Springsteen does not tell the listener what to think about the main character of each song (in "Streets of Philadelphia" a lawyer terminated from his job because he has AIDS, and in "Dead Man Walkin'" a death-row prisoner headed to his execution) but forces us to think about life from that character's perspective. By having each man describe his condition, and refraining from stating any clear conclusions or judgments, the human rights message inherent in the song can touch a larger audience and blur the prejudices and biases that can arise in more politically charged music.

Jonathan Demme, the director of *Philadelphia*, approached Springsteen and asked him to write the title song. He said that he was "making [the movie] for the malls" and Springsteen felt that Demme "wanted to take a subject that people didn't feel safe with and were frightened by and put it together with people that they did feel safe with like Tom Hanks or me or Neil Young ... I always felt that was my job" (Springsteen, quoted in Sawyers, 2004, p. 213). This is a telling statement in that Springsteen was regarded as a "safe" person (in this case a safely *heterosexual* man) to convey Demme's message of tolerance and support for people with AIDS.

In an extensive interview with the gay magazine the *Advocate* in 1996, fans saw a side of Springsteen that again challenged his macho, heterosexual image. He frankly describes the development of his views toward homosexuality from negative images as a child to acceptance and understanding as an adult. In addition to many fascinating comments on the subject, he expresses his support for gay marriage at a time when the concept was relatively new and seemingly impossible to fathom: "There is no reason I can see why gays and lesbians shouldn't get married ... It is important because those are the things that bring you in and make you feel a part of the social fabric" (quoted in Sawyers, 2004, p. 213). Out of this background, "Streets of Philadelphia" emerged as Springsteen's thoughtful musical statement on the AIDS crisis.

The song's structure is simple, consisting of three verses and a bridge. Springsteen plays all the instruments himself, and the song is marked by the use of the drum machine and synthesizer, which are used to set a vaguely hip-hop beat and fill out the texture with sustained chords that produce a sense of timelessness. The song retains a largely improvisational feel, which is a result of Springsteen composing the song on his home tape recorder and ad-libbing over the drum machine beat.[4] Harmonically, he keeps the chords relatively uncomplicated and smooth, in the verse alternating between an F major and A minor chord (both chords share two notes) and moving to a B-flat major chord when he sings the title of the song. The only diversion from this repetitive structure comes in the bridge where he enriches the harmony and builds the soundscape with background voices and some light bass and percussion. It is precisely the simple construction of the music from a formal, rhythmic, and harmonic perspective that permits the lyrics to take center stage.

Like Springsteen's earlier engagements with political themes in songs, "Streets" withholds any explicit statement of his own opinions. I would argue that the musical background, with its vaguely undirected harmonies and wash of synth sound parallel the lyrical ambiguities that build to the song's climax. The lyrics begin clearly enough, with statements about the afflicted man being "bruised and battered" and "unrecognizable to myself," but as the song progresses and the music intensifies, another character enters the story and alters the narrative in the bridge: "Ain't no angel gonna greet me/ It's just you and I my friend" and "So receive me brother with your faithless kiss/ Or will we leave each other alone like this/ On the streets of Philadelphia." Who is this other person? Is it a friend of the man, or is he speaking to society, or to the individual listener? As the ambiguities and emotional pleas increase, the music becomes busier and more intense, culminating in the chordal diversity in the bridge. Maybe the man has come to terms with his fate, or maybe he is making a plea for society to think about his life and the way he was treated as he grows sicker. And as the man "feel[s] himself fading away," the song itself fades and leaves the listener pondering the message of fair treatment and human rights.

---

[4]   Springsteen describes the process of composition in *Songs* (2003, pp. 261-3).

Springsteen's stance against capital punishment became more public after his involvement with Amnesty International, an organization well known for its ardent opposition to the death penalty. In recent years, he has allowed the organization People of Faith Against the Death Penalty to set up booths at his concerts in North Carolina, and his humane treatment of criminals in his songs has even inspired scholarship in law journals (Smith, 2005). According to Georgetown University Law Professor Abbe Smith, "'Dead Man Walkin'" may be one of the best songs ever written about being on death row" (2005, p. 789).

Springsteen casts "Dead Man Walkin'" in a traditional folk style, driven by acoustic guitar instead of keyboards and drums. The song is told from the perspective of a condemned man named Patrick Sonier scheduled to die the next morning and looking back on the crime he committed and his reasons for committing it. Based on the book *Dead Man Walking* by Sister Helen Prejean, Springsteen's song assumes even more poignancy because as in "Streets of Philadelphia," we already know the outcome of the story. As we learn from the movie and the song, the killer remains defiant to the very end, telling his spiritual advisor, "Sister I won't ask for forgiveness/ My sins are all I have." Bryan K. Garman explains that this theme of defiance in the face of devastating circumstances is a Springsteen lyrical trope, also used in the song "Johnny 99" and in "Nebraska" from the album of the same name (2000, p. 208). In "Dead Man Walkin'," the man realizes that even though he is responsible for his crime—"all I could feel was the drugs and the shotgun/ and my fear up inside of me"—he has nothing else *except* his crime and defiance to take to his execution: "Now I've got my story/ Mister no need for you to listen/ It's just a dead man talkin'."

The music of "Dead Man Walkin'" exhibits the traits described in the presentation of Springsteen's political music. The song begins with a solo acoustic guitar, set in "drop D" tuning (lowest string tuned down a step from E to D). This tuning produces a drone that pervades much of the song and causes the guitar to resonate strongly. Additionally, the introduction features a syncopated rhythm that evokes the march to the death chamber in its repetition and insistence; one may even hear the syncopation as walking with shackles and chains. Springsteen's voice is even more gravelly than usual, emphasizing certain words with a slight growl, portraying the man's weariness.

After the first verse, a dobro enters and plays a stinging riff that echoes the bluesy feel of the setting in Louisiana. Drums, percussion, and keyboards enter in the third verse ("In the deep forest"), providing some rhythm and chordal background, while the dobro continues to punctuate the musical texture. One noteworthy structural feature concerns the meter; the song is in common time (4/4) except for when the title of the song is sung and the meter is shortened by two beats (2/4). This is a striking change that alters the flow of the song. As we will see in other songs written around the same time, Springsteen uses this technique to fit in all the words.

In short, Springsteen creates the atmosphere of darkness and despair both musically and lyrically. But as always, we are not told to sympathize with the man, especially given his own admission of guilt; instead, we are invited to consider the system in general, and whether it is fair to all those involved. In a short song, Springsteen raises numerous questions and uses musical means to shed light on the need for equitable treatment of all people, even criminals.

War Song

Roosevelt wrote both of his pivotal speeches during World War II, and naturally stressed the importance of victory on the battlefield. Additionally, he was concerned about the welfare of the rest of the population during wartime, and in both speeches expresses the need to eradicate fear and want. In fact, four of the "rights" in the "Second Bill of Rights" explicitly mention jobs, fair wages, and employment, and in the "Four Freedoms" speech he explains the importance of reaching "economic understandings which will secure to every nation a healthy peace time life for its inhabitants."

One group that has often been forgotten in this American picture is veterans returning from war, especially from the Vietnam War. Many books and songs have been written about the plight of veterans and their struggles to achieve a sustainable and profitable life after serving in the military, and Springsteen has contributed several important songs to this effort. After his involvement with the Vietnam Veteran's Association in the early 1980s, he wrote his most famous song about veterans—"Born in the U.S.A."—but there is a lesser known song that explores the same subject called "Shut Out the Light" that appeared on the B-side of the "Born in the U.S.A." single (now found on the *Tracks* box set). Both songs describe the story of young men inspired to serve in the military, seeing horrifying things in battle, and then returning home to a very different world. Everything promised to them has disappeared: jobs, family, respect. And in the end, the veterans in these songs are left with fears and needs, as well as profound sadness about how they have been treated by their country.

The story of "Shut Out the Light" focuses on a veteran named Johnson Lineir— "Johnny"—who returns to his hometown and family but cannot readjust to his previous life. Despite having a wife, kids, and friends who all express excitement at his return, Johnny is haunted by his war experiences and foresees a bleak future. The warning signs include "staring at the ceiling" at 4.00 a.m. not being able to "move his hands," and being assured by his father that "they'd give him his job back down at the factory." The most disturbing image in the song appears in the chorus, where Johnny cries out for his "mama" (mother or wife?) to "throw your arms around me in the cold dark night" and to not "shut out the light." The light serves as a metaphor for hope and prosperity, which seems to elude Johnny. Instead, the song concludes with him standing in a river in a *dark*, rainy forest staring at the city lights as he "dreams of where he's been." Even with a hero's welcome home, this veteran seems destined to be forgotten and ignored by his country, thus succumbing to both want and fear.

Springsteen portrays this tragic tale musically in a variety of ways. The melody of the verse begins on only one pitch—a drone—first stated by the acoustic guitar and remains very restricted in pitch. He sings it in an emotionless manner, moving to a "blue note" on the third line. As the song builds, he adds tambourine and background vocalists, all of which enter together on the chorus. Once again, Springsteen uses the same method of "cheating" the meter to include a measure of two beats instead of four when he mentions the title of the song. Springsteen plays all instruments on this track except the violin, which enters after the first chorus and for me, evokes music of the Civil War. For example, the main character's name is "Johnny" and his friends and family unfurl a banner that says "Johnny Welcome Home," an unmistakable reference to the Civil War song "When Johnny Comes Marching Home." As the song ends, the violin wails while the droning voice continues, and a harmonica enters toward the end, another reference to historic American music. Springsteen employs music and imagery that cuts across all eras and generations to illustrate an unfortunate American human rights issue, that of the forgotten man—the veteran.

Fear Song

I wish to look briefly at "The Ghost of Tom Joad," another song in which the promises Roosevelt proposed do not materialize. Rob Kirkpatrick states that in the eponymous album, "Springsteen ... examines the lives of latter-day inhabitants of life on the fringe," all of whom have particular grievances and challenges presented to them by society (2007, p. 132). In this particular song, clearly influenced by John Steinbeck's *The Grapes of Wrath*, the characters have again been marginalized and forgotten; the lyrics mention a "shelter line stretchin' round the corner," "families sleepin' in their cars," "no home no job no peace no rest." Out of this bleak atmosphere, one of the characters waits for the "ghost" of Tom Joad, Steinbeck's character in *Grapes*, who, "confronts social injustice and is transformed into a radical" (Springsteen, as quoted by Corn, 1996). In a paraphrase of Tom Joad's famous speech toward the end of the book, Springsteen attempts to conclude the song positively—with a "smidgen of hope"—by showing how Joad will rise to help those in need. Unlike other songs set in a world of despair, there is a ray of light that shines on those who fight injustice and in support of human rights.

Musically, the song is quite bleak. The instrumentation consists of a guitar, harmonica, pedal steel guitar, bass, drums, and keyboard, but is mostly driven by the acoustic guitar. Springsteen sets the song in a minor mode (Dorian mode), which creates a serious atmosphere, reinforced by his soft but intense vocal delivery. Harmonically, the song is simple, which allows the lyrics to rise above the texture. Once again, he incorporates a truncated meter, but this time he includes a measure of three instead of four while singing the song's title. The impression left after hearing this song is one of desperation and the knowledge that while the "highway is alive tonight, where it's headed everybody knows." Springsteen channels the injustices and fears outlined by Steinbeck in *The Grapes of Wrath*, through the ideal rights espoused by Roosevelt, weaving these themes into a conflicting patchwork that epitomizes American life from the 1930s to the present.

Hope Song

Even when the outlook is dismal for characters in his songs, Springsteen usually includes a silver lining. For example, his album *Nebraska* is filled with stories about injustice, death, criminals, and poverty, but the final song on the album is titled "Reason to Believe." In this song, each character deals with crushing situations, but "at the end of every hard earned day people find some reason to believe." This uniquely American sense of optimism in the face of tragedy is another trait Springsteen shares with Roosevelt.

I conclude this look at the subject of human rights in Springsteen's music by considering the song "Livin' in the Future" from his 2007 album *Magic*. If people had any doubts where Springsteen stood on issues of the day, they only needed to tune into the *Today* show on September 27, 2007. Over an E Street Band vamp, he greeted the audience and recited a list of things that "we love about America," such as cheeseburgers, baseball, and the Bill of Rights; but then he turned serious and rattled off another type of list:

> But over the past six years we've had to add to the American picture: rendition, illegal wiretapping, voter suppression, no habeas corpus, the neglect of our great city New Orleans and its people, an attack on the Constitution. And the loss of our young best men and women in a tragic war. This is a song about things that shouldn't happen here—happening here.

This statement was met with a mixture of boos and cheers from the audience, but it demonstrates his more recent turn toward explicit political outspokenness beginning with his piece in *The New York Times*. While the mode of address is sharply different in its pointedness, the themes and issues he raises have remained consistent in his songwriting.

"Livin' in the Future" exemplifies the dichotomy between the negative and tragic events happening now, and the hope for a better future. In this story, the protagonist shares all the doubts and fears he has to his partner: of being separated, of waking up on Election Day expecting a negative result, and losing his faith. Despite these feelings, he reassures his partner not to worry or fret, "We're livin' in the future and none of this has happened yet." As Springsteen said, this song is about "what's happening now ... right now" and how if we stop embracing these deleterious policies, a brighter future awaits.

This song features the E Street Band, so the music is full and orchestrated. Many of Springsteen's most recognizable musical traits appear: layers of guitars, prominent saxophone fills played by Clarence Clemons, dueling piano and organ, a "sha na na na" coda where the whole band joins in singing, strong drumming, and of course, Springsteen's vocal guiding it all. It is fitting to conclude this analysis with a song that displays Springsteen's characteristic sound, as he is able to project important messages and themes through catchy, driving music that induces the crowd to sing along (think of "Born in the U.S.A."). Perhaps this ability is Springsteen's most impressive quality as a songwriter: he can write about our fears and dreams while expressing his desires for a better future, and the audience sings along—a true collaborative effort. This musically mirrors the collaboration within democratic communities that is necessary for the full benefits of a free society to reach all people.

Conclusions

In Springsteen's op-ed piece for *The New York Times* he explains how as a musician, he has "tried to write songs that speak to our pride and criticize our failures ... who we are, what we stand for, why we fight." He concludes by writing that "It is through the truthful exercising of the best of human qualities—respect for others, honesty about ourselves, faith in our ideals—that we come to life in God's eyes ... It is how our soul, as a nation and as individuals, is revealed." This message sounds remarkably similar to what FDR stated in his "Second Bill of Rights" speech: "America's own rightful place in the world depends in large part upon how fully these and similar rights have been carried into practice for our citizens. For unless there is security here at home there cannot be lasting peace in the world" ([1944] 1968, p. 485). Bruce Springsteen's transition into one of rock music's most outspoken advocates for justice and human rights furthers traditions and values expressed by many, notably Franklin Delano Roosevelt, in speeches that still resonate today. By forging a musical path built on a similar set of characteristics, Springsteen conveys his messages clearly and directly, all the while forcing the listener to confront his or her own beliefs and to challenge how society treats all its members. Politically and socially influenced music has a power to affect people like no other medium because it hits both the heart and the mind. And if we pay attention to the words and music, the focus on human rights can take on greater meaning. In Springsteen's words, "The country we carry in our hearts is waiting."

Chapter 12

The Vision of Possibility:
Popular Music, Women, and Human Rights

Sheila Whiteley

Freedom consists of voices that have been broken and blood that has been shed. Freedom tastes of pain ... there is no objectivity ... there is only the vision of possibility.—Sarah Maitland

It is an inexcusable fact that "significant numbers of the world's population are routinely subject to torture, starvation, terrorism, humiliation and even murder simply because they are female ... that women are discriminated against and abused on the basis of gender," that "women's rights and human rights are viewed as distinct" (Bunch, 1990, p. 486). Reports on Human Rights Watch describe how millions of women live in conditions of abject deprivation of, and attacks against, their fundamental human rights for no other reason than that they are women.[1] While it is not unusual to displace such accounts on to the all-encompassing "other" (political, religious, ethnic), it is also evident that female bodily autonomy is not necessarily an unassailable right in Western culture. As such, while the extremes of violence reported daily in the media are largely situated within the context of tribal conflicts and political extremism, as evidenced recently in reports of genocide in Ethiopia, the state-run terror campaign unleashed against supporters of the Movement for Democratic Change in Zimbabwe, and the continuing suicide bombings in Iraq, this chapter shifts the focus on to the UK, southern Ireland, and the United States, exploring women's rights to make reproductive and sexual decisions, and how such issues as pregnancy, domestic violence, rape, and the shaming of the body have been confronted by singer-songwriters.

At the time of writing, two anniversaries have shaped my thinking. On December 10, 1948 the General Assembly of the United Nations adopted and proclaimed a Universal Declaration of Human Rights (UDHR), which enshrined the principles of justice, fairness and equality. Prompted by the atrocities of the Holocaust and the horrors of World War II, it was the first global statement to recognize the inherent dignity and equality of all human beings, and its 30 articles are framed by a concern to support and promote the unalienable rights of all members of the human family, regardless of race, color, sex, language, religion, political or other

---

[1] http://www.hrw.org/en/category/topic/women%E2%80%99s-rights, accessed May 11, 2009.

opinion. The second anniversary commemorated Charles Darwin's birth in a BBC2 program which examined the abuses of his theory of evolution and how it became twisted into eugenics, and then the Nazi's Final Solution, "where bad science and bad politics turned the survival of the fittest into the murder of the weakest" in a perverted interpretation of evolution through natural selection. Six million Jews, together with gypsies, communists, Poles, Slavs, homosexuals, and political and religious dissidents were exterminated as centuries of prejudice were given a scientific gloss: the murder of the weakest (*Darwin's Dangerous Idea*, 2009).

What links the two anniversaries is the way in which the UDHR can be interpreted as a return to and confirmation of Darwinism in its assertion that all human beings are connected by common descent and hence belong to the same species, *homo sapiens*; that difference is due to culture, so placing the emphasis on nurture rather than nature (*Darwin's Dangerous Idea*, 2009). It is this emphasis on cultural difference, and its relationship to family, reproduction, and bodily autonomy that is central to my discussion of women, popular music, and human rights.

In this regard, and returning briefly to the 1948 Universal Declaration of Human Rights, it is relevant to note that its framing of equality and concern for universal dignity and justice includes the identification of the family as the "natural and fundamental group unit of society," and states that men and women are entitled to equal rights when it comes to marriage, during marriage, and at its dissolution.[2] The UDHR's identification of shared responsibility in marital decision-making underpins its concern for equality, but the issues surrounding reproductive rights are problematic.[3] While these relate to "the right to marry and found a family" (UDHR, Article 16), they can also include the right to control one's reproductive functions and to make reproductive choices free from coercion, discrimination,

---

[2] (1) Men and women of full age, without any limitation due to race, nationality or religion, have the right to marry and to found a family. They are entitled to equal rights as to marriage, during marriage and at its dissolution.

(2) Marriage shall be entered into only with the free and full consent of the intending spouses.

(3) The family is the natural and fundamental group unit of society and is entitled to protection by society and the State (http://www.un.org/en/documents/udhr/, accessed May 12, 2009).

[3] The General Assembly of the United Nations published its *Declaration of the Elimination of Discrimination* on November 7, 1967. It related to their concern that "despite the Charter of the United Nations, the Universal Declaration of Human Rights, the International Covenants on Human Rights and other instruments of the United Nations and the specialized agencies and despite the progress made in the matter of equality of rights, there continues to exist considerable discrimination against women" (http://www.unhchr.ch/html/menu3/b/21.htm, accessed May 12, 2009). Reproductive Rights were first established as a subset of human rights at the United Nation's 1968 International Conference on Human Rights. The Convention on the Elimination of All Forms of Discrimination against Women (CEDAW) was adopted in 1979 by the United Nations General Assembly and is described as an international bill of rights for women. It came into force on September 3, 1981.

and violence, issues that still remain hotly debated in their relation to bodily autonomy.[4] Two examples provide insights into why this is so important. In 1912, at the first Eugenics Conference, Winston Churchill proposed the sterilization of the feeble-minded so that they could live otherwise normal lives but without "the threat of reproduction." The Feeble-minded Person's Control Bill was thrown out in the UK, but picked up in Scandinavia and the United States, which was alarmed about the influx of refugees and immigrants, and, hence, the continuing strength of American citizens. Between 1904 and 1970, 60,000 "feeble-minded" were sterilized as part of the US Eugenics program. The role of the state in deciding who should and who should not reproduce was also part of the Nazi Eugenics Breeding Program, whereby German officers were instructed to father children by German or Nordic mothers. Ten thousand children were fathered in Norway under Nazi occupation and at the end of the war the mothers were publicly humiliated (*Darwin's Dangerous Idea*, 2009). Most recently, the trafficking of women and girls into forced prostitution, and women being sexually assaulted in war as a way of terrorizing their communities are also being taken into account (Lai and Ralph, 1995, p. 201), but the extent to which existing human rights principles can be applied to protect and promote women's sexual autonomy—including the rights of women to make decisions about when, how, and with whom to conduct their sexual lives—remains contentious, not least in situations where politics are dominated by authoritarian ideologies (such as fascism) and/or religious fundamentalism (for example, Muslim, Jewish, Christian, or tribal).[5]

It is also interesting to note that the Convention on the Elimination of All Forms of Discrimination Against Women (now in its twenty-seventh year) identifies discrimination against women as "... any distinction, exclusion or restriction made on the basis of sex [including] fundamental freedoms in the political, economic, social, cultural, civil or any other field" ("Overview of the Convention"), so highlighting the ways in which cultural self-expression can relate to political, economic, and social circumstances, including the ways in which women represent themselves. As Alice Walker recalls, "It was a punishable crime for a black person to read or write under slavery. What might have been the result if singing, too, had been forbidden by law. Listen to the voices of Bessie Smith, Billie Holiday,

---

[4]   Reproductive rights can also refer to education about contraception and sexually transmitted infections, freedom from coerced sterilization, and protection from gender-based practices such as female circumcision.

[5]   For example, when the Serbian-Montenegrin forces in the Balkans war ourred the women they raped that they would bear children who would forever be their enemies and fight against their mother and her people, they were behaving according to a particular complex of inherited social beliefs, they were speaking out of commitment to military values, paternal lineage, and a cult of male heroism. See Warner (1994, pp. 28-9).

Nina Simone, Roberta Flack and Aretha Franklin, among others, and imagine these voices muzzled for life" (1983, quoted in Ingram, 1999, p. 173).[6]

The association of "music with lived experience and the broader patterns of culture that it both mirrors and actively produces" (Brett, Wood, and Thomas, 1992, pp. vii-ix) draws attention to female artists who have provided specific insights into subjective experience and the ways in which songs "not only represent to us how things are but also help to construct the very categories of identity through which we experience them" (Middleton, 2000, p. 231). Sonya Aurora Madan's confrontational lyrics on Echobelly's debut CD *Everyone's Got One* (1994), for example, resonate with her self-perception as a strong Asian woman. The album's title creates an acronym (EGO), and its overall mood is challenging, confronting the problems of young Asian and Arab women who are subjected to forced marriage and honor-based brutality ("blame the mother/ sell the sister"), urging them to take control of their lives ("Half the population, one percent of wealth …," "Give Her a Gun"). Madan was acutely aware that her Asian parentage and upbringing could attract adverse attention, and her "I Don't Belong Here" (from the band's 1993 debut EP *Bellyache*) comes across as throwing down the gauntlet and tackling both prejudice and alienation head-on. Her awareness of being "an East-West casualty" was also confronted by wearing a Union Jack T-shirt with "My Country Too" scrawled across it, highlighting the conflicts surrounding identity, tradition, and women's rights. "Father, Ruler, King, Computer," a title inspired by Germaine Greer's *The Female Eunuch*, takes issue with the patriarchal assumptions surrounding marriage ("I was brought up, I've been told, that a husband is the goal,/ What connotations in these loaded words … I am whole all by myself") and is seen by Madan as "a celebration of independence," written at a time when "I was busy trying to discover myself" (quoted in Raphael, 1995, p. 43). Other songs explore sexist exploitation ("Insomniac"), post-abortion denial ("Bellyache"), and the paradox of being abused ("You're the evil world of the nursery rhyme," "Centipede") and loving your abuser ("You're my only friend, don't be cruel to me," "Centipede"). As Madan reflects, an abused woman is an abused woman regardless of her background and religion. "I didn't go into this to represent a minority. I did it for me" (quoted in Raphael, 1995, p. 34).

Despite the UDHR's declaration that "Everyone has the right to freedom of opinion and expression," the freedom for women to represent themselves through the arts as a form of cultural self-expression remains contentious.[7] "Cultural

---

[6]   It is interesting to note that Billie Holiday's recording company, Columbia, refused to record the anti-lynching song "Strange Fruit." Its powerful lyrics ("the bulging eyes and twisted mouth," the "black bodies swaying in the Southern breeze") were considered too controversial. A deal was made with Columbia, who loaned her to Commodore, and "Strange Fruit" was cut on April 20, 1939 at Brunswick's World Broadcasting Studios with Frankie Newton's Café Society band. See Nicholson (1996, p. 113).

[7]   Article 19 of the UDHR states, "Everyone has the right to freedom of opinion and expression: this right includes freedom to hold opinions without interference and to seek,

relativism, which argues that there are no universal human rights and that rights are culture-specific and culturally determined, is still a formidable and corrosive challenge to women's rights to equality and dignity in all facets of their lives" (Amnesty International, *Stop Violence Against Women Campaign*). At its most extreme—in the recent murder of singer songwriter Ayman Udas, whose family believed it was sinful for a woman to perform on television[8]—the persecution and sexual abuse of female artists, writers, and musicians in Pakistan and Afghanistan under Shi'ite law is symbolic of the betrayal by the international community to support women's rights.[9] And the recent case of a woman who burnt herself to death on International Women's Day evidences the hopelessness of Afghan women who are desperate to escape abusive marriages yet have no words to express their despair.[10] "Arguments that sustain and excuse these human rights abuses—those of cultural norms, 'appropriate' rights for women, or Western imperialism—barely disguise their true meaning: that women's lives matter less than men's" (Amnesty International, *Stop Violence Against Women Campaign*). The question thus arises as to how to free these silenced voices when they are denied the right to express themselves and to make their distress known.

While the media and the internet offers an opportunity to access information, the struggle against patriarchal religions and the suppression of women's voices—not least the mythologizing of motherhood and its impact on the victimization and repression of the female body—has been given pre-eminence in the flowering of women's writings across and beyond the course of the twentieth century. Virago Press, founded in 1973, was the first British publishing company to highlight the contribution made by women authors, publishing nineteenth- and

receive and impart information and ideas through any media and regardless of frontiers" (http://www.un.org/en/documents/udhr/, accessed May 12, 2009).

[8] As Daud Khattak comments, her murder "has shocked the city's artistic community because it symbolises a backlash against women and cultural freedom in an area that is increasingly dominated by Islamic fundamentalists." She was allegedly shot dead by her own brothers in the conservative city of Peshawar, Pakistan (Khattak, 2009, p. 25).

[9] President Karzai's signing of the Shia Personal Status Law contradicts both the Afghan Constitution and the Convention of the Elimination of All Forms of Discrimination against Women, to which Afghanistan is a State party. Many activists who have spoken out against the law have received threats. The fears of women activists have been compounded by the killing of a prominent women's rights campaigner and local councilor, Sitara Achakzai, who was shot dead in Kandahar after receiving death threats (Human Rights Watch, April 14, 2009, http://www.hrw.org/en/news/2009/04/14/afghanistan-new-law-threatens-women-s-freedom, accessed May 13, 2009).

[10] Self-immolation occurs across Afghanistan; its highest incidence is in Herat. The hospital had 81 cases in 2009, almost all women aged 15-25. Fifty-nine died. Attending reading and writing classes has also led to the mutilation and murder of Afghan women, including 25-year-old Nadia Anjuman who was killed by her own husband for her love of poetry (Lamb, 2009).

twentieth-century "classics," and since then there has been a proliferation of ethnically diverse literature (autobiographical, academic, feminist, fact and fiction, prose and poetry) exploring motherhood, bodily autonomy, and identity. The musico-poetic voice has been more constrained; issues such as pregnancy, miscarriage, sexual abuse, the traumas of family life, motherhood, abortion, religion, and racism are not issues usually found on a top-selling album or chart single, and where these do occur, they often tend toward the autobiographical.[11] While it is recognized that such introspection is important in voicing subjective experience, the art of creating a voice for the dead or forgotten draws on the legacy of the story-teller musician who can inhabit the pain and expand our understanding of both the victim(s) and the situation through "direct confronting speech, commingled with imagery and a caustic voice" (Whitesell, 2008, p. 77).[12] As Joni Mitchell recalls,

> In 1996 the Sisters of our Lady of Charity, the Magdalene Laundries in London, sold off 11 half acres to realtors for development and in ploughing it the realtors' tractors unearthed over 100 graves, women just thrown into the ground, named simply Magdalene of the tears, Magdalene of this and that, just anonymously and so the outrage grew ... Most towns had one—a prison for females who committed some crime—but the crimes varied, many of them were just victims, some just pregnant girls, some pregnant by their own father, by their own priest, but the worst crime of all it seems to me was that unmarried women in their late twenties, if men were still looking at them, in some parishes could be deemed jezebels and the town could incarcerate them for life—as scrub women to the nuns.[13]

The Magdalene Laundries, as they came to be known, originated in the nineteenth century as rehabilitation centers for prostitutes and other "fallen" women. Administered by the Roman Catholic Church, and supervised by nuns, the prison-like character of the asylums was justified by the creed of penitence, enforced through hard physical labor (primarily in laundries), corporal punishment, and, commonly, a strict rule of silence. Justified by the religious belief that Mary Magdalene was a reformed sinner (Luke 7: 36-50) and, as such, a good role model for prostitutes, and bolstered by strong conservative values, the Magdalene

---

[11]   See, for example, Tori Amos, "Me and a Gun," Sinead O'Connor, "My Three Babies," and Loretta Lynn, whose song "The Pill" was banned by country stations across the United States.

[12]   Joni Mitchell's encounter with Bob Dylan provided, as she recalls, "an expanded understanding of what pop songs can accomplish. ... I wrote poetry, and I had always wanted to make music. But I never put the two together ... the potential for the song had never occurred to me" (David Wilde, "A Conversation with Joni Mitchell," *Rolling Stone*, May 30, 1991, in Whitesell, 2008, p. 77).

[13]   Joni Mitchell, http://www.youtube.com/watch?v=8S2hv7uVxxY&NR=1, accessed May 15, 2009).

movement spread across southern Ireland, taking under its wing unmarried mothers and other "socially dysfunctional" girls and women.[14] Over its 150-year history it is estimated that 30,000 women were admitted to these institutions, often by family members and parish priests, the last closing in 1996. Southern Ireland was not alone in making profit out of unmarried mothers and other so-termed "social misfits." The Magdalene institutions, under the supervision of the Roman Catholic Church, were also commonplace in Europe, paralleling the practice in state-run asylums in Britain and Ireland where women were stripped of identity and subjected to sexual, psychological, and physical abuse. Little was known about the existence of the Magdalene institutions and the fate of inmates until the remains of female bodies were unearthed by developer's tractors. These were exhumed and, except for one body, cremated and reburied in a mass grave in Glasnevin Cemetery.[15]

Joni Mitchell's response to the "Magdalenes" is one of empathy and outrage, combining character portraits within a statement of social critique. "The Magdalene Laundries" (*Turbulent Indigo*, 1994) adopts an explicit, personalized voice as she takes on the persona of a 27-year-old woman, "cast in shame" into the Magdalene Laundries "for the way men looked at me." Taking on the role of storyteller, she reveals the plight of the "prostitutes and destitutes and temptresses like me ... sentenced into dreamless drudgery," contrasting their status as "fallen women" with the nuns, "these bloodless brides of Jesus," dramatizing the moment when "Peg O'Connell died," reflecting on her own destiny: "One day I'm going to die here too/ And they'll plant me in the dirt/ Like some lame bulb that never blooms ...."

The effectiveness of the song lies in its choice of language and the way in which Mitchell addresses her hypothetical listener. As Lloyd Whitesell writes,

> While in actual terms, Mitchell's songs were all intended for oral performance (either live with an actual audience present or simulated in recorded form with little authorial control over the listening situation), in fictional terms, they present themselves according to four modes of artistic enunciation; dramatic, narrative, lyric, and political. These modes can be distinguished by the different roles they assign the singer as well as to the implied audience. (2008, p. 44)

Mitchell's framing of the political content of the song through the thoughts of an (unnamed) "Magdalene" heightens its communicative power by allowing access to her state of mind and the feelings triggered by the death of Peg O'Connell. In an institutionalized setting characterized by a sense of isolation, the imaginary monologue accesses thoughts normally repressed by the rule of silence—the

---

[14]   There is no reference to Mary Magdalene's association with prostitution or adultery in the New Testament.

[15]   For more see Alexander Didden, "Magdalene Laundries: Still No Justice in the World."

certainty of dying, stuffed in a hole like Peg, never to bloom. The use of imagery and simile creates an unspoken sub-text of sterility which is heightened by a pragmatic description of girls who arrived pregnant ("Brigit got that belly by her parish priest"), the brief character sketch of Peg (a cheeky girl, a flirt), and veiled references to the mythology surrounding Mary Magdalene, where the nuns are aligned with the accusers of the anonymous woman "taken in adultery" (John 8: 3-11), stones concealed behind their rosaries. The blend of the ordinary and the poetic resonates with the reflective tone of the narrative. The restrained vocal tone of the opening verse contrasts with the emotional outburst and harsh confrontation of "this heartless place" and its association with "Our Lady of Charity"; the impassioned "Surely to God you'd think at least some bells should ring" subsides into a more muted expression of personal worth ("like some lame bulb that never blooms") before the repetitive lines of the coda ("not any spring") where over-dubbing creates the feel of a subdued chorus of "Magdalenes," a recognition of the shared plight of all the "woe-begotten-daughters."[16]

Unlike many political songs where a verse/chorus structure provides space for group singing (implying both a collective response and an affirmation of shared values), the narrative of "The Magdalene Laundries" "captures the lyric utterance of a single speaker, caught in an identifiable situation at a dramatic moment" (Whitesell, 2008, p. 47). Released in 1994, on the album *Turbulent Indigo*, it can be interpreted as a direct and personalized response to the unearthing of the graves and the silencing of the so-called "fallen women" of the Magdalene Laundries. As Joni Mitchell was only too aware in choosing her central character (identifying what she considered "the worst crime," the unmarried women in their late twenties who, if men were still looking at them, could be incarcerated for life), "There, but for the grace of God ...." As a woman constantly under media scrutiny for her numerous romantic affairs, the 1960s was still a difficult period for women when it came to bodily autonomy, and Mitchell's commitment to personal freedom is given particular poignancy in Christy Moore's cover of "The Magdalene Laundries."[17] Opening with the words, "Joni was an unmarried girl, she'd just turned twenty-seven ...," the naming of the central character creates an additional layer of meaning. Christy, as narrator, tells "Joni's story" (as author of the song, and as imagined character) drawing her into association with the "Magdalenes" and the "dreamless drudgery" of institutional life under the "brides of Christ,"

---

[16]   The Catholic Church's dominant image of the Holy Mother and Child as symbolic of nurturing spiritual values within the moral rhetoric of family values provides a religious frame of reference for the relationship between nuns (mothers) and inmates (daughters). Joni Mitchell always performed her own overdubs and here, the effective use of multi-layered voices draws into association the countless women who were lost to the Magdalene Laundries.

[17]   "When I went back to my own neighbourhood, I found that I had a provocative image. They thought I was loose because I always liked rowdies ..." (quoted in Whitesell, 2008, p. 92).

while hinting at the existence of her own child, who was given up to adoption in 1963.

The lullaby to "Little Green," on Mitchell's 1971 album, *Blue*, takes the form of a letter of farewell to her daughter, the ambiguity of its final line and the imprecision of its ongoing future tense disguising a very fresh wound in its acceptance of sorrow. Contextualized by songs which explore the cost of self-determination, and a recognition that relationships and prescribed gender roles (housewife, nurturer, submissive partner) constrict and smother personal growth, the thematically linked songs explore the conflict between belonging, freedom, and the emptiness and confusion that can accompany the lonely road of independence.[18] As Tillie Olsen (1978) writes, among the social forces that can lead to the silencing of an author, particularly a female author, including domestic responsibility, poverty, and race, it is motherhood that is the most constraining, and until recently almost all literary achievement came from childless women (Ingham, 1999).[19] Behind the self-exploration of *Blue* lies the reality of the choices Mitchell had to make if she was to achieve her ambitions as a singer-songwriter. As a personalized message to her child, loss is tempered by an underlying mood of resilience: "You're sad and you're sorry but you're not ashamed."

The dramatic focus on personal freedom and prescriptive gender roles have been recurring themes in Mitchell's body of songs,[20] but while religion is frequently at the heart of the moral imperatives surrounding motherhood,[21] violence toward women extends the frame of reference to the domestic sphere. "Not to Blame" (*Turbulent Indigo*, 1994) is, as Philip Martin writes, "an example of Mitchell's willingness to push on into darker channels" (2004, n.p.): "Six hundred thousand doctors are putting on rubber gloves/ And they're poking at the miseries made of love./ That way they're learning how to spot the battered wives/ Among all the women they see bleeding through their lives."

---

[18]   For a more detailed discussion see Sheila Whiteley, "The Lonely Road: Joni Mitchell," in Whiteley (2000, pp. 78-94).

[19]   Sylvia Plath's suicide has been attributed to the tragic conflict between her art and her responsibility to her two small children against the background of the 1950s and early 1960s ideology of women as homemakers who were meant to assume total responsibility for their children. Margaret Drabble's early 1960s novels stress the difficulties of mothering in a society where to abandon oneself to the needs of one's infant is seen as natural behavior on the mother's part. They depict the problems encountered when highly educated young women find themselves trapped by the expectations of marriage and motherhood.

[20]   "Don't Interrupt the Sorrow" (*The Hissing of Summer Lawns*, 1975), for example, exposes the concept of the "natural order as nothing but a cycle of 'sorrow' for women ('Death and birth and death and birth'), the use of religion as a tool for brainwashing ('The good slaves love the good book') and competing theological fictions and their consequences for women's lives" (Whitesell, 2008, p. 83).

[21]   "The Sire of Sorrow (Job's Sad Song)" from *Turbulent Indigo* (1994) picks up on the theme of aggressor and abused, justifying chastisement with the reprimand, "God is correcting you."

The stark imagery of the lyrics "your fist marks on her face," and the sense of personal confrontation suggests an accusatory closeness which is heightened by the reference to the husband's "buddies," betting fame and fortune on their assurance that "she was out of line," that "you were not to blame."[22] The impact of these final lines (which act almost like a chorus to the verse) is heightened by their association with blood ("these red words that make a stain on your white-washed claim") and "her lonely little grave" of the third and final verse. As a poet, Mitchell was well aware of the power of rhyme and the broad ā sounds (blame, stain, claim, grave) are drawn into poignant association. They're chilling, and like the repeated lines of "The Sire of Sorrow" (*Turbulent Indigo*, 1994), where she draws blood with repeats of a line that cuts to the emotional bone—"You make everything I dread and everything I fear come true" (Milward, 1994, n.p.)—they have a resonance that extends beyond the boundaries of the song. To paraphrase John Milward, it's irrelevant when Mitchell wrote this song of domestic violence, and its significance isn't tied to a particular time or space. Recent statistics on violence against women is on the rise, and as the Women's Aid website reveals

> at least 1 in 4 women experience domestic violence in their lifetime and between 1 in 8 and 1 in 10 women experience it annually. Viewed as physical, sexual, psychological or financial, violence against women transcends ethnicity, religion, class, age, sexuality, disability or lifestyle and can also occur in a range of relationships, including heterosexual, gay, lesbian, bisexual and transgender. The majority of abusers are men who choose to behave violently to get what they want and gain control. Less than half of all incidents are reported to the police ....[23]

* * *

... and when they arrive, they say they can't interfere with domestic affairs.— Tracy Chapman, "Behind The Wall"

---

[22]   The subject matter of the song hints at the indictment of her former friend Jackson Browne who the tabloids had accused of battering his then girlfriend Daryl Hannah. The reference to the three-year-old in the third verse has also been interpreted as a reference to Browne's son Ethan, who was three at the time of his mother's suicide (Browne's first wife, Phyllis). This has been denied by Mitchell. See Martin (2004).

[23]   On one typical day—November 2, 2006—11,310 women and 8,330 children were being supported by domestic violence services in England (both residential and non-residential). This has increased by 50 percent since 2003. On the same day, 3,615 women and 3,580 children were being supported within refuge-based services. Domestic violence accounts for between 16 percent and one quarter of all crime, and on average two women a week are killed by a male partner or former partner (http://www.womensaid.org.uk/domestic_violence_topic.asp?section=0001000100220041&sectionTitle=Domestic+violence+%28general%29, accessed May 26, 2009).

Tracy Chapman's "Behind the Wall" (*Tracy Chapman*, 1988) is still, for me, the most chilling of political songs. Written in the first person singular and sung unaccompanied, she tells of sleepless nights, the "loud voices behind the wall" that precede marital violence, the lyric association of "screaming" with "sleepless," "peace" with "sleep" creating an underlying subtext which situates the triangular relationship between the victim, the narrator/witness, and the police ("here to keep the peace ... we could all use some sleep"). The power of the song lies in repetition, with four of the five verses opening with the line "Last night I heard the screaming." The explicit, personalized voice is powerful, recording the narrator's thoughts, giving credibility to her proximity to the violence, and her cynical observation that "it won't do no good to call the police," the extended melisma on "late" creating a sense of resignation before the final phrase, "if they come at all." The structure of the song also reflects the repetitious nature of marital violence, with verse two and the final verse repeating the lyric content and melody line of the opening verse, so effecting a sense of the cyclical nature of abuse: "it never ends."

The everyday language and shaping of the melodic line adds to the impact of the song, reflecting and constructing the mood of the lyrics. Starting on top F (at the upper end of Chapman's vocal range) and ending on the octave below, there is a move from the initial shock of waking to the screams of the abused to a grudging acceptance of police inactivity. Emotional content is heightened by a variation in the melodic line of the fourth verse as "the screaming" is followed by "a silence that chilled my soul." Straining upwards to the very top of her range (the leap from C above middle C to top A on "I prayed"), the slow stepwise fall ("that I was") before the sustained tension on dreaming (top G falling to D) creates a mood of anxious instability that is heightened by the rawness of her vocal tone. Above all, it is the decision to sing alone and unaccompanied that underpins the feeling of vulnerability. Chapman "tells it how it is," without elaboration, the *a cappella* vocal creating a personal and poetic musical language of helpless aloneness in the face of aggression. Not least, the exposed vocal line emphasizes the relationship between vocal delivery and narrative representation. The *a cappella* of "Me and a Gun" (*Little Earthquakes*, 1992) has a similar effect in communicating Tori Amos's personal experience of rape and, like "The Magdalene Laundries" and "Behind the Wall" "captures the lyric utterance of a single speaker, caught in an identifiable situation at a dramatic moment" (Milward, 1994, n.p.).[24] This sense of moment is important. It situates the song in time and place, interpolating the listener into the trauma of the narrative, inviting their response. Genre is thus important in its association with musical identity. It has to speak to the listener.

While the songs so far discussed fall largely within the overarching genre of the singer-songwriter, "Thank You" (2004), by Jamelia, confronts the hopelessness and inertia of the abused women through r&b, combining elements of hip-hop

---

[24]   For a detailed discussion of "Me and a Gun" and other songs by Tori Amos see Whiteley (2005, pp. 84-103).

and soul in a catchy pop format.[25] The strength of the narrative lies in its combination of everyday speech and the stylization of its poetic language: "the fights, those nights," "my head, near dead," "my soul, so cold," "so young, so dumb." The explicit use of "I"/"you" creates an accusatory voice, "You hit, you spit, you split every bit of me," drawing the listener into the subjective experience of physical and mental abuse before the revelation "you're such a joke to me" and the realization that the narrator has moved on, "can't believe I stayed with you so long." The lift to an upbeat chorus, "you broke my world, you made me strong, thank you" is, perhaps, surprising within a song about domestic violence, but the success of "Thank You," which peaked at number two on the r&b charts and received the 2004 MOBO (Music of Black Origin) award for best single, has elicited a big response on Jamelia-associated websites. As NelleG, writes on the Thank-you Jamelia website, "there is not a lot of songs that 14 y.o's can relate to but i can relate to this." Other reviewers share their experience: "Fantastic lyric. So real to me. I've been there but now I'm out and laughing," "this song helped me to get over mi xbf john who beat me up and put me in hospital," "thank you explains exactly what I went through." What is apparent is the shared admiration for Jamelia ("great to have artists who write and perform music bout these very real issues such as domestic violence and emotional abuse") and the way in which "this song makes me start believing I actually am strong for everything he put me through." It is interesting that "Jamelia's song also has a meaning to me, not about violence or mental cruelty by a boyfriend, but can only mean a parent, and I can identify with it, as I was once an unhappy child, with a violent parent. Thank you Jamelia," so extending its relevance to the younger listener who has suffered abuse.[26]

Jamelia's popular appeal and the way in which "Thank You" challenges and deflates the often misogynistic representations of sexual violence and sexist power relations inherent in hip-hop ("I understand, to make you feel like a man, you hit, you spit ... you're such a joke to me") provides an insight into cultural self-expression and why it is important for women to represent themselves. As Germaine Greer writes, "Women can be routinely insulted and humiliated for years on end, repeatedly raped and sexually abused and yet keep silence, made to endure a life of kicks and blows ... because they are afraid ... The woman paralysed by terror exists in her own mind as well as that of her abuser to be abused. She can see no way out, no possible rescue, because fear has blinded her" (1999, p. 272). Speaking out, confronting abuse, defusing fear by offering hope and the possibility of personal freedom cannot solve the problem, but it can raise awareness of power and status in relationships by relating music to lived

---

[25]   Contemporary r&b (or urban contemporary) has evolved into a mainstream musical genre which incorporates elements of soul, funk, dance, pop, reggae, calypso, and hip-hop, so assuring both a broad-based appeal and a space for often subversive and left-field music.

[26]   All reviews from http://www.sing365.com/music/lyric.nsf/Thank-You-lyrics-jamelia/, accessed June 6, 2009.

experience, as my brief discussion of web reviews for "Thank You" shows. What is important is not whether the song is the literal truth of personal experience but rather the way Jamelia presents herself as a strong and vibrant woman who has successfully moved on from a sexually abusive relationship ("won't happen again"). It is the way in which she articulates her identity and performance in order to direct her audience to a particular interpretation of her song that is important (Negus, 1997, p. 182).

The "right to freedom of opinion and expression, and the freedom to hold opinions without interference and to seek, receive and impart information and ideas through any media and regardless of frontiers" (UDHR, Article 19) is crucial to politicized music. My choice of case studies was prompted by the ways in which they relate to the abuse and subjugation experienced by women and the contrast between those who are powerless to fight back and those who have a voice. The personal *is* political and the musico-poetic voice is important in questioning power and status, oppression and subordination.[27] Not least, it demonstrates that repression is historical and cultural while drawing attention to the fact that discrimination and exploitation continues to exist. As Germaine Greer tellingly observes, "on every side speechless women endure endless hardship, grief and pain, in a world system that creates billions of losers for every handful of winners" (1999, p. 3). What remains is the vision of possibility.

---

[27]   Joan Baez, for example, provides an unflinching example of commitment to social and political issues not only in her songs, but equally in founding the Institute for the Study of Nonviolence in Carmel, California.

Bibliography

A Concert for Hurricane Relief, Broadcast (NBC Universal, 2 Sep 2005).

Adorno, Theodor, "On Tradition," *Telos*, 94 (1993-94): 75-81.

Agamben, Giorgio, *The Coming Community*, Trans. Michael Hardt (Minneapolis: University of Minnesota Press, 1993).

Agamben, Giorgio, *Homo Sacer*, Trans. Daniel Heller-Roazen (Stanford: Stanford University Press, 1998).

Alfonso, Barry, et al., *The Illustrated Encyclopedia of Music*, Paul Du Noyer (general ed.), Ian Anderson et al. (consulting eds) (London: Flame Tree, 2003).

Allen, Deek, Interview with Kevin Dunn, April, 2009.

Alterman, Eric, *It Ain't No Sin To Be Glad You're Alive: The Promise of Bruce Springsteen* (Boston: Little, Brown, 1999).

America: A Tribute to Heroes, DVD (Warner Reprise Video, 2001).

Amnesty International, *Stop Violence Against Women Campaign* <http://www.amnestyusa.org/violence-against-women/stop-violence-against-women-svaw/page.do?id=1108417>, accessed May 15, 2009.

Andersen, Mark, and Mark Jenkins, *Dance of Days: Two Decades of Punk in the Nation's Capital* (New York: Akashic Books, 2001).

Armada, Bernard J., "Memorial Agon: An Interpretive Tour of the National Civil Rights Museum," *Southern Communication Journal*, 63 (1998): 235-43.

Aucoin, Dan, "Stars of Every Stripe Join Show of Patriotism; TV Networks, Celebs Unite in Fundraiser for Attack Relief Effort," *The Boston Globe* (September 21, 2001): C1.

Aucoin, Dan, "America Prepares the Recovery," *The Boston Globe* (September 22, 2001): A10.

Badiou, Alain, *Manifesto for Philosophy*, Trans. Norman Madarasz (Albany: State University of New York Press, 1999).

Badiou, Alain, *Ethics: An Essay on the Understanding of Evil*, Trans. Peter Hallward (London: Verso, 2002).

Badiou, Alain, *Being and Event*, Trans. Oliver Feltham (London: Continuum, 2005a).

Badiou, Alain, *Infinite Thought: Truth and the Return of Philosophy* (London: Continuum, 2005b).

Baraka, Amiri (LeRoi Jones), *Blues People: Negro Music in White America* (New York: Perennial, 2002).

Barretta, Scott, "Struggling Blues: Willie King: Backwoods Philosophy of the Blues," interview with Willie King, *Living Blues*, 31 (November-December, 2000): 24-32.

Barth, Fredrik, *Ethnic Groups and Boundaries: The Social Organization of Cultural Difference* (London: Allen & Unwin, 1969).

Beckett, Francis, and David Hencke, *Marching to the Fault Line: The 1984 Miners' Strike and the Death of Industrial Britain* (London: Constable, 2009).

Benedict, Helen, *Virgin or Vamp: How the Press Covers Sex Crimes* (New York: Oxford University Press, 1992).

Benhabib, Seyla, "The Legitimacy of Human Rights," *Daedalus*, 137 (2008): 94-104.

Benjamin, Walter, *Illuminations*, Trans. Harry Zohn (London: Fontana, 1975).

Bennett, Jill, *Empathic Vision: Affect, Trauma and Contemporary Art* (Stanford: Stanford University Press, 2005).

Berger, George, *The Story of Crass* (London: Omnibus Books, 2006).

Bhabha, Homi, "Foreword: Framing Fanon," in Frantz Fanon, *The Wretched of the Earth*, Trans. R. Philcox (New York: Grove Press, 2004): xii-xlii.

Bodnar, John, *Remaking America: Public Memory, Commemoration, and Patriotism in the Twentieth Century* (Princeton: Princeton University Press, 1992).

Boschert, Harry, "Singing in the Field," *Life in the Delta*, 12 (September, 2008): 15.

Bragg, Billy, *Back to Basics with Billy Bragg* (Essex: International Music Publications, 1985).

Bragg, Billy, *The Progressive Patriot: A Search for Belonging* (London: Black Swan, 2006).

Bragg, Billy, Interview with John Creedon, RTE (Ireland), Radio 1, June 3, 2006.

Bragg, Billy, Interview with Kieran Cashell, Dublin, December 4, 2008.

Bragg, Billy, *Independent on Sunday* (April 4, 2010): 14-17.

Bragg, Billy, Email to Kieran Cashell, November, 2010.

Bragg, Melvyn, *The Ashington Group: Lee Hall's* The Pitmen Painters, produced and directed by John Mapplebeck (London: ITV/Southbank, 2009).

Brett, Philip, Elizabeth Wood, and Gary C. Thomas (eds.), *Queering the Pitch* (New York: Routledge, 1992).

Brick, Michael, "Cultural Divisions Stretch to Relief Concerts," *The New York Times* (September 17, 2005): 7.

Brown, Dee, *Bury My Heart at Wounded Knee: An Indian History of the American West* (New York: Holt, Rinehart and Winston, 1970).

Buck-Morss, Susan, "Revolutionary Time: The Vanguard and the Avant-Garde," in Helga Geyer-Ryan (ed.), *Benjamin Studies/Studien 1: Perception and Experience in Modernity* (Amsterdam/NY: Rodopi, 2002): 209-22.

Bunch, Charlotte, "Women's Rights as Human Rights: Towards a Re-Vision of Human Rights," *Human Rights Quarterly*, 12, 4 (1990): 486-98.

Butler, Judith, "Merely Cultural," *New Left Review*, 1, 227 (January-February, 1998): 33-44.

Capps, Charles W. Jr., Interview with Charles Bolton, August 9, 1999, Charles W. Capps Jr. Oral History, OH246, Delta State University Archives, Cleveland, Mississippi.

Carthy, Martin, *A Guitar in Folk Music* (Surrey: Punchbowl, 1987).

Casey, Edward S., "Public Memory in Place and Time," in Kendall R. Phillips (ed.), *Framing Public Memory* (Tuscaloosa: University of Alabama Press, 2004): 17-44.

Child, F.J., *The Englsih and Scottish Popular Ballads* (vols 1-10) (Boston: Houghton Mifflin, 1882–98).

Christgau, Robert, *Christgau's Record Guide: Rock Albums of the Seventies* (New York: Ticknor and Fields, 1981).

Christgau, Robert, "Room for the Occasion: Working Professionals Defeat Doom on Two Benefit Comps," *Village Voice* (2002) <http://www.villagevoice.com/2002-03-19/music/room-for-the-occasion/1>, accessed April 27, 2009.

Christgau, Robert, "Charity Cases," *Barnes & Noble Review* (2009) <http://bnreview.barnesandnoble.com/t5/Rock-Roll/Charity-Cases/ba-p/1026>, accessed July, 2009.

Cleaver, Eldridge, *Soul on Ice* (New York: Delta, 1999).

Clifford, James, *The Predicament of Culture: Twentieth-Century Ethnography, Literature, and Art* (Cambridge, Mass.: Harvard University Press, 1988).

Collins, Andrew, *Still Suitable for Miners: Billy Brag, the Official Biography* (London: Virgin, 2002).

Commager, Henry Steele, and Allan Nevins, *A Pocket History of the United States of America* (New York: Pocket Books, 1981).

Corn, David, "Bruce Springsteen Tells the Story of the Secret America," *Mother Jones* (March/April, 1996) <http://motherjones.com/media/1996/03/bruce> accessed February 24, 2010.

Cornell, Drucilla, *At the Heart of Freedom* (Princeton: Princeton University Press, 1996).

Cowling, Mark, and James Martin, *Marx's Eighteenth Brumaire* (London: Pluto Press, 2002).

Critchley, Simon, *Infinitely Demanding: Ethics of Commitment, Politics of Resistance* (London: Verso, 2007).

Cullen, Jim, *Born in the U.S.A.: Bruce Springsteen and the American Tradition* (New York: HarperPerennial, 1997).

D'Ambrosio, Antonino, *Let Fury Have the Hour: The Punk Rock Politics of Joe Strummer* (New York: Nation Books, 2004).

Darwin's Dangerous Idea (BBC2, March 5, 2009).

Davies, Matt, "Do It Yourself: Punk Rock and the Disalienation of International Relations," in Marianne Franklin (ed.), *Resounding International Relations: On Music, Culture, and Politics* (New York: Palgrave, 2005): 113-40.

Dayan, Daniel, and Elihu Katz, *Media Events: The Live Broadcasting of History* (Cambridge, Mass.: Harvard University Press, 1992).

DeCurtis, Anthony, "Springsteen's Secret History," *Rolling Stone*, 801 (December, 1998) <http://www.rollingstone.com/artists/brucespringsteen/articles/story/5934951/springsteens_secret_history>, accessed March 1, 2010.

Deleuze, Gilles, "Nomad Thought," in David B. Allison (ed.), *The New Nietzsche: Contemporary Styles of Interpretation* (London: Delta Books, 1984): 142-9.

Deleuze, Gilles, *Proust and Signs*, Trans R. Howard. (Minnesota: University of Minnesota Press, 2003).

Deloria, Phillip, *Playing Indian* (New Haven: Yale University Press, 1998).

Deloria, Vine, Jr., *Custer Died for Your Sins: An Indian Manifesto* (London: Collier-Macmillan, 1969).

Deloria, Vine, Jr., "The Rise of Indian Activism," in R. Gomez, C. Collingham, R. Endo, and K. Jackson (eds.), *The Social Reality of Ethnic America* (Lexington: Heath, 1974): 179-87.

Deloria, Vine, Jr., "American Indians," in John D. Cuenker and Lorman A. Ratner (eds.), *Multiculturalism in the United States: A Comparative Guide to Acculturation and Ethnicity*, revised and expanded edition (Westport, Conn.: Greenwood Press, 2005): 23-45.

de Moraes, Lisa, "Kanye West's Torrent of Criticism, Live on NBC," *The Washington Post* (September 3, 2005): C01.

Denselow, Robin, *When the Music's Over: The Story of Political Pop* (London: Faber and Faber, 1989).

Didden, Alexander, "Magdalene Laundries: Still No Justice in the World," Historytimes.com <http://www.historytimes.com/current-affairs/magdalene-laundries-still-no-justice-in-the-world>, accessed May 27, 2009.

Donnelly, Jack, *Universal Human Rights in Theory and Practice*, 2nd edition (Ithaca: Cornell University Press, 2003).

Dunn, Kevin, Telephone interview with Pat Thetic, May 12, 2005.

Dunn, Kevin, Telephone interview with Guy Picciotto, March 30, 2007.

Dunn, Kevin, "Never Mind the Bollocks: Punk Rock and Global Communication," *Review of International Studies*, 34, S1 (2008): 193-210.

Ellison, Mary, *Lyrical Protest: Black Music's Struggle against Discrimination* (New York: Praeger, 1989).

Epstein, Joel, and Stacia Langenbahn, *The Criminal Justice and Community Response to Rape* (Darby: Diane Publishing, 1994).

Estrich, Susan, *Real Rape* (Cambridge, Mass.: Harvard University Press, 1987).

Fanon, Franz, *The Fanon Reader*, Ed. Azzedine Haddour (London: Pluto Press, 2006).

Farmer, James, and Malcolm X, "Separation or Integration," in James L. Golden and Richard D. Rieke (eds.), *The Rhetoric of Black Americans* (Columbus: Merrill, 1971): 422-39.

Fenton, Steve, *Ethnicity* (Cambridge: Polity Press, 2004).

Finding, Deborah, "'Give Me Myself Again': Sexual Violence Narratives in Popular Music" (Ph.D. Thesis: Gender Institute, London School of Economics, 2010).

Folk Britannia (BBC4 Documentary, 2006) <www.bbc.co.uk/bbcfour/music/features/folk-britannia.shtml>.

Forman, Murray, "Soundtrack to a Crisis: Music, Context, Discourse," *Television and New Media*, 3 (2002): 191-204.

Frank, Arthur W., *The Wounded Storyteller: Body, Illness, and Ethics* (Chicago: Chicago University Press, 1995).

Fraser, Nancy, "Feminism, Capitalism, and the Cunning of History," *New Left Review*, 56 (March-April, 2009): 97-117.

Freeman, Michael, *Human Rights: An Interdisciplinary Approach* (Oxford: Polity Press, 2002).

Fricke, David, "Bringing It All Back Home," *Rolling Stone*, 1071 (February, 2009) <http://www.rollingstone.com/news/coverstory/26066137> accessed March 4, 2010.

Frow, Gerald, *"Oh Yes It Is!": A History of Pantomime* (London: BBC, 1985).

Gallo, Phil, "America: A Tribute to Heroes," *Daily Variety* (September 24, 2001): 2.

Gammon, Vic, *Desire, Drink and Death in English Folk and Vernacular Song 1600-1900* (Aldershot: Ashgate, 2008).

Garman, Bryan K., *A Race of Singers: Whitman's Working-Class Hero from Guthrie to Springsteen* (Chapel Hill: University of North Carolina Press, 2000).

Garman, Bryan, "Models and Charity and Spirit: Bruce Springsteen, 9/11, and the War on Terror," in Jonathan Ritter and J. Martin Daughtry (eds.), *Music in the Post-9/11 World* (New York and London: Routledge, 2007): 71-89.

Garofalo, Reebee, "Nelson Mandela, the Concerts: Mass Culture as Contested Terrain," in Reebee Garofalo (ed.), *Rockin' the Boat: Mass Music and Mass Movements* (Boston: South End Press, 1992a): 55-65.

Garofalo, Reebee, *Rockin' the Boat: Mass Music and Mass Movements* (Boston: South End Press, 1992b).

Garofalo, Reebee, et al., "Call and Response: Who is the World?: Reflections on Music and Politics Twenty Years after Live Aid," *Journal of Popular Music*, 17, 3 (November, 2005): 324-44.

Garofalo, Reebee, "Pop Goes to War, 2001-2004: U.S. Popular Music after 9/11," in Jonathan Ritter and J. Martin Daughtry (eds.), *Music in the Post-9/11 World* (New York and London: Routledge, 2007): 3-26.

Geesling, Don, "An American Griot: Gil Scott-Heron with Don Geesling," *The Brooklyn Rail* (November, 2007): n.p.

Gill, Rosalind, *Gender and the Media* (Cambridge: Polity Press, 2007).

Gilmore, Mikal, "Bruce Springsteen's America," in June Skinner Sawyers (ed.), *Racing in the Street: The Bruce Springsteen Reader* (New York: Penguin, 2004): 266-83.

Glasper, Ian, *The Day the Country Died: A History of Anarcho Punk 1980-1984* (London: Cherry Red Books, 2006).

Goddard, Simon, "Billy Bragg: Album by Album," *Uncut* (July, 2006): 69-72.

Golden, James L., and Richard D. Rieke, *The Rhetoric of Black Americans* (New York: Merrill, 1971).

Green, Joshua, "Down in Smoke," *Washington City Paper* (1999) <http://www.washingtoncitypaper.com/display.php?id=16513>, accessed July 20, 2009.

Greer, Chris, *Sex Crime and the Media* (Devon: Willan, 2003).

Greer, Germaine, *The Female Eunuch* (New York: Bantam, 1970).

Greer, Germaine, *The Whole Woman* (London: Transworld, 1999).

Grinde, Donald, "Historical Narratives of Nationhood and the Semiotic Construction of Social Identity: A Native American Perspective," in Michael K. Green (ed.), *Issues in Native American Cultural Identity* (New York: Peter Lang, 1995): 201-22.

Gussow, Adam, *Seems Like Murder Here: Southern Violence and the Blues Tradition* (Chicago: University of Chicago Press, 2002).

Hamacher, Werner, "The Right Have Rights (Four-and-a-Half Remarks)," *South Atlantic Quarterly*, 103, 2/3 (2004): 343-56.

Hanna, Kathleen (ed.), *Bikini Kill Color and Activity Book* (Washington, DC: n.p., c. 1991).

Hansberry, Lorraine, "The Negro Writer and His Roots: Towards a New Romanticism," in Gerald Early (ed.), *Speech and Power*, vol. 2 (New York: Ecco Press, 1993): 129-41.

Harker, Ben, *Class Act: The Cultural and Political Life of Ewan MacColl* (London: Pluto Press, 2007).

Harper, Colin, *Dazzling Stranger: Bert Jansch and the British Folk and Blues Revival* (London: Bloomsbury, 2006).

Harris, John, *The Last Party: Britpop, Blair and the Demise of English Rock* (London: HarperPerennial, 2004).

Havel, Vaclav, "Kosovo and the End of the Nation-State," *New York Review of Books*, 46, 10 (June 10, 1999): 50-58.

Havel, Vaclav, "The Power of the Powerless" [1978] <http://www.vaclavhavel.cz/index.php?sec=6&id>, accessed March 4, 2009.

Hedwig and the Angry Inch, directed by John Cameron Mitchell, songs by Stephen Trask (New Line Cinema, 2001).

Hentoff, Nat, Liner notes to Gil Scott-Heron, *Small Talk at 125th and Lenox* (Flying Dutchman, 1971): n.p.

Howes, Frank, *Folk Music of Britain—and Beyond* (London: Methuen, 1969).

Hutnyk, John, *Critique of Exotica: Music, Politics and the Culture Industry* (London, Pluto Press, 2000).

Ingram, Heather (ed.), *Mothers and Daughters in the Twentieth Century: A Literary Anthology* (Edinburgh: Edinburgh University Press, 1999).

Isaacs, Harold Robert, *The New World of Negro Americans: A Study from the Center for International Studies, Massachusetts Institute of Technology* (New York: Day, 1963).

Ishay, Micheline R. (ed.), *The Human Rights Reader: Major Political Writings, Essays, Speeches, and Documents from the Bible to the Present* (New York: Routledge, 1997).

James, Caryn, "A Nation Challenged: The Benefit; Stars Gather on TV to Raise Money and Pay Tribute," *The New York Times* (September 22, 2001): B1.

Jameson, Fredric, "Marx and Postmodernism," *New Left Review*, 1, 176-7 (July-August, 1989): 31-45.

Johnson, Troy, "Roots of Contemporary Native American Activism," *American Indian Culture and Research Journal*, 20, 2 (1996): 127-54.

Johnson, Troy, Duane Champagne, and Joane Nagel, "American Indian Activism and Transformation," in Troy Johnson, Joane Nagel, and Duane Champagne (eds.), *American Indian Activism: Alcatraz to the Longest Walk* (Urbana: University of Illinois Press, 1997): 9-44.

Jones, LeRoi [Amiri Baraka], *Black Music* (New York: Morrow, 1967).

Kalra, Virinder, and John Hutnyk (eds.), *Postcolonial Studies* [Special Issue on Music and Politics], 1, 3 (1998).

Khattak, Daud, "Shot by Her Brothers for TV Sin," *The Sunday Times* (May 3, 2009): 25.

Kirkpatrick, Rob, *The Words and Music of Bruce Springsteen* (Westport, Conn.: Praeger, 2007).

Kofsky, Frank, *Black Nationalism and the Revolution in Music* (New York: Pathfinder, 1970).

Kovic, Ron, *Born on the Fourth of July* (New York: McGraw-Hill, 1976).

Kundnani, Arun, *The End of Tolerance: Racism in 21st Century Britain* (London: Pluto Press, 2007).

Kureishi, Hanif, *My Son, the Fanatic* (London: Faber and Faber, 1998).

Lacan, Jacques, *Ecrits* [1966] (London: Norton, 2006).

LaCapra, Dominic, *Representing the Holocaust: History, Theory, Trauma* (Ithaca: Cornell University Press, 1994).

Lai, Sara Y., and Regan E. Ralph, "Female Sexual Autonomy and Human Rights," *Harvard Human Rights Journal*, 8 (1995): 201-27.

Lamb, Christina, "The Defiant Poets' Society," *The Sunday Times Magazine* (April 26, 2009): 46-55.

Landau, Jon, "Records: The Concert for Bangladesh," *Rolling Stone* (February 3, 1972): 42.

Lawless, Andrew, "Must I Paint You a Picture—Billy Bragg in Interview," *Three Monkeys* (online magazine), 6 (2004) <www.billybragg.co.uk/words/words1.php?word_id=6>, accessed November 26, 2008.

Leblanc, Lauraine, *Pretty in Punk: Girls' Gender Resistance in a Boys' Subculture* (New Brunswick, NJ: Rutgers University Press, 1999).

Lee, Craig, *Hardcore California: A History of Punk and New Wave* (San Francisco: Last Gasp, 1983).

Levi, Primo, *The Search for Roots* (London: Penguin, 2001).

Lifton, Sarah, *Folk Music: The Listener's Guide* (Dorset: Blandford Press, 1983).

Lindstrom, Lamont, "Leftamap Kastrom: The Political History of Tradition on Tanna, Vanuata," *Mankind*, 13 (1982): 316-29.

Lloyd, A.L., *Coaldust Ballads (Part-songs by various composers)*. (London: Workers' Music Association).

Lloyd, A.L., *Come All Ye Bold Miners: Ballads and Songs of the Coalfields* (London: Lawrence and Wishart, 1952).

Lloyd, A.L., *Folk Song in England* (New York: International Publishers, 1967).

Löwy, Michael, *Fire Alarm: Reading Walter Benjamin's "On the Concept of History"*, Trans. Chris Turner (London and New York: Verso, 2005).

Maitland, Sarah (ed.), *Women Fly When Men Aren't Watching* (London: Virago, 1993).

Malcolm X, "Message to Grassroots" (November 10, 1963) <http://teaching americanhistory.org/library/index.asp?document=1145>, accessed March 3, 2010.

Marcus, Greil, *Lipstick Traces: A Secret History of the Twentieth Century* (Cambridge, Mass.: Harvard University Press, 1989).

Marcus, Greil, "Real Life Rock Top 10," *Salon* (2002) <http://dir.salon.com/story/ent/col/marc/2002/02/25/63/index.html>, accessed April 27, 2009.

Marsh, Dave, *Born to Run: The Bruce Springsteen Story* (New York: Doubleday, 1979).

Martin, Philip, "The Genius of Joni," *Arkansas Democrat-Gazette* (September 28, 2004), <http://jonimitchell.com/library/view.cfm?id=1409>, accessed May 26, 2009.

Marx, Karl, *Marx's Eighteenth Brumaire: (Post)modern Interpretations* [1852], Eds Mark Cowling and James Martin (London: Pluto Press, 2002).

Maslan, Susan, "The Anti-Human: Man and Citizen before the Declaration of the Rights of Man and of the Citizen," *South Atlantic Quarterly*, 103, 2/3 (2004): 357-74.

Matthiessen, Peter, *In the Spirit of Crazy Horse* (New York: Viking Press, 1983).

McAllester, David P., and Douglas F. Mitchell, "Navajo Music," in Alfonzo Ortiz (volume editor) and William C. Sturtevant (general editor), *The Handbook of North American Indians, Vol. 10: Southwest* (Washington: Smithsonian Institution, 1983): 605-23.

McGinley, Paige, "Floods of Memory (A Post-Katrina Soundtrack)," *Performance Research*, 12, 2 (2007): 57-65.

McNeil, Legs, and Gillian McCain, *Please Kill Me: The Uncensored Oral History of Punk* (New York: Grove Press, 1996).

Medevoi, Leerom, "Cold War American Culture as the Age of Three Worlds," *Minnesota Review*, 55-7 (2002): 167-86.

Middleton, Richard (ed.), *Reading Pop: Approaches to Textual Analysis in Popular Music* (Oxford: Oxford University Press, 2000).

Miller, James L., "Review of *Roman Pantomime: Practice and Politics* by Frank W.D. Reis," *Dance Research Journal*, 11, 1/2 (1978): 52-4.

Milward, John, Album review of *Turbulent Indigo* by Joni Mitchell, *Rolling Stone* (December 15, 1994) <http://www.rollingstone.com/artists/jonimitchell/albums/album/321631/review/5945724/turbulent_indigo>, accessed May 26, 2008.

Mitchell, Gail, and Bill Werde, "An Urban Music Industry Ponders a Rappers Words," *Billboard* (September 17, 2005): 5.

Moore, Michael, "Mavericks, Renegades and Troublemakers," *Rolling Stone*, 990/991 (December 29, 2005): 65-6.

Morrish, John (ed.), *The Folk Handbook: Working with Songs from the English Tradition* (New York: Backbeat, 2007).

Morse, Steve, "Tori Amos Opens Heart Onstage and Off," *The Boston Globe*, Arts Section (June 10, 1994): 63.

Murg, Wilhelm, "The Musicology of Tom Bee" [2003], *Indian Country Today* (2008) <www.indiancountrytoday.com/ archive/28179874.html>, accessed February 17, 2009.

Nagel, Joane, *American Indian Ethnic Renewal: Red Power and the Resurgence of Identity and Culture* (Oxford: Oxford University Press, 1996).

Nagel, Joane, and C. Matthew Snipp, "Ethnic Reorganization: American Indian Social, Economic, Political and Cultural Strategies for Survival," in Susan Lobo and Steve Talbot (eds.), *Native American Voices: A Reader* (Upper Saddle River: Prentice Hall, 2001): 487-503.

Nairn, Tom, "The Sound of Thunder," *London Review of Books*, 31, 19 (2009): 29-30.

Negus, Keith, "My Three Babies," in Sheila Whiteley (ed.), *Sexing the Groove: Popular Music and Gender* (London: Routledge, 1997): 178-90.

Nelson, David, "Willie King and the Liberators: Freedom Creek," *Living Blues*, 31 (November-December, 2000): 50.

Nicholson, Stuart, *Billie Holiday* (London: Indigo, 1996).

Nkrumah, Kwame, *I Speak of Freedom: A Statement of African Ideology* (New York: Praeger, 1961).

O'Connor, John J., "TV Weekend; 'Human Rights Now Tour,' on HBO," *The New York Times* (December 23, 1988) <http://www.nytimes.com/1988/12/23/movies/tv-weekend-human-rights-now-tour-on-hbo.html?pagewanted=1>, accessed February 26, 2010.

Olsen, Tillie, *Silences* [1978] (London: Virago, 1980).

Omi, Michael, and Howard Winant, *Racial Formation in the United States: From the 1960s to the 1990s* (New York: Routledge, 1994).

O'Neal, Jim, Liner notes to Willie King, *Freedom Creek* (Rooster Blues Records, 2000).

"Overview of the Convention," Convention on the Elimination of All Forms of Discrimination against Women (CEDAW) <http://www.un.org/womenwatch/daw/cedaw/>, accessed May 12, 2009.

Pareles, Jon, "Critic's Notebook; Star-Spangle or Reflective, Pop Captures the Mood," *The New York Times* (December 20, 2001) E3.

Peddie, Ian, "Love of Labor," *PopPolitics.com: The Work Issue* (2000), <www. poppolitics.com/archives/2000/10/Love-of-Labor/>, accessed November 20, 2009.

Peddie, Ian (ed.), *The Resisting Muse: Popular Music and Social Protest* (Aldershot: Ashgate, 2006).

Pegley, Kip, and Susan Fast, "'America: A Tribute to Heroes': Music, Mourning and the Unified American Community," in Jonathan Ritter and J. Martin Daughtry (eds.), *Music in the Post-9/11 World* (New York and London: Routledge, 2007): 27-42.

Pekar, Harvey, *American Splendor: Our Movie Year* (New York: Ballantine Books, 2004).

Perry, Jonathan, "Crime and Punishment: Country Stars Steve Earle and Jon Langford Speak Out," *Boston Phoenix* (2002) <http://www.bostonphoenix. com/boston/music/top/documents/02413171.htm>, accessed April 27, 2009.

Phillips, Kendall R., "Introduction," in Kendall R. Phillips (ed.), *Framing Public Memory* (Tuscaloosa: University of Alabama Press, 2004): 1-14.

Poole, Scott W., "Memory," in Charles Reagan Wilson (ed.), *Myth, Manners, and Memory: The New Encyclopedia of Southern Culture, Vol. 4* (Chapel Hill: University of North Carolina Press, 2006): 104-7.

Press, Joy, "Where the Girls Are," *George* (January, 1996): n.p.

Ralli, Tania, "Who's a Looter? In Storm's Aftermath, Pictures Kick Up a Different Kind of Tempest," *The New York Times* (September 5, 2005): C1.

Rancière, Jacques, *Disagreement*, Trans. Julie Rose (Minneapolis: University of Minnesota Press, 1999).

Rancière, Jacques, "Who is the Subject of the Rights of Man?," *South Atlantic Quarterly*, 103, 2/3 (2004): 297-310.

Rancière, Jacques, *Hatred of Democracy*, Trans. Steve Corcoran (London: Verso, 2006).

Raphael, Amy, *Never Mind the Bollocks: Women Rewrite Rock* (London: Virago Press, 1995).

Reily, Ross, "Blues Royalty," *Delta Democrat Times* (June 1, 2005): A1, A8.

Rogers, Charles E., "Kanye West Calls Out Bush for Curious Neglect of Poor and Blacks," *The New York Amsterdam News* (September 8-14, 2005): 21.

Rolling Stone, *Bruce Springsteen: The Rolling Stone Files* (New York: Hyperion, 1996).

Romanowski, Patricia, and Holly George-Warren (eds.), *The New Rolling Stone Encyclopedia of Rock & Roll* (New York: Fireside, 1995).

Rooksby, Rikki, "The Music of English Folk Song," in John Morrish (ed.), *The Folk Handbook: Working with Songs from the English Tradition* (New York: Backbeat, 2007): 54-61.

Roosens, Eugene, *Creating Ethnicity: The Process of Ethnogenesis* (Newbury Park, Calif.: Sage, 1989).

Roosevelt, Franklin D., "F.D. Roosevelt's 'Four Freedoms' Speech" [1941] in Henry Steele Commager and Milton Cantor (eds.), *Documents of American History* (New York: Appleton-Century-Crofts, 1968): 446-9.

Roosevelt, Franklin D., "An Economic Bill of Rights" [1944] in Henry Steele Commager and Milton Cantor (eds.), *Documents of American History* (New York: Appleton-Century-Crofts, 1968): 483-5.

Rural Members Association <http://www.alabamablues.org/Willie%20King/RMA/RMAindex.htm>, accessed March 15, 2009.

Salewicz, Chris (with Adrian Boot), *Midnights in Moscow* (London: Omnibus, 1989).

Savage, Jon, *England's Dreaming: Anarchy, Sex Pistols, Punk Rock, and Beyond* (London: Faber and Faber, 1991).

Sawyers, June Skinner (ed.), *Racing in the Street: The Bruce Springsteen Reader* (New York: Penguin, 2004).

Sawyers, June Skinner, *Tougher than the Rest: 100 Best Bruce Springsteen Songs* (New York: Omnibus Press, 2006).

Scaggs, Austin, "Kanye West [Interview]," *Rolling Stone*, 990/991 (December 29, 2005): 72.

Scales, Christopher A., Interview with Tom Bee, July 28, 2009.

Scarry, Elaine, *The Body in Pain: The Making and Unmaking of the World* (New York: Oxford University Press, 1985).

Scott-Heron, Gil, *Small Talk at 125th and Lenox: A Collection of Black Poems* (New York: World Publishing Company, 1970).

Scott-Heron, Gil, *So Far, So Good* (Chicago: Third World Press, 1990).

Scott-Heron, Gil, *The Vulture* and *The Nigger Factory* (Edinburgh: Canongate, 1996).

Scott-Heron, Gil, *Now and Then: The Poems of Gil Scott-Heron* (New York: Canongate, 2000).

Shackel, Paul A., "Introduction: Contested Memories and the Making of the American Landscape," in Paul A. Shackel (ed.), *Myth, Memory and the Making of the American Landscape* (Gainesville: University Press of Florida, 2001): 1-16.

Sharma, Sanjay, and John Hutnyk (eds.), *Theory, Culture & Society*, 17, 3 (2000).

Sharma, Sanjay, John Hutnyk, and Ash Sharma, *Dis-Orienting Rhythms: The Politics of the New Asian Dance Music* (London: Zed Books, 1996).

Sharma, Sanjay, and Ash Sharma, "'So Far So Good, So Far So Good ...': *La Haine* and the Poetics of the Everyday," *Theory Culture and Society*, 17, 3 (2000): 103-16.

Sharp, Cecil J., *English Folk Song: Some Conclusions* (London: Mercury Books, 1965).

Shelter from the Storm: A Concert for the Gulf Coast, Broadcast (American Broadcasting Company, 2005).

Shepp, Archie, "Foreword," in Ben Sidran, *Black Talk* (New York: Da Capo, 1981): ii-xii.

Sidran, Ben, *Black Talk* (New York: Da Capo, 1981).

Sillers, Walter, Sr., "Historical," in William F. Gray (ed.), *Imperial Bolivar* (Cleveland, Miss.: Bolivar Commercial, 1923): 7-10.

Sinclair, John, "The Secret History of the Blues," Liner notes to Willie King, *Living in a New World* (Rooster Blues Records, 2002).

Sinker, Daniel, *We Owe You Nothing: Punk Planet: The Collected Interviews* (New York: Akashic Books, 2001).

Smith, Abbe, "The Dignity and Humanity of Bruce Springsteen's Criminals," *Widener Law Journal*, 14 (2005): 787-835.

Soothill, Keith, and Sylvia Walby, *Sex Crimes in the News* (London: Routledge, 1991).

Sorkin, Alan, *The Urban American Indian* (Lexington, Ky.: Lexington Press, 1978).

Spigel, Lynn, "Entertainment Wars: Television Culture after 9/11," in Dana Heller (ed.), *The Selling of 9/11: How a National Tragedy Became a Commodity* (New York: Palgrave Macmillan, 2005): 119-54.

Spitz, Marc, and Brendan Mullen, *We Got the Neutron Bomb: The Untold Story of L.A. Punk* (New York: Three Rivers Press, 2001).

Spivak, Gayatri Chakravorty, "Can the Subaltern Speak?," in Cary Nelson and Lawrence Grossberg (eds.), *Marxism and the Interpretation of Culture* (Urbana: University of Illinois Press, 1985): 271-313.

Spivak, Gayatri Chakravorty, *A Critique of Postcolonial Reason: Toward a History of the Vanishing Present* (Cambridge, Mass.: Harvard University Press, 1999).

Springer, Robert, "The Regulatory Function of the Blues," *The Black Perspective in Music*, 4 (1976): 278-88.

Springsteen, Bruce, *Songs* (New York: HarperCollins, 2003).

Springsteen, Bruce, "Chords for Change," *The New York Times* (August 5, 2004) <http://www.nytimes.com/2004/08/05/opinion/05bruce.html?pagewanted=1>, accessed January 9, 2010.

Stabile, Carol A., "No Shelter from the Storm," *South Atlantic Quarterly*, 106, 4 (Fall, 2007): 683-708.

Stanford, Peter, "Free Radical: Why It's Showtime for Billy Bragg," *Independent on Sunday* (April 4, 2010): 14-17.

"Stars Offer Heartfelt Performances in Benefit: Aaron Neville, Harry Connick, Faith Hill Sing to Help Raise Funds for Victims" (September 5, 2005) <http://www.msnbc.msn.com/ib/9146525>, accessed May 13, 2009.

Steinbeck, John, *The Grapes of Wrath* [1939] (New York: Penguin, 1992).

Straus, Terry, and Debra Valentino, "Retribalization in Urban Indian Communities," in Susan Lobo and Kurt Peters (eds.), *American Indians and the Urban Experience* (New York: Altamira Press, 2001): 85-94.

Sunstein, Cass R., *The Second Bill of Rights: FDR's Unfinished Revolution and Why We Need It More Than Ever* (New York: Basic Books, 2004).

Taylor, Timothy, *Global Pop: World Music, World Markets* (New York: Routledge 1997).

Tucker, Mark, "Our Man in England: Interview with Martin Carthy," *Acoustic*, 1 (2005): 16-20.

Ullestad, Neal, "Diverse Rock Rebellions Subvert Mass Media Hegemony," in Reebee Garofalo (ed.), *Rockin' the Boat: Mass Music and Mass Movements* (Boston: South End Press, 1992): 34-54.

U.S. Census Bureau (2000), American FactFinder, Memphis Town, Alabama <http://factfinder.census.gov>, accessed March 15, 2009.

U.S. Census Bureau (2007), State and County Quickfacts, Pickens County, Alabama <http://quickfacts.census.gov/qfd/states/01/01107.html>, accessed March 15, 2009.

Varelas, Nicole, and Linda Foley, "Blacks' and Whites' Perceptions of Interracial and Intraracial Date Rape," *Journal of Social Psychology*, 138 (1998) 392-400.

Von Eschen, Penny, *Race against Empire: Black Americans and Anticolonialism 1937-1957* (Ithaca: Cornell University Press, 1997).

Wald, Elijah, *Escaping the Delta: Robert Johnson and the Invention of the Blues* (New York: HarperCollins, 2004).

Walker, Alice, *In Search of Our Mother's Gardens: Womanist Prose* (New York: Harcourt Brace, 1983).

Warner, Marina, *Six Myths of Our Time: Managing Monsters. The Reith Lectures 1994* (London: Vintage, 1994).

Weiss, Peter, *The Aesthetics of Resistance Vol. 1*, Trans. Joachim Neugroschel (Durham, NC: Duke University Press, 2005).

Welch, Matt, "Velvet President: Why Vaclav Havel is Our Era's George Orwell," *Reason*, May 2003 <http://www.reason.com/news/show/28781.html>, accessed March 4, 2009.

Werner, Craig, *A Change is Gonna Come: Music, Race and the Soul of America* (New York: Penguin, 1998).

Whiteley, Sheila, *Women and Popular Music: Sexuality, Identity and Subjectivity* (London: Routledge, 2000).

Whiteley, Sheila, *Too Much Too Young: Popular Music, Age and Gender* (London: Routledge, 2005).

Whitesell, Lloyd, *The Music of Joni Mitchell* (New York: Oxford University Press, 2008).

Willhardt, Mark, "Available Rebels and Folk Authenticities: Michelle Shocked and Billy Bragg," in Ian Peddie (ed.), *The Resisting Muse: Popular Music and Social Protest* (Aldershot: Ashgate, 2006): 30-48.

Williams, Granville, *Shafted: The Media, the Miners' Strike and the Aftermath* (London: Campaign for Press and Broadcasting Freedom, 2009).

Williams, Leonard, "Anarchism Revived," *New Political Science*, 29, 3 (2007): 297-312.

Willie King: Down in the Woods, directed by Saskia Rietmeijer and Bart Drolenga (Visible World Films, 2007).

Wilonsky, Robert, "Hunger Strike: Can a Non-9/11 Album Make Any Noise?," *San Francisco Weekly* (2001) <http://www.sfweekly.com/2001-12-05/culture/hunger-strike/> accessed July 20, 2009.

Wilson, Amit, *Dreams, Questions, Struggles: Asian Women in Britain* (London: Pluto Press, 2006).

Winterson, Jeanette, *Written on the Body* (London: Jonathan Cape, 1992).

Wypijewski, JoAnn, "Blue Notes," *The Nation*, 264 (May 26, 1997): 35-7.

Zelizer, Barbie, "Reading the Past against the Grain: The Shape of Memory Studies," *Critical Studies in Mass Communication*, 12 (1995): 214-39.

Žižek, Slavoj, "Resistance is Surrender," *London Review of Books*, 29, 22 (2007) <www.lrb.co.uk/v29/n22/zize01_.html>, accessed August 18, 2009.

Žižek, Slavoj, "Why Cynics Are Wrong: The Sublime Shock of Obama's Victory," *In These Times, November 13, 2008* <www.inthesetimes.com/article/4039>, accessed August 18, 2009.

Zuberi, Nabeel, *Sounds English: Transnational Popular Music* (Urbana and Chicago: University of Illinois Press, 2001).

Discography

7 Worlds Collide, *The Sun Came Out* (Sin, 2009).

America: A Tribute to Heroes (Interscope, 2001).

Amos, Tori, *Little Earthquakes* (Atlantic, 1992).

Artists United Against Apartheid, "Sun City" (Manhattan, 1985).

Artists United Against Apartheid, *Sun City* (Manhattan, 1985).

Bad Brains, "Banned in D.C.," *Bad Brains* (ROIR, 1982).

Bad Brains, "Pay to Cum," *Bad Brains* (ROIR, 1982).

Bad Brains, "Destroy Babylon," *Rock for Light* (Caroline, 1983).

Bad Brains, "We Will Not," *Rock for Light* (Caroline, 1983).

Bad Brains, *Attitude—The ROIR Sessions* (Relativity, 1989).

Bad Brains, "God of Love," *God of Love* (Maverick, 1995).

Bad Brains, "Give Thanks and Praises," *Build a Nation* (Megaforce, 2007).

Band Aid, "Do They Know It's Christmas?," *The Christmas Compact Disc* (EMI, 1986).

Bikini Kill, "Double Dare Ya," *Bikini Kill* (Kill Rock Stars, 1992).

Bikini Kill, "Resist Psychic Death," *Yeah Yeah Yeah Yeah* (Kill Rock Stars, 1993).

Bikini Kill, "This Is Not a Test," *Yeah Yeah Yeah Yeah* (Kill Rock Stars, 1993).

Born to Choose (Rykodisc, 1993).

Bragg, Billy, *Life's a Riot with Spy Vs. Spy* (Utility/Go! Discs, 1983).

Bragg, Billy, *Brewing Up with Billy Bragg* (Go! Discs, 1984).

Bragg, Billy, *Between the Wars* EP (Go! Discs, 1985).

Bragg, Billy, *Days Like These* EP (Go! Discs, 1985).

Bragg, Billy, *Talking with the Taxman about Poetry* (Go! Discs, 1986).

Bragg, Billy, *Back to Basics* (Go! Discs, 1987).

Bragg, Billy, *Workers' Playtime* (Go! Discs, 1988).

Bragg, Billy, *The Internationale* (Utility, 1990).

Bragg, Billy, *Don't Try This at Home* (Go! Discs, 1991).

Bragg, Billy, *William Bloke* (Cooking Vinyl, 1996).

Bragg, Billy, *Bloke on Bloke* (Cooking Vinyl, 1997).

Bragg, Billy, *Mermaid Avenue* (Elektra, 1998).

Bragg, Billy, *Mermaid Avenue Volume II* (Elektra, 2000).

Bragg, Billy, *England, Half English* (Elektra, 2000).

Bragg, Billy, *Mr Love and Justice* (Cook CD, 2008).

The Bridge: A Tribute to Neil Young (Caroline, 1989).

Briggs, Anne, *A Collection* (with notes by Colin Harper) (Topic, 1999).

Carthy, Martin, *Martin Carthy* (Fontana, 1965).

Carthy, Martin, *Shearwater* (Pegasus, 1972).

Carthy, Martin, *Crown of Horn* (Gama, 1976).

Carthy, Martin, *Out of the Cut* (Gama, 1981).

Chapman, Tracy, *Tracy Chapman* (Elektra, 1988).

The Clash, "White Riot," *The Clash* (CBS/Epic, 1977).

The Clash, "Clampdown," *London Calling* (CBS/Epic, 1979).

The Clash, *London Calling* (CBS/Epic, 1979).

The Clash, "Spanish Bombs," *London Calling* (CBS/Epic, 1979).

The Clash, "Stop the World," *The Call Up 7"* (CBS, 1980).

The Clash, "Broadway," *Sandinista!* (CBS/Epic, 1981).

The Clash, "The Call Up," *Sandinista!* (CBS/Epic, 1981).

The Clash, *Sandinista!* (CBS/Epic, 1981).

The Clash, "Washington Bullets," *Sandinista!* (CBS/Epic, 1980).

The Clash, *Combat Rock* (CBS/Epic, 1982).

The Clash, "Know Your Rights," *Combat Rock* (CBS/Epic, 1982).

The Clash, "Rock the Casbah," *Combat Rock* (CBS/Epic, 1982).

The Clash, "Straight to Hell," *Combat Rock* (CBS/Epic, 1982).

Coltrane, John, *Kulu Se Mama* (Polygram, 1965).

The Concert for Bangladesh (Apple, 1971).

The Concert for New York City (Columbia, 2001).

Concerts for the People of Kampuchea (Atlantic, 1981).

Cooke, Sam, "A Change Is Gonna Come," *Ain't That Good News* (RCA, 1964).

Crass, "Angels," *The Feeding of the 5000* (Small Wonder, 1978).

Crass, "Do They Owe Us a Living?," *The Feeding of the 5000* (Small Wonder, 1978).

Crass, "So What," *The Feeding of the 5000* (Small Wonder, 1978).

Crass, "Big Man, Big M.A.N.," *Stations of the Crass* (Crass, 1979).

Crass, "White Punks on Hope," *Stations of the Crass* (Crass, 1979).

Crass, *Penis Envy* (Crass, 1981).

Crass, "Reality Asylum," *The Feeding of the 5000: The Second Sitting* (Crass, 1981).

Crass, *Christ—The Album* (Crass, 1982).

Crass, "You Can Be Who?," *Christ—The Album* (Crass, 1982).

Crass, *Best Before* (Crass, 1986).

Dark Was the Night: Red Hot Compilation (4AD, 2009).

Dickies, The, *We Aren't the World!* (Combat, 1986).

Dylan, Bob, *Freewheelin' Bob Dylan* (Colombia, 1963).

East Timor Benefit Album (Idols of the Marketplace, 2000).

Echobelly, *Bellyache* EP (Pandemonium, 1993).

Echobelly, "Centipede," *Insomniac* CD single (Fauv, 1994)

Echobelly, *Everyone's Got One* (Rhythm King, 1994).

For the Lady (Rhino, 2004).

Fun-da-Mental, "Tribal Revolution," *Tribal Revolution EP* (Nation, 1994).

Fun-da-Mental, "Dog Tribe," *Seize the Time* (Nation, 1996).

Fun-da-Mental, "GODEVIL," *GodEvil* EP (Nation, 1997).

Fun-da-Mental, *Erotic Terrorism* (Nation, 1998).

Fun-da-Mental, *America Will Go to Hell* (Nation, 1999).

Fun-da-Mental, *All Is War* (Nation, 2006).

Gaughan, Dick, *Kist O'Gold* (Topic, 1976).

Gaughan, Dick, *Gaughan* (Topic, 1978).

Gaughan, Dick, *Handful of Earth* (Topic, 1981).

Gaughan, Dick, *True and Bold: Songs of the Scottish Miners* [1986] (Celtic Music, 1988).

Genocide in Sudan (Waxploitation, 2004).

God Bless America (Sony, 2001).

Green Day, *American Idiot* (Reprise, 2004).

Groundwork: Act to Reduce Hunger (Hear Music/Starbucks, 2001).

Help: A Charity Project for the Children of Bosnia (Polygram, 1995).

Ian Campbell Folk Group, *The Coaldust Ballads* (Transatlantic, 1967).

The Impressions, "Keep on Pushing," *Keep on Pushing* (Paramount, 1964).

The Impressions, "We're a Winner," *We're a Winner* (Universal, 1968).

Indie Aid Abroad (Drive-In/Library, 2000).

The Jackson Five, *Maybe Tomorrow* (Motown, 1971).

Jackson, Michael, "Man in the Mirror," *Bad* (Epic, 1987).

Jamelia, "Thank You," *Thank You* (EMI, 2004).

Killen, Louis, Colin Ross, and Johnny Handle, *Along the Coaly Tyne* (Topic, 1968).

King, Willie, *Freedom Creek* (Rooster Blues Records, 2000).

King, Willie, *I Am the Blues* (Willie King, 2000).

King, Willie, *Living in a New World* (Rooster Blues Records, 2002).

King, Willie, *Jukin' at Bettie's* (Freedom Creek Music, 2004).

King, Willie, *One Love* (Freedom Creek Music, 2006).

The Last Poets, "Niggers Are Scared of Revolution" (Varese Sarabande, 1970).

Light of Day: A Tribute to Bruce Springsteen (Discmedi, 2003).

Lincoln Street Exit, *Drive It* (Mainstream, 1970).

Lynn, Loretta, "The Pill," *Back to the Country* (MCA, 1975).

Mingus, Charles, *Mingus Ah Um* (Columbia, 1959).

Mitchell, Joni, *Blue* (Warner, 1971).

Mitchell, Joni, *The Hissing of Summer Lawns* (Warner, 1975).

Mitchell, Joni, *Turbulent Indigo* (Warner, 1994).

Moore, Christy, "The Magdalene Laundries," *Burning Times* (Sony, 2006).

No Alternative (Red Hot Organization/Arista, 1993).

No Boundaries: A Benefit for the Kosovar Refugees (Sony, 1999).

Pine Valley Cosmonauts, *The Executioner's Last Songs* (Bloodshot, 2002).

Ramones, "Bonzo Goes to Bitburg" (Beggars Banquet, 1985).

Red Hot + Blue: A Tribute to Cole Porter (Chrysalis, 1990).

Rhythms del Mundo Classics (Universal, 2009).

Roach, Max, *We Insist: Freedom Now* (Candid, 1960).

Rock the Net: Musicians for Network Neutrality (Thirsty Ear, 2008).

Rollins, Sonny, *Freedom Suite* (Riverside, 1958).

Scott-Heron, Gil, *Small Talk at 125th and Lenox* (Flying Dutchman, 1971).

Scott-Heron, Gil, *Free Will* (Flying Dutchman, 1972).

Scott-Heron, Gil, *The First Minute of a New Day* (Arista, 1975).

Scott-Heron, Gil, *From South Africa to South Carolina* (Arista, 1976).

Scott-Heron, Gil, *Bridges* (Arista, 1977).

Scott-Heron, Gil, *Secrets* (Arista, 1978).

Serve3: The Hard Rock Benefit Album (The Orchard, 2008).

Simon, Paul, *Graceland* (Warner, 1986).

Songs for Sudan (Big Noise Music, 2004).

Springsteen, Bruce, *Greetings from Asbury Park, NJ* (Columbia, 1973).

Springsteen, Bruce, *Born to Run* (Columbia, 1975).

Springsteen, Bruce, *The River* (Columbia, 1980).

Springsteen, Bruce, *Nebraska* (Columbia, 1982).

Springsteen, Bruce, *Born in the U.S.A.* (Columbia, 1984).

Springsteen, Bruce, *The Ghost of Tom Joad* (Columbia, 1995).

Springsteen, Bruce, *Tracks* (Columbia, 1998).

Springsteen, Bruce, *Magic* (Columbia, 2007).

Sweet Relief: A Benefit for Victoria Williams (Thirsty Ear/Chaos, 1993).

'Til Things Are Brighter: A Tribute to Johnny Cash (Red Rhino/Fundamental, 1988).

USA for Africa, *We Are the World* (Polygram, 1985).

Various Artists, *Philadelphia: Original Soundtrack Music* (Epix Soundtracks, 1994).

Various Artists, *Music from and Inspired by the Motion Picture Dead Man Walking* (Columbia, 1996).

War Child Presents Heroes (Astralwerks, 2009).

Wed-Rock (Centaur, 2006).

XIT, *Plight of the Redman* (Rare Earth, 1972) [reissued SOAR 1989].

XIT, *Silent Warrior* (Rare Earth, 1973) [reissued SOAR 1989].

Index

www.ingramcontent.com/pod-product-compliance
Lightning Source LLC
Chambersburg PA
CBHW050646280326
41932CB00015B/2805